Glorying in Tribulation

SOJOURNER TRUTH.

Glorying in Tribulation

The Lifework of Sojourner Truth

Erlene Stetson
Linda David

MICHIGAN STATE UNIVERSITY PRESS | *East Lansing*

Michigan State University Press
East Lansing, Michigan 48823-5245

Library of Congress Cataloging-in-Publication Data
Stetson, Erlene, 1949-
Glorying in tribulation : the lifework of Sojourner Truth/
Erlene Stetson, Linda David. p. cm.
Includes bibliographical references (p.) and index.
ISBN 0-87013-337-4 (cloth); ISBN 978-1-61186-501-1 (paper);
ISBN 978-1-62895-190-5 (ePub); ISBN 978-0-87013-908-6 (PDF)
1. Truth, Sojourner, d. 1883. 2. Afro-Americans-Biography. 3. Abolitionists-United States-
Biography 4. Social reformers-United States-Biography. I. David, Linda. II. Title.
E185.97T8S741994
305.5'67'092-dc20
[B] 94-14577 CIP

Cover design by Anastasia Wraight

Visit Michigan State University Press at www.msupress.org

To Nell Gattiker, Ora Lee Johnson, and Naomi Long Madgett
Creative Spirits

Contents

Illustrations

Frontispiece: Frontispiece from the 1850 edition of *Narrative of Sojourner Truth*. Courtesy of the Lilly Library, Indiana University.

Facing chapters 1, 2, 3, and 6: Sketches by James Wells Champney (1843- 1903), a painter and illustrator who accompanied Edward Smith King through the South in 1873-74. King's articles appeared in the *Scribner's Monthly* between December 1872 and April 1875. They were revised and published in book form with Champney's illustrations as *The Great South* (Hartford: American Publishing Company, 1875). The original sketches are reproduced courtesy of the Lilly Library, Indiana University.

Facing chapters 4 and 5: Engravings from Edward Smith King's *The Great South* (1875). Courtesy of the Lilly Library, Indiana University.

Page 202: Pencil sketch by Charles C. Burleigh Jr., of Sojourner Truth as a laundress. Courtesy Historic Northampton, Northampton, Massachusetts.

Foreword

LaShawn D. Harris

The genre of biography is a useful analytical approach to understanding Black women's fascinating and complex lives as activists, intellectuals, institution builders, and mothers and wives. It also presents writers and readers the opportunity to explore women's views on labor and politics, womanhood, and equality, as well as examine national, social, and political movements from women's perspectives. Biographies, whether cradle-to-the-grave stories or thematic and analytical accounts, humanize Black women—those historically objectified, debased, and silenced in histories written about the American past. Furthermore, biography becomes useful to exploring Black women's longstanding tradition of testimony. In disclosing various aspects of their life stories to family and friends and journalists and writers, women articulated their joys, fears, and disappointments. They also relived painful moments of exclusion, oppression, and violence. Survivors of discriminatory practices, to borrow from poet and activist Audre Lorde, had "come to believe over and over again that what is most important to [them] must be spoken, made verbal and shared, even at the risk of having it bruised or misunderstood."[1] Disclosure about harm and violence was a way to reclaim one's body and humanity, advocate for social and legal justice, and mobilize communities on behalf of Black womanhood.[2] Testimony generated the opportunity to publicly document victimization and share with listeners the aftershocks of violence and harm. And for many Black women, like nineteenth century abolitionist and women's rights advocate Sojourner Truth, speaking the truth became a weapon against slavery, white supremacy, and inequality.

In *Glorying in Tribulation: The Lifework of Sojourner Truth*, the former enslaved woman, who became a national symbol of freedom for African Americans and women, speaks her truth. "Talking aloud," according to scholars Erlene Stetson and Linda David, was Truth's calling. Testifying was part of Truth's personal, political, and religious ministries. Stetson and David's work is a major contribution to scholarship on Black women. At the time of its publication in 1994, *Glorying in Tribulation*, standing alongside the seminal work of Black women historians such as Darlene Clark Hine, Evelyn Brooks Higginbotham, Stephanie Shaw, and Deborah Gray White, cemented its place as a contributor to the burgeoning historiography on African American women.[3] During the 1990s, Stetson and David and other scholars did the painstaking work of unearthing Black women's forgotten histories and archival footprints, proving that women were (and continue to be) central historical actors. *Glorying in Tribulation* is also part of a growing list of seminal biographies on enslaved women; some of these pioneering monographs include Jean Fagan Yellin's *Harriet Jacobs: A Life* (2004), Catherine Clinton's *Harriet Tubman: The Road to Freedom* (2004), Nikki Taylor's *Driven Toward Madness: The Fugitive Slave Margaret Garner and Tragedy on the Ohio* (2016), and Erica Armstrong Dunbar's *Never Caught: The Washingtons' Relentless Pursuit of the Their Runaway Slave, Ona Judge* (2017).

Writing an engaging study, Stetson and David use the genre of biography and literary analysis to explore Truth's lifework, her personal and public histories, to deconstruct her 1850 narrative and white women's scripting of that narrative and to examine the various intersections between race and gender and freedom. Moreover, Stetson and David illuminate the making of a radical reformer who was committed to living in a just nation.

Stetson and David take a unique and careful approach to excavating Truth's many lives. The authors' eloquent prose and insightful analysis of some of Truth's well-known speeches, including her 1851Women's Rights Convention speech in Akron, Ohio, reveals a masterful storyteller, a resilient activist, and an inspiring public intellectual working toward the liberation of African Americans and women. Describing Truth's activist circles and friendships, Stetson and David beautifully narrate the correspondences and exchanges between Truth and various Black and white abolitionists, politicians, and women's rights activists, such as Oliver Johnson, Frederick Douglass, Harriet Tubman, and President Abraham Lincoln. In October 1864, Truth alongside white abolitionist Lucy Colman visited the president. Truth's account of her White House visit was published in several newspapers, including William Loyd Garrison's *Liberator*, a weekly abolitionist newspaper published in Boston.

Stetson and David's account on Truth's lifework shines in its description of northern racism or what many twentieth century scholars call Jim Crow North.

Truth's lived experiences and fight for Black freedom and women's rights are situated against the backdrop of racial exclusion. Living in New York and in other northern spaces, Truth came to witness and understand the historical roots of racial segregation. Segregation was omnipresent in these spaces. Free Blacks faced a regime of racial proscriptions that would emerge in southern states several decades after the close of the American Civil War. Within a multi-layered system of racial segregation, African Americans were subjected to political disenfranchisement, carceral confinement, and white violence and excluded from public schools and skilled labor jobs.

Glorying in Tribulation's strength lies in its exploration of Truth's role in controlling her narrative and public image. Employing a myriad of primary documentation, including correspondences between Truth and reformers such as Amy Post and Rowland Johnson and her 1850 autobiography, *Narrative of the Life of Sojourner Truth*, Stetson and David meticulously demonstrate Truth's agency over her life story. Like many Black women activists of her generation, Truth's thoughts about controlling her public persona were rooted in a desire to "leav[e] a legacy [and story] of her choosing." Historically, the crafting and curating of personal narratives has always been important to Black women. Personal stories were used as a liberation strategy against anti-Black rhetoric and legal statutes that denied Black freedom. And speaking in defense of themselves, women's narratives were employed to show Black respectability while countering minstrelsy caricatures and racist American print culture that imagined women as hypersexual and as criminals.

Scholarship on Truth has grown exponentially since the publication of *Glorying in Tribulation*. New books and essays, while acknowledging Stetson and David's many interventions and cogent analysis, offer scholars, students, and a general audience new insights and portraits of the Black abolitionist. For instance, Nell Irvin Painter's *Sojourner Truth: A Life, a Symbol* (1996) and Margaret Washington's *Sojourner Truth's America* (2009) are brilliantly researched and written biographies on Truth. Both delve deep into her personal and public life and her commitment to race and gender equality. More broadly, Painter, Washington, and other scholars of the nineteenth century offer nuanced ways of understanding histories of Black women from slavery to freedom, as well as new ways of analyzing the antebellum era's socioeconomic and political landscape.

Erlene Stetson and Linda David tell a remarkable story about one of the nation's most iconic figures. Everyone should read this book. It reminds us how important

Sojourner Truth's voice and extraordinary lifework was to the liberation struggles of African Americans and women and to radically transforming the nation.

Notes

1. Audre Lorde, *Sister Outside: Essays and Speeches* (Berkeley: Crossing Press, 1984), 40.
2. Danielle McGuire, *At the Dark End of the Street. Black Women, Rape, and Resistance—A New History of the Civil Rights Movement from Rosa Parks to the Rise of Black Power* (New York: Vintage, 2010), xix.
3. Evelyn Brooks Higginbotham, *Righteous Discontent: The Women's Movement in the Black Baptist Church, 1880–1920* (Cambridge, MA: Havard University Press, 1994); Stephanie J. Shaw, *What a Woman Ought to Be and to Do: Black Professional Women Workers during the Jim Crow Era* (Chicago: University of Chicago Press, 1996); Darlene Clark Hine, *Hine Sight: Black Women and The Re-Construction of American History* (Bloomington: Indiana University Press, 1994); Deborah Gray White, *Too Heavy a Load: Black Women in Defense of Themselves, 1894–1994* (New York: W. W. Norton, 1999).

Acknowledgments

Our work grew out of a convergence of separate endeavors and we have first of all to thank each other for the sustenance and joy we found in our collaboration. A circle of friends helped the work to grow over a long period and we thank each member of it. The assistance of Jean Phoenix Laurel and Phyllis Guskin was crucial, as was the long-term support of Harriet McCombs, coeditor of Sojourner: A Third World Women's Research Newsletter, Elizabeth Kennedy, Barbara Halporn, Fritz Senn, Gayle Margherita, Mischa Senn, Joan M. Zirker, Angelina Maccarone, Rob Fulk, Joanna G. Williams, Fatima El-Tayeb and Fareedah Allah. We are grateful as well to Melanie Walder, Virginia Munroe, Tom Karr, Geraldine White, Judith Rose Gettelfinger, Sylvia Escher, Kathryn Crittenden, and Brigit Keller.

Our families helped us and we warmly thank Al David and Gerd Knoblauch, La Nicerra Stetson, La Quetta Stetson, and Benjamin David. Throughout the writing of this book we were paying tribute to the memory of our mothers, Rose Green Hawkins and Alma Louise Utz.

Thanks are due to Karl Kabelac, Manuscripts Librarian, and to Molly Solazzo of the Department of Rare Books and Special Collections, University of Rochester Library, and to Laura V. Monti, Keeper of Rare Books and Manuscripts and to R. Eugene Zepp, Reference Librarian in the Division of Rare Books and Manuscripts of the Boston Public Library. We are especially grateful to Sue Presnell, Head of Reference Services and to Heather Munro of the Manuscripts Department of the Lilly Library, Indiana University. For helping us to eliminate a false lead we thank Cathy Cherbosque, Curator of Literary Manuscripts, and Karen Kearns, Archivist, at The Henry Huntington Library. Much of our research originated under the expert guidance of the late Wilmer Baatz of the Indiana University Black Culture Center Library; he was a learned and tireless friend to scholarship.

Julie L. Loehr of the Michigan State University Press has consistently supported the book. Kristine M. Blakeslee has been an ideal editor, thoughtful, questioning, and ceaselessly encouraging. It is our great pleasure to see our book appear alongside MSU Press's Lotus Poetry Series. Our collaboration really began in a rare books library reading together the poetry of Naomi Long Madgett.

Erlene Stetson, Berlin
Linda David, Bloomington

Glorying in Tribulation

One

Speaking of Shadows

> *I sell the shadow to support the substance.*
> Sojourner Truth[1]

On the first day of October 1865 Sojourner Truth dictated a letter from Washington, D.C. to her friend Amy Post in Rochester, New York:

> I have heard nothing from my children for a long time, neither from my grandchildren since they left me. I take this occasion to inquire after their whereabouts and health, as well as your own prosperity, and to inform you of my own. I spent over six months at Arlington Heigths [sic], called the Freedmen's village, and served there as counciller for my people, acceptably to the good but not at all times to those who desire nothing higher than the lowest and the vilest of habits. For you know I must be faithful Sojourner everywhere.

Six months after the formal ending of the Civil War, Truth felt that the nation was still wandering like the Israelites in the wilderness with no promised land in sight.

> I have generally received the kindest attention from those in Authority even to the President. But I see dark spots still in the great cloud that leads us by day, and occasional angry flashes in the pillar of fire that guides through this long dark night. Yet my comfort in all this is in the thought that God rules.

The dark spots by day were easy enough to account for in her constant confrontation with the racism that persisted after the abolition of slavery.

A few weeks ago I was in company with my friend Josephine S. Griffing, when the Conductor of a street car refused to stop his car for me, although closely following Josephine and holding on to the iron rail they draged me a number of yards before she succeeded in stoping them. She reported the conductor to the president of the City Rail Way who dissmissed him at once; and told me to take the number of the car wherever I was mistreated by a conductor or driver, and report to him and they should be dismissed. On the 13th inst. I had occasion to go for blackbury wine, and other necessieares for the patients in the Freedmen's Hospital in this city where I have been *doing* and advising, for a number of months under sanction of the Bureau. As they had often refused to stop for me, I thought now I would get a ride without trouble as I was in company with annother Friend Laura S. Haviland of Mich.. As I assended the platform of the car, a man just leaving it, called out, "Have you got room for niggers here?" as the conductor then noticed my black face, pushed me, saying "go back—get off here." I told I was not going off, "then I'l put you off," said he furiously, with clenching my right arm with both hands, using such violence that he seemed about to succeed, when Mrs Haviland reached us and told him, he was not going to put me off, placing her hands on both of us. "Does she belong to you? if she does, take her in out the way" said he, in a hurried angry tone. She replied "She does not belong to me, but she belongs to Humanity and she would have been out of the way long ago, if you had have let her alone." The number of the car was noted, and conductor dismissed at once upon the report to the President (Mr Gideon) who advised his arrest for Assault and Battery as my shoulder was sprained by the wrench given by the conductor in his effort to put me off. Accordingly I had him arrested and the case tried before Justice Thomson who refered the case to the Grand Jury of the United States, and placed James C. Weedon, the conductor under bonds for his appearance to court which opens next Wednesday. My shoulder was very lame and swolen, but is better, but I sometimes fear it will trouble me for a long time, if I ever get entirely over it. It is hard for the old slave-holding spirit to die. But *die* it *must*. Write *immediately*, tell me where my children are, and *how* they are.[2]

"Mrs Haviland is here on business, and will remain a week or ten days longer," added Truth in a postscript; "She does the reading and writing for me while here."

Although Truth's powerful oratory created her public reputation (J. Miller McKim, the corresponding secretary for the Pennsylvania Anti-

Slavery Society, thought that a person could "as well attempt to report the seven apocalyptic thunders" as to recapture the effect of Truth's eloquence[3]), scholarly interest in her has often centered around an attempt to assess her role in producing written records of her own words. Again and again this effort hinges on the question of her *lack* of literacy. Yet clearly it is Truth's experience of illiteracy that functions as an authorizing strategy in her stories about her life and that forms the bridge between her lived experience and the development of her mature political thought. "You know, children," she is reported to have said, "I don't read such small stuff as letters, I read men and nations."[4] This was strictly true. This was the source of her efficacy as a spokesperson for the right to political self-determination for millions of formerly enslaved people whose conception of social organization had been formed out of their own experience under a legal prohibition against literacy.

Illiteracy did not exclude Truth from political discourse, and the concept is of little utility in understanding her work. "She is a woman of strong religious nature," wrote a correspondent after the war, "with an entirely original eloquence and humor, possessed of a weird imagination, of most grotesque but strong, clear mind, and one who, without the aid of reading or writing, is strangely susceptible to all that in thought and action is now current in the world" (*NarBk*, 237).

In evaluating the authenticity of the work of the first English autobiographer, Margery Kempe, the fifteenth-century woman who also relied on scribes and intermediaries to put her words into written form, historian Karma Lochrie has argued for a category somewhere between literacy and illiteracy, "a quasi-literacy defined by its *access* to the written word." For Truth, as for many people in medieval times and since, "reading was more often linked with hearing or listening than it was with seeing" and many written texts would be "read aloud for their 'readers.'"[5] During the 1820s, when Truth had escaped slavery to stay with the Van Wagenens, she was probably being read to from the Bible on a regular basis for the first time, while many an illiterate English laborer went regularly to a pub to hear the editorials of Cobbett read aloud.[6]

We can identify the two crucial elements in the print culture that served as a conduit into Truth's ears and a vehicle for the words she spoke to circulate in the world beyond her immediate audience. These were the Bible and newspapers. We have many images of her methods of interaction with both.

Truth's political primer was the Bible. The power struggles of a people under the eye of a partisan god were models for a marginalized culture. The *Narrative* allows us to hear her listening to Genesis, to Isaiah, to the passage in which Paul claims that Jesus had a Bride (the Church). Truth expropriated the moral center of white Christianity, emptying out the stores of biblical imagery in the service of her race. She could use the Bible to withering effect. Her speaking strategy on the abolitionist stage was to convert the white man's rationale for slavecatching as soul-saving into the topsy-turvy argument that the civilizing of the whites was now the black person's burden. Playing on the white Christian's convention of wonder that Christ could love man, Truth would ask from the platform, "Isn't it wonderful that the Ethiopians can love you?" She said of the thieving bureaucrats managing the refugee programs in Washington that "the people here (white) are only here for the *loaves* and *fishes* while the freedmen get the *scales* and crusts."[7] Speaking her politics in biblical terms, Truth wrote in outrage to the *National Anti-Slavery Standard* in 1867: "I have just heard an extract of a letter read from Gerrit Smith to Mr. Garrison, which makes all my nerves quiver." She reminded Smith, who was urging reconciliation, that the South had "robbed and starved and butchered for centuries," like those "workers of iniquity" to whom Jesus said "I was hungry and ye fed me not." She asked of Smith, "Has he forgot Andersonville and Fort Pillow?"[8]

Truth was a sophisticated listener who grasped how difficult it is to get a straightforward reading, since every reading is both a presentation and an interpretation; and to this could be added the burden of the reader's analysis. In Truth's *Narrative* it is explained that

> when she was examining the scriptures, she wished to hear them without comment; but if she employed adult persons to read them to her, and she asked them to read a passage over again, they invariably commenced to explain, by giving her their version of it; and in this way, they tried her feelings exceedingly. In consequence of this, she ceased to ask adult persons to read the Bible to her, and substituted children in their stead. Children, as soon as they could read distinctly, would re-read the same sentence to her, as often as she wished, and without comment;—and in that way she was enabled to see what her own mind could make out of the record, and that, she said, was what she wanted, and not what others thought it to mean. (*NarBk*, 108-9)

Scribes as well as interpreters presented problems for the speaker-hearer. Before God taught her to keep her own records, Rebecca Cox Jackson experienced the problem of the unfaithful recorder in the person of her authoritarian brother:

> So I went to get my brother to write my letters and to read them. So he was awriting a letter in answer to one he had just read. I told him what

to put in. Then I asked him to read. He did. I said, "Thee has put in more than I told thee." This he done several times. I then said, "I don't want thee to *word* my letter. I only want thee to *write* it."[9]

Truth understood that the Bible had been "worded" rather than written. Following her careful hearing/reading of the Bible, she always tested its authority.

> She wished to compare the teachings of the Bible with the witness within her; and she came to the conclusion, that the spirit of truth spoke in those records, but that the recorders of those truths had intermingled with them ideas and suppositions of their own. (*NarBk*, 109)

If the spirit of truth found only intrusive scribes, the human speaking voice could be expected to have problems as well. To separate the recorded word from the speaking spirit of truth in Holy Scripture was an act of searching analytical skill to which Truth felt authorized by the text of her experience. When Lyman Beecher asked her if she preached "from the Bible," Truth asserted that she did not, because she could not "read a letter." She explained that she preached only one text, that of her experience: "*My* text is, 'WHEN I FOUND JESUS!'"[10] The conversion experience that had thrown the organizing textual grid over her preaching had liberated Truth from the tyranny of written doctrine, even that expounded in the Bible itself.

After the Bible Truth read newspapers, and her political consciousness developed in dialogue with the circulating record of abolitionist opinion. She corresponded with white abolitionist Oliver Johnson, who edited the official organ of Garrisonian abolitionism, *The National Anti-Slavery Standard*, from 1858 to 1865. A letter dated 29 July 1863, written to her by Johnson after the murderous anti-black riots in New York City, gives some of the quality of their exchange:

> Yours by the hand of J. M. Peebles came promptly. I thank you for the photographs, though they are poor compared with the one you sent me first. It is a pity you did not preserve the negative of that instead of this. Not only is the likeness better, but the work also.
>
> The mob did not disturb the *Anti-Slavery* office, nor me. The fact is the *Standard* is scarcely known to the vile class composing the mob, having but a small circulation in the city. But it would have taken only a hint to direct their attention to us, and then my life would have been in danger, and the office would probably have been destroyed. A good

Providence seems to have watched over us. Mr. Leonard, the colored clerk, was obliged to hide, but no harm came to him. Many of the colored people were dreadfully abused, but a very healthful reaction has already set in; and I believe the condition in this city will be better than it was before. Upwards of $30,000 has been raised for the relief of the sufferers, and they will get pay from the city government for the property they lost. I shall send the *Standard* as you request. (*NarBk*, 258-59)

From Washington in 1864 Truth wrote a careful description of her work with the freedpeople and of her visit to Lincoln to her Quaker friend Rowland Johnson: "You may publish my whereabouts, and anything in this letter you think would interest the friends of Freedom, Justice, and Truth, in the *Standard* and *Anglo-African,* and any other paper you may see fit." The surviving files of the New York weekly *Anglo-African,* the most important of the black newspapers of the Civil War period, are incomplete, so a source for information about the most interesting of Truth's print interactions is lacking; still we know from this letter that she read it and that its readers probably read about her in its pages. In the same letter she wrote, "Ask Mr. Oliver Johnson to please send me the *Standard* while I am here, as many of the colored people like to hear what is going on, and to know what is being done for them. Sammy, my grandson, reads for them."[11]

How Truth related to printed accounts of herself reveals much about her awareness of her public image and much about the extent to which she controlled it. Some of the power of the press was on her side. Garrison's *Liberator,* Marius Robinson's *Anti-Slavery Bugle,* and Oliver Johnson's *National Anti-Slavery Standard* sought copy for their antislavery crusade and were willing to give her space on some other subjects—religion, temperance, woman suffrage, and her petition for land grants to post-war blacks—as well. Truth understood the power of newspaper reporters and editors to tailor the message she wanted to convey.

Elizabeth Cady Stanton recounts a compelling scene after the Equal Rights Association meetings in New York City on 9-10 May 1867, which were intended to serve the alliance between feminists and abolitionists. Truth had spoken three times at the convention, delivering arguably her greatest statement on black woman's rights. Stanton wrote to the Democratic editor of the New York *World* that she had been "entertaining Mrs. Stowe's 'Lybian Sybil' at our home for the last week":

The morning after the Equal Rights Convention, as the daily journals one by one made their appearance, turning to the youngsters of the household, she said: "Children, as there is no school to-day, will you read Sojourner the reports of the Convention? I want to see whether these young sprigs of the press do me justice.

"Sojourner then gathered up her bag and shawl, and walked into the parlor in a stately manner," Stanton wrote, "and there, surrounded by the children, the papers were duly read and considered."

Stanton's witty portrait of Truth seated among the newspapers, being read to by the children who reproduce the written word with straightforward unmediated voice, without the editorializing of adults, renders remarkably Truth's dynamic and dramatic interaction with the printed word. It also gives a sense of Truth's ongoing activity as the keeper of her own image.

"I think," said one of the group, "the press should hereafter speak of you as Mrs. Stowe's Lybian Sybil [sic], and not as 'old church woman.'" "Oh, child, that's good enough. The *Herald* used to call me 'old black nigger,' so this sounds respectable. Have you read the *Herald* too, children? Is that born again? Well, we are all walking the right way together."[12]

Attending to what Karma Lochrie has called "the fundamentally vocal experience of the written text,"[13] Truth experienced the presentation of print in terms of her own oral presentations. Breaking up passages, Truth said, "gives the reporter time to take breath and sharpen his pen, and think of some witty thing to say." Truth had a shrewd eye for dramatic format.

She said she liked the wit of the *World's* reporter; all the little texts running through the speeches, such as "Sojourner on Popping-Up," "No Grumbling," "Digging Stumps," "Biz," to show what is coming, so that one can get ready to cry or laugh, as the case may be—a kind of signboard, a milestone, to tell where we are going, and how fast we go.

When her readers pointed out "the solid columns of the other papers," Truth said that "she did not like the dead calm." She preferred, instead, "the breaking up into verses, like her songs."

The thesis of Stanton's letter to the *World* is that Truth "understands the whole question of reconstruction, all its 'quagmires and pitfalls,' as she says, as well as any man does." In Stanton's account, Truth, taking in the reports from the *Express*, the *Post*, the *Commercial Advertiser*, the *World*, the *Times*, the *Herald*, the *Tribune*, and the *Sun*, is an activist monitor of the subtleties of political coverage of the universal suffrage issue, which saw the defection of long-standing allies like Horace Greeley's *Tribune* and the opportunistic courting of the woman's rights activists by Democratic papers like the *World*. Truth is sarcastic about the shift:

> "But, children, why did you not send for some of those wicked Democratic papers that abuse all good people and good things?" "They are all here," said the readers in chorus. "We have read you all the Republicans and the Democrats say." "Why, children, I can't tell one from the other. The millennium must be here, when one can't tell saints from sinners, Republicans from Democrats. Is the *World* Horace Greeley's paper?" "Oh, no; the *World* is Democratic!" "Democratic! Why, children, the *World* does move! But there is one thing I don't exactly see; if the Democrats are all ready to give equal rights to all, what are the Republicans making such a fuss about? Mr. Greeley was ready for this twenty years ago; if he had gone on as fast as the Democrats he should have been on the platform, at the conventions, making speeches, and writing resolutions, long ago."

Horace Greeley had made his influential New York *Tribune* a strong voice against slavery and had given early, friendly support to the woman's rights movement, but like many abolitionists, he believed that the campaign for woman suffrage would hurt the cause of black male suffrage. Greeley's emphasis on tariffs and protective duties reflected the general shift away from the reformist issues of reconstruction. Truth played with Greeley's free trade argument, adapting its rhetoric of trade relations to her greater text, the reconstruction of human relations:

> Yes, I go for everything free. Let nature, like individuals, make the most of what God has given them, have their neighbors to do the same, and then do all they can to serve each other. There is no use in one man, or one nation, to try to do or be everything. It is a good thing to be dependent on each other for something, it makes us civil and peaceable.

Truth's call for interdependence as the enabling structure of freedom resonated against the prevailing view among abolitionists that the end of slavery was equal to freedom and that freedpeople could function without organized assistance.

When Truth asked for Theodore Tilton's paper, the children reminded her that "the *Independent* is a weekly, it came out before the Convention." Truth's rejoinder is pointed: "But Theodore is not a weekly; why did he not come to the Convention and tell us what he thought?" Theodore Tilton and Henry Ward Beecher had transformed the New York *Independent*, a Congregationalist weekly, into the most prominent religious newspaper with a strong abolitionist stance. The paper was now equivocal on the expanding movement for woman suffrage.

> "Well, here is his last paper [Tilton's *Independent*], with a grand editorial," and Sojourner listened to the end with interest. "That's good," said she, "but he don't say woman." "Oh, he is talking about sectarianism, not suffrage; the Church, not the State." "No matter, the Church wrongs woman as much as the State: 'Wives, obey your husbands,' is as bad as the common law: 'The husband and the wife are one, and that one the husband.' I am afraid Theodore and Horace are playing bo-peep with their shadows."[14]

From its 1850 publication Truth carried copies of her *Narrative* to sell, and during the war she sold photographs of herself, captioned "I sell the shadow to support the substance" (*NarBk*, 203). In a luminous moment, Truth took up the trope of the shadow:

> "Speaking of shadows," said Sojourner, "I wish the *World* to know that when I go among fashionable people in the Church of the Puritans, I do not carry 'rations' in my bag; I keep my shadow there. I have good friends enough to give me clothes and rations. I stand on principle, always, in one place, so everybody knows where to find Sojourner, and I don't want my shadow even to be dogging about here and there and everywhere, so I keep it in this bag."

The *World*'s insulting image of her as a kind of vagrant with "rations" in her bag, roaming the convention floor in the Church of the Puritans is countered by Truth with her own image of herself as a figure strongly rooted in a community of friends (even if they are, she admits mordantly, "fashionable"). In her bag she carries her "shadow," her recorded life history and her photographs. Unlike the newspapers, which do not stand "in one place," Sojourner is always standing "on principle." The male editors have "shadows" too: their printed words and recorded images cast across the public path and onto history. In her fascinating locution, their shadows have come loose: Greeley and Tilton are "playing bo-peep with their shadows," losing their old principles or leaving them alone to come home on their own.

Truth is not such a faithless shepherd: "I don't want my shadow even to be dogging about here and there and everywhere, so I keep it in this bag." The shadow loosed in the external world, figured in words and pictures, in *Narrative* and in speeches and newspaper accounts, is after all moral conscience, the essence of a person's spirit. Truth stands by her own representations of it.

On that day in Stanton's parlor, Truth was satisfied with the reports of her performances but was considering separate publication of her speeches.

> I'll tell you what I'm thinking. My speeches in the Convention read well. I should like to have the substance put together, improved a little, and published in tract form, headed "Sojourner Truth on Suffrage."[15]

Actually, in composing the narrative, "Sojourner Truth on the Press," and in addressing it to the editor of the Democratic *World*, Elizabeth Cady Stanton was already packaging some of Truth's opinions for her own purposes. We must look, as always, to the agenda of the framer to try to guess for what purpose the story has been framed. In her portrait of Truth as a savvy ally, Stanton was strategically associating Truth with the white feminist opposition to the extension of suffrage to black and immigrant males unless it was at the same time granted to women. Truth's view was similar but not identical, looking toward the rights of black women without turning away from the rights of black men. In her speeches Truth argued that the vote was crucial for black women as well as for black men because the economic situation of black women prevented them from achieving even the limited degree of autonomy allowed to black men. But in calling "slavery partly destroyed; not entirely,"[16] she acknowledged to the convention what Stanton and her allies would not: that the abolition of slavery had not placed blacks, male or female, on a level of parity with white women. The conflicted nature of Truth's stance can be caught in her enigmatic reformulation of Henry Ward Beecher's recommendation to the convention to "Bait your trap with the white woman, and I think you will catch the black man."[17] Truth recast Beecher's line to say that "if you bait the suffrage-hook with a woman, you will certainly catch a black man," the sense of which cut many ways.[18]

In the next few months, infuriated by the indifference to woman suffrage of their former allies among Republicans and abolitionists, Stanton and Susan B. Anthony abandoned their universalist rhetoric, campaigning in Kansas with the racist Democrat George Francis Train ("Woman first, and negro last, is my programme").[19]

Stanton's strategies for liberating *her* people, a certain segment of middle-class white womanhood, would always find some use for black women; but Stanton conceptualized their relations implicitly in her famous "Solitude of Self" address to a Senate committee considering the woman suffrage amendment in 1894: "In discussing the rights of woman, we are to consider, first, what belongs to her as an individual, in a world of her own, the arbiter of her own destiny, an imaginary Robinson Crusoe with her woman Friday on a solitary island."[20] The strategies of interdependence that Truth held to were rooted in a very different sense of community.

Although Sojourner Truth lived in a print culture in which books were being dissociated from oral production, she herself remained an oral producer, and it is misguided to see Truth's orality as a pathology, a condition of negation. "She has rare natural gifts; a clear intellect; a fine moral intuition and spirited insight, with much common sense," wrote Lucy Stone in the official organ of the American Woman's Suffrage Association; "She never could read, and often said, that all the great trouble of the world came from those who could read, and not from those who could not, and that she was glad she never knew how to read."[21] This view lay at the heart of Truth's political vision. Perhaps in agreement with Audre Lorde that *"the master's tools will never dismantle the master's house,"*[22] Truth seems never to have believed that what was taught by the white patriarchal culture could be unlearned; it was best not to learn it at all. Truth saw "through a millstone" that Western culture hung around the neck of her people; looking around her, seeing who had literacy and who did not, she rightly saw it not as a condition of human adequacy but as an effect of dominance.[23] Acquiring literacy did not mean moving from defective humanity to plenitude; it meant acquiring a political tool that could be useful in negating racist theories that enslaved Africans could be defined by their inability to decipher Western print. Truth had chosen a different tool for the hoeing of this field. She used her speaking voice as the unalienated inheritor of a great oral tradition.

Sterling Stuckey has argued that Harriet Beecher Stowe recorded one of the first blues performances when Truth visited her at Stone Cottage in Andover:

> Her great gloomy eyes and her dark face seemed to work with some undercurrent of feeling; she sighed deeply, and occasionally broke out,—
> "Oh Lord! O Lord! Oh, the tears, an' the groans, an' the moans! O Lord!"[24]

As the enslaved child Isabella, Truth was mothered in this tradition by Mau Mau Bett, who performed the grief of her lineage as a way of binding her children to a communal fate:

> At times, a groan would escape her, and she would break out in the language of the Psalmist—"Oh Lord, how long?" "Oh Lord, how long?" And in reply to Isabella's question—"What ails you, mau-mau?" her only answer was, "Oh, a good deal ails me"—"Enough ails me." (*NarBk*, 17-18)

Although Truth grew up believing that the god "high in the sky" saw her and "wrote down all her actions in a great book," she did not think that he could get inside her head: "she had no idea that God knew a thought of hers till she had uttered it aloud" (*NarBk*, 59). When she wanted to meet God, she went to where she thought he might be and talked out loud to him. Truth told Stowe that, having heard a story in which someone had met God on a threshing floor (perhaps the biblical story of Boas and Ruth), she "threshed down a place real hard, an' I used to go down there every day, an' pray an' cry with all my might."[25]

Her need to speak aloud to God was in conflict with the constraints imposed on the speech of enslaved people, but Truth became certain that if she "were to present her petitions under the open canopy of heaven, speaking very loud," that God would hear her. So that "she could speak louder to God, without being overheard," she built herself a shelter on an island in a stream "by pulling away the branches of the shrubs from the centre, and weaving them together for a wall on the outside, forming a circular arched alcove, made entirely of the graceful willow" (*NarBk*, 60).[26] On such a training ground one of the great orators of the nineteenth century perfected her skills.

Talking aloud was Truth's calling, and her audience was broad. "She held almost hourly converse with, as she supposed, the God of the universe," wrote Lucy Colman.[27] From the refugee camp at Mason's Island in the Potomac during the Civil War, Truth wrote, "I do not know but what I shall stay here on the Island all winter and go around among the Freedmen's camps. They are all *delighted* to hear me talk."[28] With the characteristic reserve of literate black men toward Truth, William Still wondered at her audacity: "She would dauntlessly face the most intelligent and cultivated audiences, or would individually approach the President of the United States as readily as she would one of the humblest citizens."[29] Wendell Phillips praised her power "to move and bear down a whole audience by a few simple words."[30] Her improvisatory style used the material of the moment to incorporate the shifting needs of her audiences into her performances.

At a celebration of the West Indies' Emancipation Day in Abington, Massachusetts in the 1850s Truth appeared on the platform with Charles Lenox Remond, two unnamed enslaved men who were en route to Canada on the Underground Railroad, and "many of the old line [white] abolitionists," including Wendell Phillips, William Lloyd Garrison, Abby Kelley Foster and her husband Stephen, Parker Pillsbury, and Henry C. Wright. One of the fugitive men "arose and in a brief manner expressed his appreciation" to the audience. His words are not recorded. Garrison then announced that Truth would speak in her "peculiar manner":

> Sojourner began by improvising a song, commencing, "Hail! ye abolitionists." Her voice was both sweet and powerful, and as her notes floated away through the tree-tops, reaching the outermost circle of that vast multitude, it elicited cheer after cheer. She then made some spicy remarks, occasionally referring to her fugitive brethren on the platform beside her. At the close of her address, in which by witty sallies and pathetic appeals, she had moved the audience to laughter and tears, she looked about the assemblage and said, "I will now close, for he that cometh after me is greater than I," and took her seat. Mr. Phillips came forward holding a paper in his hand containing notes of Sojourner's speech, which he used as texts for a powerful and eloquent appeal in behalf of human freedom. Sojourner says, "I was utterly astonished to hear him say, 'Well has Sojourner said so and so'; and I said to myself, Lord, did I say that? How differently it sounded coming from his lips! He dressed my poor, bare speech in such beautiful garments that I scarcely recognized it myself." (*NarBk*, 310-11)

Because her words were so often recorded in somebody else's garments, we have lost most of the music of Truth's performance; only certain words remain, here and there. In 1854, in her scathing assessment of white reformers who supported colonizing blacks in Africa, Mary Ann Shadd Cary preserved a fragment of the lost music, referring to "those whom Sojourner Truth delights in calling the 'Shaxon race.'"[31] It seems likely that Stowe's memory of Truth's saying "*amberill*" for "umbrella" is another such sound fragment. Every attempt to textualize Truth is a sort of performance in itself. We cannot expect to recover some unified original text as if it were the woman; but neither should we reject the attempts to perform her by Olive Gilbert, Stowe, Stanton, Frances Gage, or the newspapers.

The most extensively realized attempt to perform Truth up to 1849 is *Narrative of Sojourner Truth, A Northern Slave Emancipated From Bodily Servitude By The State of New York in 1828*,[32] recorded, shaped, and filled with scribal interpolations by Olive Gilbert. Gilbert, a friend of William Lloyd Garrison, had met Truth in the 1840s through the Northampton Association of Education and Industry, a utopian community located in Massachusetts where Truth had gone to live, attracted by its diversified population of reformists. Gilbert shared with such other middle-class white women as Amy Post and Lydia Maria Child a desire to bring the voices of black women before an audience as part of their dedication to abolitionism; but in the voices of articulate black women like Harriet Jacobs and Sojourner Truth, these white experimenters in interracial shared authorship also found opportunities to express themselves. In a self-effacing act of generosity or shyness, Gilbert did not put her own name into *Narrative* in any capacity, not as scribe, compiler, editor, and certainly not as author.

Truth was a storyteller within an African American woman's tradition, and it is surely the echoes of these women we should listen for in her speaking voice. Olive Gilbert had no ear for the kind of "hungry listening" that Zora Neale Hurston knew "helped Janie to tell her story" in *Their Eyes Were Watching God*, although Gilbert may have felt Pheoby's eagerness "to feel and do through Janie."[33] Unable to report what she could not hear, Truth's scribe often missed the resonance of ancestral voices in her utterances. Nevertheless, mediated and filtered through white voices, Truth's *Narrative* is part of the enduring traditional search for a black voice.[34] From the moment the child Isabella is brutally whipped because, although she has a language it is the wrong language, to the moment of her religious conversion when the sound of her speaking voice captivates the divine spirit, the book is a chronicle of developing eloquence.

Narrative's most significant activity is that of transforming an oral tradition into written form, a kind of preservation. An oral story exists in the precise historical moment and in the precise historical situation in which it is told. Writing the story down, in some senses, cuts it loose from history, opens up its use values to individual readers in different historical moments. The complexity of this process converges in the reader's role as a participant in the activity of preservation. There is a need for "hungry listening" on our part, too. Truth was looking for an enabling language, but she was not looking to be entrapped. She itinerates in *Narrative* subverting the text. When we link up with her we become a movement.

Against the grain of the form, Truth can be seen recreating a culture that is separate, unique, and authentic, with its own unique structures of living relationships. Gilbert often does not understand what Truth tells her, and thus cannot fully suppress it. *Narrative* is marked by its element of struggle to render the growth and development of an individual within a marginalized culture to a listener who cannot comprehend the vitality of the culture. For Truth the story-telling form in *Narrative* is natural; she carries within the voices of women who do not write down their experiences, naming them instead to each other with the careful descriptiveness of folk language. A pen-tied Gilbert, trying to record at least some of the reverberations, sensed the importance of the voice and knew that she herself had no letters to express it, that it was not "possible to give the tones and manner with the words; but no adequate idea of them can be written while the tones and manner remain inexpressible" (*NarBk*, 60).

Narrative foregrounds the properties of narrative as acts of memory. Truth tells her story from the "I" perspective, which is then reflected and commented on by Gilbert in the third person. Truth's "I" becomes Gilbert's "she," although this is by no means a simple metamorphosis. Their contending dialogue reveals itself throughout, in interruptions of chronology and through corrections, amplifications, clarifications, second thoughts and deliberate suppressions. As an interactive document, *Narrative* highlights a dynamic of corrective unrest and retrospective remembering of remembering in its self-conscious attempts to establish an authentic and enduring identity for its speaker through the medium of its anonymous scribal voice. Their efforts are both collaborative and resisting, as Truth's recollection, reconstruction, and reconstitution strive against Gilbert's censoring authorial control.

As Gayle Margherita has written, "the beginning of a textualized life is always an aesthetic decision."[35] Gilbert begins with doubt. At the opening point of *Narrative*, "Her Birth and Parentage," Truth's revisionary declaration of her origin in self-naming is called into question: "The subject of this biography, Sojourner Truth, as she now calls herself, but whose name originally was Isabella. . . ."[36] Gilbert searches for Truth's story as a slave woman. Truth enacts herself as a free woman of color. The unequivocal past that Gilbert needs to make Truth intelligible in the slave narrative form is never available to Truth, for whom the past is past and thus no longer unequivocal, but modulated by the pleasures of freedom, the luxuries of forgetting, of enhancing the bittersweet and the bearable, of nostalgia. While Gilbert probed for the nullifying of the human under the slave system, Truth answered for the continuity of value and meaning in the life of the woman, enslaved or free. Olive Gilbert is an anonymous narrator not of the tale of Truth but of the narrative of "Isabella"; Isabella is an unreliable narrator who keeps her counsel, the speaking likeness of Truth's past negotiated between herself and her present interlocutor.

✤   ✤   ✤

The 1850 *Narrative*, published with an unsigned preface by Garrison, consisted of 128 pages. In 1870, Truth's friend Dr. James Boyle made her a gift of the stereotype plates of the book (*NarBk*, 264). The Quaker Frances Titus then entered the story of *Narrative*, providing a second part to Truth's life history. The revised and expanded book was published in 1875.

Perhaps influenced by Harriet Beecher Stowe's documentary approach in *A Key to Uncle Tom's Cabin* (1853), Titus used Truth's correspondence and newspaper accounts, facsimile signatures of famous people from Truth's "Lamb's Book of Life," and a collection of personal anecdotes to establish and document an official activist identity for the woman whose slave identity dominated Gilbert's *Narrative*. She also added the famous essay by Stowe and the account by Frances Gage of Truth's "Ain't I a Woman" speech.

Olive Gilbert had cast the 1850 *Narrative* in the form of a slave narrative, intending, as Garrison wrote in his preface, "that the perusal of the following Narrative may increase the sympathy that is felt for the suffering colored population of this country, and inspire to renewed efforts for the liberation of all who are pining in bondage on the American soil."[37] Frances Titus's rhetorical strategy in 1875 focused on this people's successful passage through the Red Sea out of "the Egypt of their captivity." In her preface, written shortly before Rutherford B. Hayes withdrew the troops from the South and Reconstruction ended, Titus argued that "the promised land" could now "by their own efforts, be obtained":

> Slavery has been swallowed up in a Red Sea of blood, and the slave has emerged from the conflict of races transformed from a chattel to a man. Holding the ballot, the black man enters the halls of legislation, and his rights are recognized there. (*NarBk*, vi-vii)

Frances Watkins Harper saw the historical moment differently in her 1875 address to the Pennsylvania Society for Promoting the Abolition of Slavery. Acknowledging that since "slavery is dead, the colored man has exchanged the fetters on his wrist for the ballot in his hand," Harper still found behind the veil of Southern society "the smell of blood, and our bones scattered at the grave's mouth."

> And yet with all the victories and triumphs which freedom and justice have won in this country, I do not believe there is another civilized nation

under Heaven where there are half as many people who have been brutally and shamefully murdered, with or without impunity, as in this
republic within the last ten years.[38]

Titus's "Part Second," is attached with little ceremony to Gilbert's
Narrative. Thus the reader of the composite *Narrative* and "Book of Life"
leaves Truth on page 122 as a simple primitive with a "naturally powerful
mind," whose "fearlessness and child-like simplicity" and "native enthusiasm" nevertheless add up to a lack, something missing that causes her to
fall short of Joan of Arc (*NarBk*, 121-22). A reader might be surprised to
find Truth on page 130 "in the marble room" of the Senate chamber, then
crusading in the company of the renowned abolitionist orator George
Thompson, and soon afterward entering into history at the Akron
Woman's Rights Convention.

This effect was intentional. In a remarkable opening paragraph, Titus's
gesture of repositioning actually functions as a repudiation of Gilbert's
work:

> The preceding narrative has given us a partial history of Sojourner
> Truth. This biography was published not many years after her freedom
> had been secured to her. Having but recently emerged from the gloomy
> night of slavery, ignorant and untaught in all that gives value to human
> existence, she was still suffering from the burden of acquired and trans-
> mitted habits incidental to her past condition of servitude.

Gilbert's *Narrative,* Titus argues, recorded the false consciousness of a
slave. Titus thus repudiated not just the *Narrative,* but the fifty-three-year-
old Truth who had shaped it. *That* woman had lived in a "moral gutter"
(*NarBk*, 129); Titus proposed to replace her with the story of Truth's second life. Titus's new Truth was a significant reformer among abolitionists
and woman's rights activists, with many testimonials to demonstrate this.
Titus maintained an ongoing friendship with Truth, but had not ceased to
be keenly alert to Truth's rise "from the dregs of social life, like a phenix
[sic] from its ashes, to become the defender of her race" (*NarBk*, 253).

From this opening paragraph issues Titus's struggle for possession of
her subject. Titus's additions and revisions to *Narrative* read as a kind of
future to Gilbert's past, altering the meaning of its muted ending by
embedding it in a new text of triumph and publicity. Presenting the Truth
of 1850 as an incipient celebrity, the author of her own fate, Titus mentions no other author. In a fascinating passive-aggressive arrangement of
correspondence, Titus prints an 1874 letter from Samuel May, inquiring

about Truth's whereabouts and her "health and circumstances." To satisfy "the library of a public institution" he asked "Can you inform me who wrote out (or otherwise compiled) and edited the narrative of Sojourner Truth's life?" (*NarBk*, 276).

Directly following May's letter, Titus placed without comment two brief letters written by Olive Gilbert to Truth fifteen or more years after the publication of *Narrative*. They are rather repressively designated by Titus "Extract From A Letter" and "Another Letter From The Same Person." The letter Titus prints second is undated, but it is probably the earlier of the two, written soon after the end of the Civil War, which brought "the great deliverance of your people from the house of bondage," and it suggests that for many years most of what Gilbert learned of Truth had come from newspapers and magazines. Their distance is marked out in Gilbert's wistful reference to their great collaboration: "Of the little book I wrote for your benefit, some of the copies I took are sold; others I gave to my friends as keep-sakes, &c." (*NarBk*, 278).

In the letter written from Leeds, Massachusetts, 17 January 1870, Gilbert wrote:

> You and I seem to move around as easily as soap bubbles—now here—now there—making our mark, I suppose, everywhere, though mine is a very quiet mark compared to yours. I get a glimpse of you often through the papers, which falls upon my spirit like bright rays from the sun. There is a wee bit of a chapel here, pulpit supplied by a Mr. Merritt, and one evening last fall he repeated something that "Sojourner Truth" had said. I was not there, so I cannot tell what it was. I did not think you were laying the foundation of such an almost world-wide reputation when I wrote that little book for you, but I rejoice and am proud that you can make your power felt with so little book-education. (*NarBk*, 276-77)

The name "Sojourner Truth" seems to echo as if from a great distance in Gilbert's ear. As an interested observer of the making of Truth's reputation, Gilbert details its shaping through the printed word.

> Your call upon Mrs. Stowe, and our dear, sainted president, and your labors connected with the army, and the Freedmen's Bureau, gave you a publicity that enabled me to observe you at your old vocation of helping on and doing good to your fellow-creatures, both physically and mentally. I was much pleased with Mrs. Stowe's enthusiasm over you. You really almost received your apotheosis from her. She proposed, I think, that you should have a statue and symbolize our American Sibyl. (*NarBk*, 277-78)

Ironically, Gilbert's role in producing Truth's *Narrative* was to be effaced by Stowe. Lucy Stone wrote in *Woman's Journal* in 1876 that "For the past few years she has lived in Michigan, supported mainly by the sale of the narrative of her life which was written for her by Mrs. Stowe, and which, during the last year, has been enlarged by Mrs. Frances Titus, of Battle Creek, Michigan."[39] The reputation of the famous essay had overtaken *Narrative* itself, without doing harm to Frances Titus's contribution. On 27 November 1883, the New York *Tribune* carried a dispatch from Battle Creek announcing the death of "Sojourner Truth the colored lecturer and sibyl"; it noted that

> Some years ago Mrs. Harriet Beecher Stowe wrote what is known as Sojourner Truth's "Book of Life," a volume that had an extensive sale among anti-slavery people. In 1876 this book was enlarged and reprinted at the expense of Mrs. Francis W. Titus, of Battle Creek, Mich., where Sojourner lived for many years.[40]

William Wetmore Story's statue of the "Libyan Sibyl," produced after hearing Stowe's description of her visit with Truth (and from which Stowe then borrowed the name to use in her essay), loomed over Frances Titus's conception of Truth.[41] Under the spell of both Story and Stowe, Titus saw the older Truth as "true to the character of sibyl."

> And when her free black hands were raised to heaven, invoking blessings upon her country, it was a fairer sight to see and a surer guarantee of its permanence and glory than was the imposing spectacle of that beauteous "queen of the East," upon whose snowy, perfect hands the golden chains of slavery shone, as she entered the gates of the eternal city, leading the triumphant procession of a Caesar. (*NarBk*, 254-55)

Titus's fantastical juxtaposition of the supplicating Truth's "free black hands" with the "snowy" (sic) hands of the enchained Cleopatra referred to the (white) marble Libyan Sibyl and its companion piece, the (white) marble statue of Cleopatra exhibited by Story at the World Exposition in London in 1862. A reader might feel that the Truth of Olive Gilbert's time had been wholly crushed under the weight of Titus's titanic prose.

As members of overlapping circles of spiritualists, woman's rights activists, and reform-minded workers for black refugees, Titus and Truth came to know each other well after Truth moved to Michigan around

1857. Titus traveled with Truth to Kansas to see the Exodusters in 1879.[42] Her selection of newspaper clippings and letters allow wonderful insight into the surprising webs of interest that bound together a hetero-geneous and far-flung group of reform-minded activists during a historic period of Truth's life, although we always wish we could know what she elected not to include. Paradoxically, Titus's documentary approach to Truth's history is belied by her prose, in which Truth is exhibited as a mystery shrouded in facts, a creature of prehistory on whom a history is being imposed.

Sometimes Titus seemed deaf to history. Her continual tampering with Truth's age is a heedlessly cruel play on one of the worst realities of slav-ery, the absence of any birth record with its implication of the exclusion of the enslaved from the processes of history. In her deliberate revision of Gilbert's dating, Titus buried Truth's birth in the far reaches of time:

> She is as ignorant of its date as is the fossil found in the limestone rock or the polished pebble upon the sea-shore, which has been scoured by the waves ever since the sea was born. (*NarBk*, 307)

Truth recognized that writing fossilizes. When Theodore Tilton pro-posed to write her life, Truth "replied in effect that she expected to live a long time yet, and was going to accomplish 'lots' before she died, and didn't wan't to be 'written up' at present" (*NarBk*, 234). Unlike Harriet Jacobs, who was able to prevent Harriet Beecher Stowe from using inci-dents from her life in *A Key to Uncle Tom's Cabin*, Truth had to live with the romantic racialist portrait of her produced by "the Great Lady." Stowe wrote, "I do not recollect ever to have been conversant with any one who had more of that silent and subtle power which we call personal presence than this woman"; Truth had "a strong sphere," she added, using the lan-guage of spiritualism. "So, this is *you*," had been Truth's response directly on meeting Stowe. Stowe could see Truth only through many stages of mediation:

> She was evidently a full-blooded African, and though now aged and worn with many hardships, still gave the impression of a physical devel-opment which in early youth must have been as fine a specimen of the torrid zone as Cumberworth's celebrated statuette of the Negro Woman at the Fountain. Indeed, she so strongly reminded me of that figure, that, when I recall the events of her life, as she narrated them to me, I imagine her as a living, breathing impersonation of that work of art.[43]

Statues! Not just a work of art, but an "impersonation" of a work of art! Perhaps hearing this, Truth felt something of Robert Purvis's dismay in 1852 when he read Stowe's endorsement of colonization in the closing chapter of *Uncle Tom's Cabin*: "Alas!" he exclaimed, "save us from our friends."[44]

Speaking to a correspondent to the *Advertiser and Tribune* in 1864, Truth expressed exasperation with the persistence of Stowe's image of her as the "Libyan Sibyl":

> She would never listen to Mrs. Stowe's Libyan Sibyl. "Oh!" she would say, "I don't want to hear about that old symbol; read me something that is going on *now*, something about this great war."

"She was then full of intense interest in the war," the correspondent continued, "and foresaw its result in the emancipation of her race. It was touching to see her eager face when the newspapers were read in her presence" (*NarBk*, 174).

The flexible, shifting, shared foci of consciousness (observer-reporter, observer-participant, observer-observed) in *Narrative* incorporated the triad of voices of Truth, Gilbert, and then Titus. The mythmaking rhetoric of Titus invites us to imagine them as triple goddesses of the past, present, and future, shaping the life history of *Narrative*, spinning, measuring, splicing the loose threads of the lived life into a whole. Truth, mythologized as older than time, acted as the spinner, Gilbert and Titus apportioned the episodes and brought the story to its conclusion with a description of Truth's last illness and death, recounted in the memorial chapter Titus added to the 1884 edition.

Yet the hard facts of production were otherwise. While the book was composed by Gilbert and by Titus, Truth spoke much of it and collected most of its documentary materials. Abolitionist supporters such as Garrison, James Boyle, and Olive Gilbert may have wanted the book to exist for the good it would do the antislavery cause; advocates of various reform causes, the New York *Herald* sneered in 1853, were "continually advertising from their platforms some 'Thrilling Narrative.'"[45] But the book was a product of Truth's labor both in its making and its distribution. The cost of its production was ultimately borne by Truth. Like Jarena Lee, who had paid thirty-eight dollars for the printing of her narrative in 1836 and distributed it on the street and at camp meetings, Truth sold her book at abolitionist and feminist meetings wherever she traveled.[46] "I had been publishing my *Narrative*," she wrote about her decision in 1851 to travel and speak with the British antislavery speaker George Thompson, "and now indebted to Mr. Yerrington for the printing," she wrote at the end of the summer to William Lloyd Garrison, anxious that she had sold only a few books but expecting to sell as many as six hundred at upcoming conventions.[48]

When Truth wrote to James Redpath at *The Commonwealth* following the publication of Stowe's essay in 1863, she sent him copies of *Narrative*, which he excerpted for his readers. She was not at the time able to travel to sell her book.

> I have sold my books for twenty-five cents apiece. I will send you six copies today, and I am much obliged to you. You will find them correct, they are Sojourner herself. Isaac Post's wife from Rochester, has sent for two dozen of my photographs, and now that I cannot do anything, I am living on my shadow. I used to travel and sell my books, but now I am not able to do that, I send whatever is requested of me. If you can dispose of any for me I would be very much obliged to you. I will put no price on them, let them give whatever they choose to. Please let me know if you received my books. I remain your friend. May heaven bless us.
>
> Yours Respectfully,
> Sojourner Truth.

In her late seventies, having mortgaged her Battle Creek house to pay for the funeral of her grandson, a beloved companion who had been her favorite reader and writer, Truth was advertising the new expanded edition of *Narrative*, hoping "that she may be able to liquidate old debts, and have a little competency for coming days."

> Sojourner Truth now appeals to *true friends*, wherever they are to immediately assist her, in selling her *new work* which has just been printed and is now in the hand of the binder. It is an *octavo volume* of 320 pages, good paper, and well bound, correct portrait, and has three pages of engraved autographs of the women and men who have aided her in her work. Price of the work $1.25, post paid.[49]

She wrote to William Still in 1876 that she hoped to sell the enlarged edition of *Narrative* during the Centennial celebration in Philadelphia, explaining that she owed Frances Titus several hundred dollars for the printing expenses. She referred to Frances Titus as "the lady that wrote my book."[50]

Writing in 1808, the period of Truth's childhood, the biographer Anne Grant laid out the problem of constructing a truthful narrative of her friend Margarita Schuyler, a Dutch settler living in eighteenth-century Albany. In *Memoirs of An American Lady*, Grant stressed the biographer's "dread of being inaccurate":

> Embellished facts, a mixture of truth and fiction, or what we some-
> times meet with, a fictitious superstructure built on a foundation of real-
> ity, would be detestable on the score of bad taste, though no moral sense
> were concerned or consulted. 'Tis walking on a river half frozen that
> betrays your footing every moment. By these repulsive artifices no person
> of real discernment is for a moment imposed upon. You do not know
> which part of the narrative is false; but you are sure it is not all true, and
> therefore distrust what is genuine where it occurs. For this reason a fic-
> tion, happily told, takes a greater hold of the mind than a narrative of
> facts, evidently embellished and interwoven with inventions.[51]

We embrace her fears gladly. It was exactly the climate of distrust engendered by the interplay of invention and fact that opened some space for the chief embellisher and weaver of fantasies in the printed accounts of Truth—Truth herself. Olive Gilbert could not make up her mind about Truth, whose complexly shifting shadow scattered under her pen. On the one hand, Gilbert admired her "bright, clear, positive, and at times ecsta-tic" religion, which "is not tinctured in the least with gloom." On the other hand, on a personal level, she saw that Truth "has set suspicion to guard the door of her heart" (*NarBk*, 122), an alarming tendency in the subject of a biography.

Truth's guarded interiorization disturbed Gilbert. Suppressed interior-izations of black women populate the pages of abolitionist literature. Elizabeth Cady Stanton described an encounter at the house of abolitionist Gerrit Smith, which was a depot of the Underground Railroad:

> One day Mr. Smith summoned all the young girls then visiting there,
> saying he had a great secret to tell them if they would sacredly pledge
> themselves not to divulge it. Having done so, he led the way to the third
> story, ushered us into a large room, and there stood a beautiful quadroon
> girl to receive us. "Harriet," said Mr. Smith, "I want you to make good
> Abolitionists of these girls by describing to them all you have suffered in
> slavery." He then left the room, locking us in. Her narrative held us

spell-bound until the lengthening shadows of the twilight hour made her departure safe for Canada. One remark she made impressed me deeply. I told her of the laws for women such as we then lived under, and remarked on the parallel condition of slaves and women. "Yes," said she, "but I am both. I am doubly damned in sex and color. Yes, in class too, for I am poor and ignorant; none of you can ever touch the depth of misery where I stand to-day."[52]

Complexities of framed response emerge. Gerrit Smith had authorized a paternalist discourse in which the white girls locked into the room with the "beautiful quadroon" were to be made into abolitionists. He framed them as subject to his will and as objects of his efforts at moral improvement. They were to order their relation to the black woman as liberator to exemplary slave, perhaps on the model of the famous abolitionist slogan, "Am I not a woman and a sister?" Stanton, the white female narrator (locked in), reordered the scene in terms of woman's rights, citing "the parallel condition of slaves and women," disobeying patriarchal law by repositioning the women side by side instead of hierarchically. Then, in a startling rejection of both these constructions, the objectified enslaved woman rejects their inscription of her in their stories and speaks her own story: "none of you can ever touch the depth of misery where I stand to-day."

Having been authorized to speak as an abolitionist's model slave and then as a white woman's sister in suffering, Harriet rejected ventriloquism to speak her own truth about race, gender, and class. Even when framed by the expectations of white recorders, black women like Harriet and Truth knew how to step out of the frame. They cast their own shadows. They raised their own voices. This is what we watch for, what we listen for.

Notes

1. [Sojourner Truth with Olive Gilbert and Frances Titus], *Narrative of Sojourner Truth; A Bondswoman of Olden Time, Emancipated by the New York Legislature in the Early Part of the Present Century; With a History of Her Labors and Correspondence Drawn from Her "Book of Life"* (New York: Arno Press and The New York Times, 1968 [1878]), 203. Unless otherwise noted, all references are to this edition and are abbreviated *NarBk*. This edition is still available from Ayer Company Publishers, Inc., Salem, New Hampshire.
2. Sojourner Truth to Amy Post, 1 October 1865, The Isaac and Amy Post Family Papers, Department of Rare Books and Special Collections, University of Rochester Library, Rochester, New York. Subsequent references to this collection are abbreviated IAPFP, UR.

3. Quoted in Lillie Buffum Chace Wyman, *American Chivalry* (Boston: Clarke, 1913), 107.

4. Elizabeth Cady Stanton, et al., eds., *History of Woman Suffrage* (New York: Fowler & Wells, 1881-1922), 2:926.

5. See Karma Lochrie, *Margery Kempe and Translations of the Flesh* (Philadelphia: University of Pennsylvania Press, 1991), 102. Chapter three, "From Utterance to Text: Authorizing the Mystical Word" (97-134) is especially useful. See also Erlene Stetson, "Studying Slavery: Some Literary and Pedagogical Considerations on the Black Female Slave," in *All the Women Are White, All the Blacks Are Men, But Some of Us Are Brave*, edited by Gloria T. Hull, Patricia Bell Scott, and Barbara Smith (Old Westbury, New York: The Feminist Press, 1982), 68-69.

6. See E. P. Thompson, *The Making of the English Working Class* (New York: Vintage Books, 1966), 711-13.

7. Truth to "My Dear Daughter," 3 November 1864, IAPFP, UR.

8. *National Anti-Slavery Standard*, 27 April 1867.

9. Rebecca Cox Jackson, *Gifts of Power: The Writings of Rebecca Jackson, Black Visionary, Shaker Eldress*, edited by Jean McMahon Humez (Amherst: University of Massachusetts Press, 1981), 107.

10. Harriet Beecher Stowe, "Sojourner Truth, the Libyan Sibyl," *Atlantic Monthly* 11 (April 1863): 474.

11. *National Anti-Slavery Standard*, 17 December 1864.

12. Stanton, et al., *History of Woman Suffrage*, 2:926-28.

13. Lochrie, *Margery Kempe and Translations of the Flesh*, 102-4.

14. Stanton, et al., *History of Woman Suffrage*, 2:926-27.

15. Ibid., 2:927-28.

16. Ibid., 2:193.

17. Ibid., 2:219.

18. Ibid., 2:928.

19. Ibid., 2:245. For the Kansas campaign, see Eric Foner, *Reconstruction: America's Unfinished Revolution 1863-1877* (New York: Harper & Row, 1988), 447-48.

20. Gerda Lerner, ed. *The Female Experience: An American Documentary* (Indianapolis: Bobbs-Merrill, 1977), 490-93.

21. *Woman's Journal*, 5 August 1876, 252. For a fascinating discussion of Anna Murray Douglass's refusal to learn to read and Frederick Douglass's commitment to "heroic literacy," see Jenny Franchot, "The Punishment of Esther: Frederick Douglass and the Construction of the Feminine," in *Frederick Douglass: New Literary and Historical Essays*, edited by Eric J. Sundquist (Cambridge: Cambridge University Press, 1990), 141-65, especially 162-63n.26.

22. Audre Lorde, "The Master's Tools Will Never Dismantle The Master's House," in *Sister Outsider: Essays & Speeches* (Freedom, California: The Crossing Press, 1984), 112.

23. Stanton, et al., *History of Woman Suffrage*, 2:926. See the discussion of literacy as "Western culture's trope of dominance over the peoples of color it had

'discovered,' colonized, and enslaved since the fifteenth century," in Henry Louis Gates, Jr., *The Signifying Monkey: A Theory of Afro-American Literary Criticism* (New York: Oxford University Press, 1988), 165; chapter four, "The Trope of the Talking Book" (127-69) is relevant here.

24. Stowe, "Sojourner Truth, the Libyan Sibyl," 474. For Truth as a blues performer see Sterling Stuckey's Foreword in [Sojourner Truth, with Olive Gilbert and Frances Titus], *Narrative of Sojourner Truth: A Bondswoman of Olden Time, Emancipated by the New York Legislature in the Early Part of the Present Century With a History of Her Labors and Correspondence Drawn from her Book of Life* (Chicago: Johnson Publishing Company, 1970 [1878]), vii-viii.

25. Stowe, "Sojourner Truth, the Libyan Sibyl," 475.

26. See the description of "hush-harbors" for secret prayers and meetings in Lawrence W. Levine, *Black Culture and Black Consciousness: Afro-American Folk Thought from Slavery to Freedom* (New York: Oxford University Press, 1977), 41-42. Isabella's prayer shelter is reminiscent of the "little booth, made neatly of palm-leaves and covered in at top, a regular African hut," built by the soldiers as a place to conduct their "shout," described in Thomas Wentworth Higginson, *Army Life in a Black Regiment* (East Lansing: Michigan State University Press, 1960 [1870]), 13.

27. Lucy N. Colman, *Reminiscences* (Buffalo: H. L. Green, 1891), 65. Colman, like Stowe, regarded Truth as "what the Spiritualists call mediumistic, but her 'control' was God."

28. Truth to "My Dear Daughter," 3 November 1864, IAPFP, UR.

29. Stowe, "Sojourner Truth, the Libyan Sibyl," 480.

30. *Evening Bulletin*, 28 July 1876.

31. This is from Mary Ann Shadd Cary's "The Humbug of Reform," an editorial originally published in *Provincial Freeman* on 27 May 1854, quoted in C. Peter Ripley, et al., eds., *The Black Abolitionist Papers* (Chapel Hill: University of North Carolina Press, 1985), 2:286.

32. [Sojourner Truth with Olive Gilbert], *Narrative of Sojourner Truth, A Northern Slave Emancipated From Bodily Servitude By The State of New York in 1828* (Boston: Printed for the author, 1850). The "writer" is identified only as a "lady." A printer's note facing the opening page states simply: "It is due to the lady by whom the following Narrative was kindly written, to state, that she has not been able to see a single proof-sheet of it; consequently, it is very possible that divers errors in printing may have occurred, (though it is hoped none materially affecting the sense,) especially in regard to the names of individuals referred to therein. The name of Van Wagener should read Van Wagenen."

33. Zora Neale Hurston, *Their Eyes Were Watching God* (New York: Harper & Row, 1990 [1937]), 10 and 6.

34. Gates, *The Signifying Monkey*, 169.

35. Gayle Margherita, *The Romance of Origins: Language and Sexual Difference in Middle English Literature* (Philadelphia: University of Pennsylvania Press, 1994), chapter one, "Marjery Kempe and the Pathology of Writing."

36. [Truth with Gilbert], *Narrative of Sojourner Truth* (1850).

37. Garrison's preface is reprinted as an appendix in the excellent new edition of *Narrative of Sojourner Truth*, edited by Margaret Washington (New York: Vintage Classics, 1993), 124.

38. "Address to the Centennial Anniversary of the Pennsylvania Society for Promoting the Abolition of Slavery," 14 April 1875, in Janey Weinhold Montgomery, *A Comparative Analysis of the Rhetoric of Two Negro Women Orators—Sojourner Truth and Frances E. Watkins Harper* (Hays: Fort Hays Kansas State College, 1968), 107-10.

39. *Woman's Journal*, 5 August 1876.

40. *Tribune*, 27 November 1883.

41. For Story's description of the statues, see Henry James, *William Wetmore Story and His Friends* (Boston: Houghton, Mifflin & Co., 1904), 2:70-73.

42. Kathleen Collins discusses Titus's interest in artistic images of Truth, providing fascinating information on Truth's last years ("Shadow and Substance: Sojourner Truth," *History of Photography* 7, no. 3 [July-September 1983]:192-93). See Carlton Mabee and Susan Mabee Newhouse, *Sojourner Truth: Slave, Prophet, Legend* (New York: New York University Press, 1993), 200-8, for details of the Titus-Truth relationship and the "network of Michigan friends" of which Titus and Truth were a part.

43. Stowe, "Sojourner Truth, the Libyan Sibyl," 473. For Harriet Jacobs's discouraging contact with Stowe, see the letters printed in Harriet A. Jacobs, *Incidents in the Life of a Slave Girl, Written by Herself*, edited by Jean Fagan Yellin (Cambridge: Harvard University Press, 1987), 233-35. Harriet Jacobs referred to Stowe as "the Great Lady."

44. Robert Purvis to Oliver Johnson, *Pennsylvania Freeman*, 29 April 1852, quoted in Ripley, et al., *The Black Abolitionist Papers*, 4:124. Truth did complain to James Redpath that Stowe had misrepresented her style: "I related a story to her and she has put it on me, for I never make use of the word honey." (*The Commonwealth*, 3 July 1863).

45. Stanton, et al., *History of Woman Suffrage*, 1:556.

46. See William L. Andrews, ed. *Sisters of the Spirit: Three Black Women's Autobiographies of the Nineteenth Century* (Bloomington: Indiana University Press, 1986), 6.

47. Truth to William Lloyd Garrison, 11 April 1864, Boston Public Library.

48. Truth to William Lloyd Garrison, 28 August 1851, Boston Public Library.

49. Quoted by Collins from a newspaper clipping pasted inside the 1875 edition of the *Narrative* in the Pattee Library of Pennsylvania State University ("Shadow and Substance," 200).

50. Mabee and Newhouse, *Sojourner Truth*, 210-11.

51. Anne MacVicar Grant, *Memoirs of An American Lady. With Sketches of Manners and Scenes in America As They Existed Previous to the Revolution* (New York: Dodd, Mead and Co., 1903).

52. Stanton, et al., *History of Woman Suffrage*, 1:471.

Two

The Country of the Slave

I come from another field—the country of the slave.
Sojourner Truth, 1867[1]

When Sojourner Truth spoke of her ancestors, she spoke in a general way as many African Americans might speak: We came from Africa. What she allowed her audience, for example in the remarks Harriet Beecher Stowe attributed to her in their 1853 meeting, was the general truth of African American historical experience.

> You see we was all brought over from Africa, father an' mother and I, an' a lot more of us; an' we was sold up an' down, an' hither an' yon.[2]

Truth wrote to James Redpath of the Boston *Commonwealth* shortly after the publication of Stowe's essay to correct the assertion that "she was evidently a full-blooded African"[3]:

> The history which Mrs. Stowe wrote about me, is not quite correct. There is one place where she speaks of me as coming from Africa. My grandmother and my husband's mother came from Africa, but I did not; she must have misunderstood me, but you will find my book a correct history.[4]

In a New York newspaper account of one of her later lectures, which dwelled on her autobiographical statements, Truth is said to have "narrated the history of her mother-in-law, who was stolen from her native land in Africa and brought to this country and sold into bondage" (*NarBk*, 209). Although Truth sent Redpath her *Narrative* and called it "correct," it is correct simply because it does not consider her ancestry. Olive Gilbert was not interested in establishing Truth's *African* roots or antecedents, specifically or generally. She was interested only in their function in her moral tale of slavery and its effects. Abolitionists were, above all, interested in the stories of white people: the *American* stories of white enslavers.[5]

Sojourner Truth was born to Elizabeth, the third wife of James Bomefree, in the state of New York at the end of the eighteenth century. Since her parents were enslaved, the infant, named Isabella, was enslaved at birth under a New York state law dating from 1706. Although there is no record of it, Truth placed her birth "as near as she can calculate between the years 1797 and 1800."[6] The year 1797 is likely based on the testimony of her former masters. A letter dated 1834 by her last owner-employer, Isaac S. Van Wagenen of Wahkendahl in Ulster County, mentions that he had known her since infancy, and another by her New Paltz, Ulster County owner John J. Dumont comes closest to suggesting a birth year. Writing on 13 October 1834, Dumont said that Isabella had lived with him "since the year 1810" and that "at the time she came here she was between 12 and 14 years of age."[7]

If Truth was born in 1797, she could have been Phillis Wheatley's daughter or granddaughter. By any accounting she would have been only recently emancipated at the time of Nat Turner's slave insurrection in Virginia in 1831. She was a nearly exact contemporary of Maria Miller Stewart, who was born in 1803 and died four years before Truth in 1879.

The estate of Isabella's first owner, the Dutchman Colonel Johannes Hardenburgh, was located on the banks of the North River in Hurley, not far from Swatakill in Ulster County. Hurley, a hilly upland town, was originally called Nieu Dorp (New Village) by Dutch settlers who created it from an Indian treaty around 1660, which was ratified by the English government after 1667. The Hardenburgh family was among seventy-five families who petitioned for land grants as early as 1706, and the historic Hardenburgh Patent, granted in 1708-1709, included mainly the county of Sullivan and part of Delaware. By the time of Truth's birth, the Hardenburghs had been nearly a century in the founding and settlement of Hurley.[8]

When Hardenburgh died, his son Charles became the owner of Isabella's family. The misery of the damp cellar where they came to live is described in the *Narrative*:

> Among Isabella's earliest recollections was the removal of her master, Charles Ardinburgh [sic], into his new house, which he had built for a

hotel, soon after the decease of his father. A cellar, under this hotel, was assigned to his slaves, as their sleeping apartment,—all the slaves he possessed, of both sexes, sleeping (as is quite common in a state of slavery) in the same room. She carries in her mind, to this day, a vivid picture of this dismal chamber; its only lights consisting of a few panes of glass, through which she thinks the sun never shone, but with thrice reflected rays; and the space between the loose boards of the floor, and uneven earth below, was often filled with mud and water, the uncomfortable splashings of which were as annoying as its noxious vapors must have been chilling and fatal to health. (*NarBk*, 14)

They were a closely-knit extended family; Isabella's Uncle Caesar, brother of Bett, and his wife Betsey lived on the Hardenburgh property. Isabella's parents talked among themselves about slavery and their servitude. They were realists first and foremost.

She distinctly remembers hearing her father and mother say that their lot was a fortunate one, as Master Charles was the best of the family,—being, comparatively speaking, a kind master to his slaves. (*NarBk*, 13)

"Strangers in a strange land," as Truth would often refer to her people, her parents endowed the present with the living quality of the past during story times in "their dark cellar lighted by a blazing pine-knot" (*NarBk*, 16).

Stories of the past were the devices by which Isabella's mother instilled in the children a sense of connection and through which she attempted to bridge the intolerable gaps in their relations opened up by the violence of slave masters. They often told "histories of those dear departed ones," the little brother and sister forcibly taken for sale elsewhere:

Among the rest, they would relate how the little boy, on the last morning he was with them, arose with the birds, kindled a fire, calling for his Mau-mau to "come, for all was now ready for her"—little dreaming of the dreadful separation which was so near at hand, but of which his parents had an uncertain, but all the more cruel foreboding. There was snow on the ground, at the time of which we are speaking; and a large old-fashioned sleigh was seen to drive up to the door of the late Col. Ardinburgh. This event was noticed with childish pleasure by the unsuspicious boy; but when he was taken and put into the sleigh, and saw his little sister actually shut and locked into the sleigh box, his eyes were at once opened to their intentions; and like a frightened deer he sprang from the sleigh and running into the house, concealed himself under a bed. (*NarBk*, 16)

Such created memories, with their concrete details and poignant narrative associations were inscribed in Isabella's memory, as closely written as a birth certificate or bill of sale. Frances Smith Foster has noted the integral function of the episode of "tearing of children from their parents" in the depiction of black women as victims in slave narratives told by men.[9] In Truth's *Narrative* the episode functions instead to show the extraordinary resilience of a black family, encircled by "the chain of family affection" forged by Bett's stories. The post-emancipation New York City drew like a magnet four of the siblings, Truth, Sophia, Nancy ("the self same sister that had been locked in the great old fashioned sleigh-box, when she was taken away, never to behold her mother's face again this side of the spirit-land"), and Michael ("the brother who had shared her fate"). Nancy died before Truth learned her identity, but at the African Zion Church Truth had "recognized her as a sister in the church, with whom she had knelt at the altar, and with whom she had exchanged the speaking pressure of the hand, in recognition of their spiritual sisterhood." Truth remembers that touch: "and was I not, at the time, struck with the peculiar feeling of her hand—the bony hardness so just like mine?" (*NarBk*, 80-81). In the intensity of her grief she memorializes the material achievement of her mother in passing on flesh, bone, and spirit.

African traditions shaped Isabella's sacred world view, which was dominated not by concepts and symbols, but by sacred place and sacred personage. "Her mother often told her of God, and her impressions were that God was a very large human being, who sat in the skies" (*NarBk*, 208). The description of Mau Mau Bett introducing her children to the God that lives in the sky is a compelling one:

> In the evening, when her mother's work was done, she would sit down under the sparkling vault of heaven, and calling her children to her, would talk to them of the only Being that could effectually aid or protect them. Her teachings were delivered in Low Dutch, her only language, and, translated into English, ran nearly as follows:—
>
> "My children, there is a God, who hears and sees you." "A *God*, mau-mau! Where does he live?" asked the children. "He lives in the sky," she replied; "and when you are beaten, or cruelly treated, or fall into any trouble, you must ask help of him, and he will always hear and help you." (*NarBk*, 17)

This God, the children were told, had made the moon and stars, by which they could situate themselves, even if they were all sold far from each other. By fixing their physical presence under the "canopy," however far they might be separated from each other, Mau Mau Bett enabled her children to position themselves in the world of their present experiences and prepare them for its particular horrors.

Although Gilbert writes that the children were taught "to kneel and say the Lord's prayer," a reader may wonder if Bett's God was closer to the God known to the Moslem Abu Bakr al-Siddiq of Timbuktu (1790-1841). Al-Siddiq, "a slave for nearly thirty years in Jamaica," prayed

> As God Almighty Himself has said, "Nothing can befall us unless it is written for us." He is our Master. In God, therefore, let all the faithful put their trust.[10]

Bett's solitary, outdoor, evening prayers (her "groans," as they are described in the *Narrative*), in the pantheistic context of moon and stars, issued from deeply-rooted African Traditional or Islamic religion. Through interaction between past and present, these traditions were being transformed into a new African American Christianity, as displaced African peoples converted the Christian God to themselves.[11]

When Isabella was nine or ten years old, Charles Hardenburgh died. Hardenburgh's heirs freed Isabella's father James, who was now too frail to work, and they considered selling Mau Mau Bett; in the end it seemed more expedient to "free" her to care for James in the "dark, humid cellar" (*NarBk*, 19). Isabella and her younger brother Peter were sold away. Isabella was auctioned off for the price of one hundred dollars and a flock of sheep to John Nealy of Ulster County. Nealy, a Yankee from Massachusetts, was by Isabella's own account a cruel and sadistic master, who chiefly wanted, by owning a slave, to improve his relations with his Low Dutch neighbors.

> Then she suffered "*terribly—terribly*," with the cold. During the winter her feet were badly frozen, for want of proper covering. They gave her a plenty to eat, and also a plenty of whippings. One Sunday morning, in particular, she was told to go to the barn; on going there, she found her master with a bundle of rods, prepared in the embers, and with cords. When he had tied her hands together before her, he gave her the most cruel whipping she was ever tortured with. He whipped her till the flesh was deeply lacerated, and the blood streamed from her wounds—and the scars remain to the present day, to testify to the fact.

The child spoke only Dutch, angering her English-speaking mistress: "If they sent me for a frying-pan, not knowing what they meant, perhaps I carried them the pot-hooks and trammels. Then, oh! how angry mistress would be with me!" (*NarBk*, 26). After remaining only a few months with Nealy, Isabella asked her father to find her a new owner.

> When she had been at Mr. Nealy's several months, she began to beg God most earnestly to send her father to her, and as soon as she commenced to pray, she began as confidently to look for his coming, and, ere it was long, to her great joy, he came. She had no opportunity to speak to him of the troubles that weighed so heavily on her spirit, while he remained; but when he left, she followed him to the gate, and unburdened her heart to him, inquiring if he could not do something to get her a new and better place. In this way the slaves often assist each other, by ascertaining who are kind to their slaves, comparatively; and then using their influence to get such an one to hire or buy their friends; and masters, often from policy, as well as from latent humanity, allow those they are about to sell or let, to choose their own places, if the persons they happen to select for masters are considered safe *pay*. (*NarBk*, 27-28)[12]

Isabella's description of returning again and again to the place where they had last spoken evokes a young child's trust in her father and has the quality of ritual, as if re-performance could effect a favorable outcome to her suit.

> He promised to do all he could, and they parted. But, every day, as long as the snow lasted, (for there was snow on the ground at the time,) she returned to the spot where they separated, and walking in the tracks her father had made in the snow, repeated her prayer that "God would help her father get her a new and better place." (*NarBk*, 27-28)

Her father was successful. Before long a man came to Nealy's farm and asked "if she would like to go and live with him."

> She eagerly answered "Yes," nothing doubting but he was sent in answer to her prayer; and she soon started off with him, walking while he rode; for he had bought her at the suggestion of her father, paying one hundred and five dollars for her. (*NarBk*, 28)

No other story in the *Narrative* captures more fully the qualities of strength of will, optimism, and seemingly ineradicable trust in tomorrow that so characterized the adult Truth.[13]

Isabella's new owner, Martin Schryver, an Ulster County tavern-keeper, farmer, and fisherman who lived six miles from Nealy, took her to "a rude, uneducated family, exceedingly profane in their language, but, on the whole, an honest, kind, and well-disposed people" (*NarBk*, 28). Isabella helped Schryver in his tavern, where she first heard the dancers singing the song "Washington's Ball," which features the planting of a liberty tree, and which she sang long after.[14] Here she lived "a wild, out-of-door kind of life"; she carried fish, hoed corn, and searched the woods for roots and herbs to be used in beer-making. When she was sent "to the Strand for a gallon of molasses or liquor," she would "browse around." She had spent a year and a half with Schryver when he suffered a financial setback and sold her "for the sum of seventy pounds," about three hundred dollars, to John J. Dumont of New Paltz (*NarBk*, 28-29).

The moral imperative that shaped Gilbert's narrative did not allow Truth the leisure to cast her mind back to family or friends except to exhibit them as victims, not survivors. Although *Narrative* does not clarify this, Truth later said "I have had two husbands yet I never possessed one of my own."[15] It is probable that Isabella had a marital relation to Bob, a man enslaved at a neighboring farm, and that Bob was the father of her first child, Diana.[16] The existence of the child may explain why their relation was brutally terminated by Robert's master, who was "anxious that no one's property but his own should be enhanced by the increase of his slaves." When Bob tried to see Isabella, his master beat him so sadistically that blood covered him "like a slaughtered beast" and he was tied up and forced back to his master's farm (*NarBk*, 34-35). Truth seems to have been referring to this when she told an audience in 1853 that "her husband's blood had flowed till it could be traced for a mile on the snow."[17]

Around 1817, Isabella was married to Thomas, a man much older than herself who was enslaved by Dumont. Olive Gilbert's disapproval of what she saw as the travesty of slave marriage allows us to see through to Thomas's tragedy; he "had previously had two wives, one of whom, if not both, had been torn from him and sold far away."

We have said, Isabella was married to Thomas—she was, after the fashion of slavery, one of the slaves performing the ceremony for them; as no true minister of Christ *can* perform, as in the presence of God, what he knows to be a mere *farce*, a *mock* marriage, unrecognized by any civil law, and liable to be annulled any moment, when the interest or caprice of the master should dictate. (*NarBk*, 36-37)

Her strong feeling about the issue of slave marriage provokes Gilbert to make a rare reference to her personal experience: "the writer of this knows from personal observation, that such is the custom among slaveholders at the present day; and that in a twenty months' residence among them, we never knew any one to open the lip against the practice; and when we severely censured it, the slaveholder had nothing to say; and the slave pleaded that, under existing circumstances, he could do no better" (*NarBk*, 36). Although Gilbert sees such slave marriages as promiscuous, historians have better characterized the relationships of people like Thomas, whose companions were repeatedly sold away, as serial monogamy.[18] Dumont's practice of selling off family members emerges in the story of Thomas, who had rebelled "after one of *his* wives had been sold away from him," escaping to New York City, where he had managed to live as a fugitive for one or two years until the slave catchers caught him and returned him to the farm (*NarBk*, 82). After emancipation, Thomas lived in the abjectest poverty "and died in the poorhouse" (*NarBk*, 71).

Besides Diana, Isabella gave birth to four other children, Peter, James, Elizabeth, and Sophia.[19] Continuing the family naming practices that insured a kind of continuity in their constantly fragmenting world, Elizabeth carried on the name of Truth's mother, James was named for Truth's father; Diana and Sophia were named for Truth's sisters; Peter carried on the name of Truth's youngest brother.

As both a reproductive producer and a field worker, Isabella kept her children with her in the fields; perhaps an African tradition survived in Isabella's way of keeping her child when she worked in the fields:

> When Isabella went to the field to work, she used to put her infant in a basket, tying a rope to each handle, and suspending the basket to a branch of a tree, set another small child to swing it. It was thus secure from reptiles, and was easily administered to, and even lulled to sleep, by a child too young for other labors. (*NarBk*, 38)

Whether simply a mother's inventiveness, a Native American practicality, or a useful syncretistic African adaptation to an American reality,[20] the ingenuity of the practice struck Gilbert, who viewed it with curious eyes.

Gilbert says little about the births of the children except as illustrations of Isabella's "state of chattelism":

> In process of time, Isabella found herself the mother of five children, and she rejoiced in being permitted to be the instrument of increasing the property of her oppressors! Think, dear reader, without a blush, if you

can, for one moment, of a *mother* thus willingly, and with *pride*, laying her own children, the "flesh of her flesh," on the altar of slavery—a sacrifice to the bloody Moloch! But we must remember that beings capable of such sacrifices are not mothers; they are only "things," "chattels," "property." (*NarBk*, 37)

Fanny Kemble also believed this unlikely assurance from her husband's obliging female slaves that they were proud to produce infant slaves for Massa: "They have all of them a most distinct and perfect knowledge of their value to their owners as property."[21] "I have had five children," Truth said in 1856, "and never could take any one of dem up and say 'my child,' or 'my children,' unless it was when no one could see me."[22]

If little is written about Isabella's relationship with her husband and children in the *Narrative*, much is said about her relationships with her master Dumont and his jealous wife.[23] In one of the lively set pieces of *Narrative*, the "dingy potato" episode, the struggle between Truth and Olive Gilbert for the story line is palpable. Gilbert does not want to relate this incident, which shows Isabella as a knowing participant in the marital discontent of her master and mistress. Truth insists that Gilbert record her vindication after the mistress, enraged by her husband's praise of Isabella's work, tried to discredit her in the house. Bad feeling intensified until one morning, "all at once, the potatoes that Isabel cooked for breakfast assumed a dingy, dirty look." When the dingy potatoes became the focus for Isabella's censure by master, mistress, and the white indentured servant Kate, the little Dumont daughter Gerty sympathized with Isabella and offered to watch the kettle, "and they would see if they could not have them *nice*":

When Isabella had put the potatoes over to boil Gerty told her she would herself tend the fire, while Isabel milked. She had not long been seated by the fire, in performance of her promise, when Kate entered, and requested Gertrude to go out of the room and do something for her, which she refused, still keeping her place in the corner. While there, Kate came sweeping about the fire, caught up a chip, lifted some ashes with it, and dashed them into the kettle. Now the mystery was solved, the plot discovered! Kate was working a little too fast at making her mistress's words good, at showing that Mrs. Dumont and herself were on the right side of the dispute, and consequently at gaining power over Isabella. Yes, she was quite too fast, inasmuch as she had overlooked the little figure of justice, which sat in the corner, with scales nicely balanced, waiting to give all their dues.

Isabella is cast as a black Cinderella, falsely accused of slovenly work
habits by a wicked step-sister and step-mother and then saved by the
unlikely "little figure of justice," Gerty:

> "Oh, Poppee! oh, Poppee!" said she, "Kate has been putting ashes in
> among the potatoes! I saw her do it! Look at those that fell on the outside
> of the kettle! You can now see what made the potatoes so dingy every
> morning, though Bell washed them clean!" (*NarBk*, 30-32).

Gilbert thought this a "comparatively trifling incident," but Truth
insisted she relate it "as it made a deep impression on her mind at the
time"; no wonder. The institutional structure of slavery is virtually mapped
in the story with its patriarchal master whose potatoes will be made dirty
or clean by four women in varying conditions of legal and emotional servitude: a wife, a daughter, a white indentured servant, a black enslaved
woman. His favor is the key to their well-being, and to attain it each
woman sets herself against the others. Some shifting alliances are possible
(mistress-indentured servant, white child-black woman), but no sense of
solidarity can emerge. Isabella, who must ordinarily hold her tongue, feels
vindicated when the mistress "remained dumb"; but the mistress can be
both blind (to her own interest as a woman) and dumb (in not protesting
her own place in the tormented triangle of master-enslaved woman-mis-
tress) and still ably perform her essential facilitating function in the institution. When the Dumonts sell Isabella's son Peter, the mistress uses her
tongue well enough:

> *Ugh!* a *fine* fuss to make about a little *nigger!* Why, have n't you as
> many of 'em left as you can see to and take care of? A pity 'tis, the niggers
> are not all in Guinea!! Making such a halloo-balloo about the neighbor-
> hood; and all for a paltry nigger!!!

The white woman denies identity on any level, seeing the black woman
as a breeder (not a mother) of "niggers" (not children); even though
Isabella is by then a freed woman, the white wife conceives her as without
the power to act because she does not have her own money (which is, in
fact, an accurate assessment of the white woman's powerlessness in her
marriage).

> Isabella heard her through, and after a moment's hesitation, answered,
> in tones of deep determination—"*I'll have my child again.*" "Have *your
> child* again!" repeated her mistress—her tones big with contempt, and

scorning the absurd idea of her getting him. "How can you get him? And what have you to support him with, if you could? Have you any money?" "No," answered Bell, "I have no money, but God has enough, or what's better! And I'll have my child again."

When Isabella (that thing that should be silent) speaks to Mrs. Dumont (that thing that can speak when allowed to by her husband) she identifies her possibilities for action with her personal sovereignty. Measuring her words, as another might count out money, Isabella "felt so *tall within*—I felt as if the *power of a nation* was with me!" (*NarBk*, 44-45). Characteristically, her sense of personal autonomy is expressed in a communal figure of solidarity. The equivocal positioning of Mrs. Dumont in the slaveholding hierarchy, forever dirtying and making white again the dingy potatoes of patriarchally enforced domesticity, will keep her solitary and never sovereign.

Truth's gradation of cruelties puzzled Gilbert. When asked if Dumont ever whipped her, she answered, "Oh yes, he sometimes whipped me soundly, though never cruelly. And the most severe whipping he ever give me was because *I* was cruel to a cat" (*NarBk*, 33). Gilbert avers that "There are some hard things that crossed Isabella's life while in slavery, that she has no desire to publish, for various reasons," including the reason that "they are not all for the public ear, from their very nature" (*NarBk*, 81). The slave narrative form aroused its audience's desire to have its myths about black women's sexuality confirmed. As with other enslaved women, Truth's sexual exploitation included at least producing children who, at birth, were transformed into the chattel of her master. If other sexual abuse took place, Truth did not regard it as defining, and she would not further satisfy her audience's cultivated taste for the sensational. She turned their knowing expectations against them by insisting that if she told "God's truth" that "it would seem to others, especially the uninitiated, so unaccountable, so unreasonable, and what is usually called so unnatural" that people would not believe it (*NarBk*, 82). Thus with the tactical reversal that was her defining intellectual strategy, Truth anticipated her audience's fascination with the enslaved woman's life as a secret, enculted, gothic existence, compounded of torture and forced sex; then between herself and this audience she drew a homespun curtain, around which they could not peek because *they* were the "uninitiated," *they* could not deal with the "unaccountable," *they* could not cope with the "unnatural," as if they were themselves too simple, too naive, too unschooled to read the horrific book they had written themselves. Perhaps she measured her own experience against her listeners' expectations and decided that her life was not their fiction.

Shaping the story of her life after the appearance of the male slave narratives of the 1840s, with their lurid set pieces of the sexual torture of black women, but before Harriet Jacobs's *Incidents in the Life of a Slave Girl* (1861), with its brilliant deconstruction of the enslaved black woman's sexual vulnerability, Truth seems to have carved out a little space of privacy around her body.[24] In its recounting of the atrocities required by the slave narrative form, stories that form themselves around the issue of control of the enslaved body, *Narrative* retains the traces of Truth's dialogic strivings with her interpreter. The strange chapter "Gleanings" seems like a black-white duel for position with Gilbert. Black women are disappearing. Truth's father had two wives before Bett, "one of whom, if not both, were torn from him by the iron hand of the ruthless trafficker in human flesh"; Truth's husband had some wives who were sold away. For some reason, Gilbert cannot keep track of these women; their stories "have been omitted through forgetfulness," she confesses. Truth's insistent voice becomes increasingly audible in the principle of selection for these stories as an atmosphere of giddy reversal begins to characterize "Gleanings."

A slave master dashes out the brains of a child; a passing Indian sees the bloody corpse and cries, "If I had been here, I would have put my tomahawk" in the master's head. The "civilized" and the "uncivilized" are reversed, and we get the pleasure, if only in fantasy, of seeing the master's head bashed in. In another hectic tale, a master abuses the sickly child ("tough as a moccasin") of a consumptive enslaved woman. The child, who could neither walk, talk, or cry, making "a constant, piteous, moaning sound," inspires the master's sadism. But when the child is dead, the master himself sickens, "his reason fled"; now he can no longer walk, talk, or cry. Soan, the black nurse, "was very strong, and was therefore selected to support her master, as he sat up in bed, by putting her arms around, while she stood behind him." She squeezes "his feeble frame in her iron grasp, as in a vice," in a macabre parodic embrace under the very eye of the white mistress:

> If his breathing betrayed too tight a grasp, and her mistress said, "Be careful, don't hurt him, Soan!" her ever-ready answer was, "Oh no, Missus, no," in her most pleasant tone—and then, as soon as Missus's eyes and ears were engaged away, another grasp—another shake—another bounce.

When Isabella asked Soan "if she were not afraid his spirit would haunt her," Soan answered that "the devil will never let him out of hell long enough for that" (*NarBk*, 82-84). In "Gleanings" we see the flailing of victim against tormentor in bizarre fields of cruelty ripe for a hateful harvest.

The turning extended to subsets of distorted human pairings and triplings: black woman enslaved to white woman (Isabella-Mistress Dumont), black woman and white woman both under the power of the same white man (Isabella-Mistress Dumont-Master Dumont). Olive Gilbert contributed the story of the brutal murder of Tabby, beaten to death and buried in the garden by her white mistress in far-off Kentucky. Gilbert's abstract antislavery vision is suddenly focused on a simple dyad: black woman-white woman. Absent the veil, the black teller and the white re-teller of *Narrative* seem to see each other face to face.

Frances Titus wrote that "Sojourner had known the joys of motherhood—brief joys, for she had been cruelly separated from her babes, and her mistress's children given to occupy the place which nature designed for her own" (*NarBk*, 194). Whether Isabella was a wet nurse for the Dumont children, the *Narrative* does not say. In 1857, in "the border-ruffian Democracy of Indiana," Truth exposed her breasts to a heckling crowd, tauntingly claiming that "her breasts had suckled many a white babe, to the exclusion of her own offspring" (*NarBk*, 137-39). Although this is the stormiest of the occasions on which she spoke of wet-nursing white children, Truth referred to it in other speeches. Whether it was a serviceable motif for her presentation of herself in traditional antislavery rhetoric or whether it referred to her actual experience cannot be said.[25]

Images of motherhood offered a potent rhetorical strategy to use against a hostile slave-holding society besotted with the ideal of the maternal. Certainly her biographers made symbolic motherhood a moral point in their arguments against slavery. Frances Titus dovetailed two popular abolitionist-feminist appeals when she wrote that "Sojourner, robbed of her own offspring, adopted her race" (*NarBk*, 194). The image of the grief-stricken slave mother, watching her children sold away on the auction block, melded with the image of woman as the eternal embodiment of maternal tenderness. Titus divined that a short-circuited maternal instinct had brought this deprived woman to adopt four million (child-like) freedpeople.

For eighteen years Isabella worked day and night in the Dumont house at domestic tasks and at such field work as binding wheat. Dumont boasted to his friends that "'*that* wench' (pointing to Isabel) 'is better to me than a *man*—for she will do a good family's washing in the night, and be ready in the morning to go into the field, where she will do as much at raking and binding as my best field hands'" (*NarBk*, 33).

The Dumonts had several other slaves living in a room behind the kitchen. The other slaves found Isabella hard to like, for she not only over-worked herself in relation to their efforts and output, she also had an unpleasant habit of reacting with contempt toward anyone who "talked to her of the injustice of her being a slave." Her fellow slaves "taunted her with being the *'white folks' nigger.'*" Gilbert wrote that Isabella looked upon Dumont as god-like in his power over her and believed herself always under his surveillance (*NarBk*, 33).

In 1817 the date of 4 July 1827 had been set by law as the time slavery was to end in New York State. Dumont promised Isabella freedom a full year before her legal emancipation if she would "do well, and be faithful." In 1826 he reneged on his promise, refusing to free her on the pretext that an injury she had suffered had kept her from working to his standard.

> She plead that she had worked all the time, and done many things she was not wholly able to do, although she knew she had been less useful than formerly; but her master remained inflexible. (*NarBk*, 39)

No explanation is given of Truth's "badly diseased hand" in Gilbert's account, but only an injury of some magnitude could have so seriously affected the output of such a worker. In 1864 at the Women's Loyal National League in New York City, Susan B. Anthony followed a speaker's remarks on the increasing level of violence against blacks by using an image of Truth as an object lesson:

> Miss Anthony held up two photographs to the view of the audience. One represented "Sojourner Truth," the heroine of one of Mrs. H. B. Stowe's tales, and the other the bare back of a Louisiana slave. Many of the audience were affected to tears. "Sojourner Truth" had lost three fin-gers of one hand, and the Louisiana slave's back bore scars of whipping. She asked every one to suppose that woman was her mother, and that man her father.[26]

This is a fascinating tableau: Susan B. Anthony holds in one hand the well-known image, *The Scourged Back*, a *carte-de-visite* of an unnamed enslaved man with a hideously scarred back which had become an abolitionist icon, and in the other hand an image of "the heroine of one of Mrs. H. B. Stowe's tales." The writer encloses "Sojourner Truth" in quotation marks as if this were no real person but another iconic phenomenon. Like the scarred back, Truth's three lost fingers are a horrific sign of the slave mas-ter's brutality.

Three years later, at the National Convention of the Equal Rights Association 10 May 1867, Truth's maimed hand is mentioned again:

> Mrs. Anthony announced that they would have another opportunity to hear Sojourner Truth, and, for the information of those who need not know, she would say that Sojourner Truth was for forty years a slave in this state. She is not a product of the barbarism of South Carolina, but of the barbarism of New York, and one of her fingers was chopped off by her cruel master in a moment of anger.[27]

Susan B. Anthony was often face to face with Truth during these years and could have discovered for sure whether she had nine fingers or seven, or even ten. Truth was often seen by people who saw only a sign.

With Isabella, Thomas had been promised his freedom a year earlier than the legal date of emancipation, at which time they were to live in a cabin provided by Dumont. Perhaps because of his earlier bitter experience as a fugitive, Thomas chose to remain behind when Isabella escaped, taking only her youngest child with her.

Isabella did not accept her master's moral injustice in breaking his word to her about her "free papers."

> Isabella inwardly determined that she would remain quietly with him only until she had spun his wool—about one hundred pounds—and then she would leave him, taking the rest of the time to herself. (*NarBk*, 39)

Perhaps her spinning of the wool suggests that she saw more than moral injustice in Dumont's action. By choosing to stay and do this amount of work, she psychologically severed any sense of working as a slave: she had paid for her time. It is an arresting picture, the strong black woman not quite thirty years old, seated in a farm house in the cooling New York autumn of 1826, spinning the wool to be used in the domestic manufacture of homespun, like many a New York matron before her.[28] There she sits, the perfect (revolutionary) housewife, spinning, planning her escape.

When Isabella walked away from Dumont's farm in the dawn, carrying her infant in her arms, she was not unassisted. After she "told God she was afraid to go in the night" and knowing in the day "everybody would see her," God conspired with Isabella like an Underground Railroad conductor, supplying her with the practical steps to freedom.

> At length, the thought came to her that she could leave just before the day dawned, and get out of the neighborhood where she was known before the people were much astir. "Yes," said she, fervently, "that's a good thought! Thank you, God, for *that* thought!" (*NarBk*, 41)

Gaining more than "the summit of a high hill, a considerable distance from her master's," Isabella was gaining the horizon; like Zora Neale Hurston's Janie, "She had been getting ready for her great journey to the horizons in search of *people;* it was important to all the world that she should find them and they find her."[29]

The Van Wagenens, to whom a kindly Quaker acquaintance had directed her, gave Isabella her first real bed, paid her wages, and, when Dumont came after her, bought her services for the remaining year, "for which her master charged twenty dollars, and five in addition for the child" (*NarBk*, 43).

It was during her time with the Van Wagenens that Isabella learned that her son Peter, a child of about five years old, had been illegally sold out of New York state into the Deep South. Dumont sold Peter to a Dr. Gedney, who found the boy too small to be of service and sent the child on to his brother Solomon. Solomon Gedney sold Peter to his brother-in-law, a man named Fowler in Alabama, who was the husband of Gedney's sister Eliza.

With the financial help of Quakers in the area, Isabella fought in a Kingston court for the return of her son, managing to convince white lawyers to undertake the case.[30] Supporting herself as a domestic in the town, Isabella persisted through long delays, at one point declining a shameful offer of reparations: in lieu of her "lost" son she was offered $300, half the bond required of an owner who illegally sold a slave child out of state. By the end of 1828, when Peter was finally produced in court, he had been terrorized into denying his mother's identity. The judge nevertheless ordered that the "boy be delivered into the hands of the mother—having no other master, no other controller, no other conductor, but his mother" (*NarBk*, 53).[31]

Truth's legal victory forcing Solomon Gedney to return her son to her as a *free* person is a mother-child story paralleled within the *Narrative* by the story of old Mrs. Gedney and her daughter Eliza. Employing a familiar rhetorical strategy by which free white women identified their disposition in marriage with the status of the slave, Mrs. Gedney compared the situation of her daughter Eliza, who has married this Fowler of Alabama and is under his power, with the situation of Isabella's little Peter, enslaved by Fowler:

Dear me! What a disturbance to make about your child! What, is *your* child better than *my* child? My child is gone out there, and yours is gone to live with her, to have enough of everything, and to be treated like a gentleman!

Condemning Mrs. Gedney's comparison, Isabella clearly states the distinction between white wives and slaves: "*Your* child has gone there but she is *married* and my boy has gone as a *slave*, and he is too little to go far from his mother" (*NarBk*, 45). White women left their families for new families (a gain), while slaves were taken from their families to serve strangers (a loss). A sympathetic editorial voice seems to suggest that white married women and slaves shared something under patriarchy. Truth seems to reply that it is their difference that matters, a difference starkly mirrored in the relation of the black mother Isabella to the white mother Mrs. Gedney.

Jenny Franchot has examined Frederick Douglass's "rhetorical exposure of the black woman's suffering body."[32] Douglass described a whipping scene he witnessed as a child which presents the reader with a specular view of the whipped woman as an isolated other. Truth offers a revision of such a scene. When Isabella uncovers the scars of Fowler's brutal beatings on Peter's body, she prays a terrible prayer for vengeance on the slave master's family that is complexly answered: "render unto them double." The doubling has already begun, as we see when Peter situates his own torture in a grotesquely duplicating spectacle of brutalization:

> Oh, this is nothing, mammy—if you should see Phillis, I guess you'd *scare!* She had a little baby, and Fowler cut her till the milk as well as blood ran down *her* body. You would *scare* to see Phillis, mammy. (*NarBk*, 54)

The un-mothered child looks at the violent spilling of mother's milk. The cruel master Nealy had whipped the nine-year-old Isabella "till the flesh was deeply lacerated, and the blood streamed from her wounds"(*NarBk*, 26). The child Isabella's lacerated flesh is refigured in "the callosities and indurations" on *her* child Peter's body, just as the Isabella-Peter relation is refigured in the Phillis-infant dyad. Superimposed over the infinite repetition of scarred black mother, scarred black child is a complexly disturbing element of whiteness. The white daughter Eliza, cut off so barbarously both from her mother and from her own "labors and watchings as a tender mother" (*NarBk*, 57) had been represented as a stealthy comforter of the black son Peter:

When Isabella inquired, "What did Miss Eliza say, Pete, when you were treated so badly?" he replied, "Oh, mammy, she said she wished I was with Bell. Sometimes I crawled under the stoop, mammy, the blood running all about me, and my back would stick to the boards; and sometimes Miss Eliza would come and grease my sores, when all were abed and asleep." (*NarBk*, 54)

Eliza's forlorn wish that Peter was with his mother Isabella can be understood to encompass her wish that she herself was with her own mother, temporarily allying the white child and the black child in their misery. The terms Isabella-Mrs. Gedney, Eliza-Peter, white-black, mother-child, wife-child, wife-slave oscillate with an ominous instability.

Isabella is present when the Gedney family learns that God has indeed "rendered them double." Old Mrs. Gedney receives a letter saying that Fowler, in a spectacular display of Southern gothic sadism, has beaten and killed her daughter Eliza: "'He knocked her down with his fist, jumped on her with his knees, broke her collar bone, and tore out her wind-pipe!'" (*NarBk*, 56). The country of the slave and the country of the free woman seem to be the same country.

By 1850 the slave narrative form into which Gilbert cast Truth's story had a structuring power of its own. The public acceptance of the form conferred an authority on the speaking subject that would not have been available to that subject writing of a private self: the protagonist had to meet the expectations of the audience for stories as examples. In telling her own story, Truth accepted the authorization of the slave narrative form, but she played with it to subvert its hierarchical structuring myth, that the drama of escape from slavery was a white-black drama.

As Truth tells her story, her escape had an ambiguous climax: when Dumont discovered her missing and came after her, the benevolent white Van Wagenens intervened and purchased her freedom and that of her child. Harriet Jacobs later wrote of the significance of her own sale to friendly intercessors that "The bill of sale is on record, and future generations will learn from it that women were articles of traffic in New York, late in the nineteenth century of the Christian religion."[33] Truth is able to subvert this subversion of her escape by embedding the scenes with her master within a second independent narrative that runs alongside the slave narrative: the narrative of her surprising conversion.

The slave narrative form with its myth of the slave escaping from a white tyranny to fight for acceptance in a (new) white tyranny vies with the conversion narrative, in which the drama of salvation is never a white-black drama. The slave narrative works its way out from a dependency myth in which freedom is a passage into the ways of the white world. The white audience for the slave narrative condoned freedom but not the political and social integration that might have followed it. The freed person is situated at the bottom of the social hierarchy in which freedom is the commencement of the attempts to scale each rung upward toward white acceptance. The conversion narrative, which was especially congenial to black women, is an independence myth with more radical implications. It proposed a radical challenge to race, class and gender oppression. Although white Christianity functioned as the principal support for the slave-holding state, an ideal Christianity did not authorize this. The ideal Christian could not, as Julia Foote knew, "say to the poor and the colored ones among them, 'Stand back a little—I am holier than thou.'"[34]

When the first page of Truth's story is written down, she is speaking retrospectively of slavery. "Of her first master, she can give no account, as she must have been a mere infant when he died" (*NarBk*, 13). At the end of her narrative she visits her impoverished former master, who once held her as "any other property" (*NarBk*, 124). In this concluding episode Isabella appears transformed in her master's eyes as Truth.[35] Although Truth had returned to Dumont's farm in the past to visit her daughters, the "last interview with her master" in the spring of 1849 is selected as the telling moment with which to end her story. The episode is almost a parody of the slave narrative form, in which the slaveholder's tale becomes a chapter in a conversion experience. Dumont was blind and deaf before to what he can see and hear now:

> For, now, the sin of slavery is so clearly written out, and so much talked against,—(why, the whole world cries out against it!)—that if any one says he don't know, and has not heard, he must, I think, be a liar. (*NarBk*, 124)

Truth thus refashions the slave master's world in 1850, the year of the Fugitive Slave Law, as a world in which slave masters can repudiate slavery; moreover the speaker of the *Narrative* is an agent bringing about this repudiation as one of those who has "so clearly written out, and so much talked against" slavery. In the freedom scene of the slave narrative, Truth was purchased from the pursuing master. In this recapitulated freedom scene the master disavows his right to ownership.

Gilbert remarks dryly that those in need of "a louder note" must be "very hard of hearing." Truth shows her new mastery by hearing her former master's "confession"; he has "turned into a brother!" In a tragi-comical parody of Isabella's absconding with the master's property (herself and her baby), the *Narrative* closes with Dumont having "gone West" with the "few articles of furniture" Truth had left with him. The happy reversal of their situations is marked out in Truth's Christian words, confirming that her dealings, as ever, are with only one Master: "Never mind," says Sojourner, "what we give to the poor, we lend to the Lord."

This scene provides the right conclusion to the conversion narrative: the high are brought low. The Christian values so long perverted are now revalued. In a reversal of the traditional narrative movement from innocence to experience, innocence was always experience. In her innocent story, Truth would let her children cry for bread but would not steal it; in her experienced story it was Dumont who stole: "he taught us not to lie and steal, when *he* was stealing all the time himself and did not know it!" (*NarBk*, 125).

The dramatic point of convergence of the slave narrative and the conversion narrative in Truth's book occurs in the central episode in which Dumont visits the Van Wagenens and Isabella decides to return with him for Pinkster, the great Africanized festival that had accreted around the Dutch Christian celebration of Pentecost. Shaping the episode into the slave narrative form, Gilbert builds it around the master-slave relation, implying that Isabella's longing for her old life extends to a longing for her old master. To Gilbert, Dumont appears out of the blue or, in the undercurrent of Gilbert's suspicion, at Isabella's bidding. There is a hint of sexual repartee in their exchange:

> It seemed to have been one of those "events that cast their shadows before;" for, before night, Mr. Dumont made his appearance. She informed him of her intention to accompany him home. He answered, with a smile, "I shall not take you back again; you ran away from me." Thinking his manner contradicted his words, she did not feel repulsed, but made herself and child ready; and when her former master had seated himself in the open dearborn, she walked towards it, intending to place herself and child in the rear, and go with him. (*NarBk*, 65)

Gilbert models her response to Isabella's desire to attend the Pinkster festival on her understanding of the slaveholders' victimizing practices. After the death of Isabella's father from exposure and neglect, the master's family sent "some black paint for the coffin, and—a jug of ardent spirits," intending that these "should act as an opiate on his slaves, rather than on his own seared conscience" (*NarBk*, 25). Noting that "slaves in this country have ever been allowed to celebrate the principal, if not some of the lesser festivals observed by the Catholics and Church of England," Gilbert sees these as occasions for "parties and balls," leading to "the lowest dissipation" (*NarBk*, 63).

Gilbert quotes from Frederick Douglass's condemnation of holidays manipulated by the slave masters to undermine the enslaved community's will to resistance. Douglass's argument that Southern slaveholders used holidays as "a safety-valve" to manipulate and discharge the hostile energies of their slaves is a radical critique of slave management and co-optation, but it is not readily transferable to Pinkster, which had been shaped from within the black community to transmit traditional African values and foster community coherence.[36] Gilbert's attitude toward the holiday reflects her general denial in *Narrative* of the significance of a viable black culture in the formation of Isabella's consciousness.

The members of Isabella's community looked forward to Pinkster more eagerly than to Christmas or New Year. In Judaism the feast of Pentecost, which concluded with offerings representing the first fruits of the harvest, was celebrated on the fiftieth day after Passover. After the Jewish Diaspora it functioned as a great feast of pilgrimage, for which the faithful scattered throughout the Roman world returned to worship in Jerusalem. On Pentecost, Jesus's disciples prayed after his ascension and were filled with the Holy Spirit, which descended like a mighty wind and settled on them with tongues of fire, causing them to speak in other languages. Enslaved Africans and their descendants in the New York area transformed the Christian observance of Pentecost, in which inspiration by divine spirit is a central feature, into the syncretistic festival of Pinkster. The Christian festival that had emerged from the Judaic festival was Africanized by victims of a new Diaspora.

In his description of Pinkster in *Satanstoe* (1845), James Fenimore Cooper remarked that the distinguishing features of the three-day festival, which he called "the great Saturnalia of the New York blacks," were African.[37] In Albany, Pinkster was a week-long celebration overseen by a "King Charles." The requirement that this man be a native-born African is of special significance; American-born blacks used the occasion to emulate and learn from African-born blacks. The fusion of pain and pleasure figured by the king's temporary autonomy reminds us, as Sterling Stuckey has said, that during Pinkster "a place should be found on the other side of laughter, or perhaps at its lower registers, for sadness."[38] Festive stalls and booths served food and spirits, there were sideshows and dancing accompanied by drums and wind and stringed instruments. The vitality of African traditions found a conduit in the Christian feast, celebrated in the aftermath of the Easter season, with its own associations of fertility and new life. The Pinkster festival was an occasion for black solidarity, an aspect trivialized by Gilbert's account in *Narrative*.

> When Isabella had been at Mr. Van Wagener's a few months, she saw in prospect one of the festivals approaching. She knows it by none but the Dutch name, Pingster, as she calls it—but I think It must have been Whitsuntide, in English. She says she "looked back into Egypt," and everything looked "so pleasant there," as she saw retrospectively all her former companions enjoying their freedom for at least a little space, as well as their wonted convivialities, and in her heart she longed to be with them. (*NarBk*, 64)

The poignant phrase "looked back into Egypt" is double-edged: on the one hand, she looked back as a weary Israelite wandering in the desert might look back on the security of Egyptian bondage with some nostalgia. Only a degraded spirit, Gilbert seems to imply, could look back from "freedom" into "slavery" with longing. Egypt also stands for what is pagan and libertine. Gilbert casts this episode as an opposition between the revel of the slaves and the sober life of the Van Wagenens: Isabella's heart is tempting her toward old pleasures. Her longing for the complex social network of her own people, "enjoying their freedom for at least a little space," her memory of "their wonted convivialities," is caught up in the phrase, resonating with Biblical meaning, "everything looked 'so pleasant there.'" Gilbert mistakes what is in fact a profound cultural yearning for the boredom of an ignorant young woman:

> With this picture before her mind's eye, she contrasted the quiet, peaceful life she was living with the excellent people of Wahkendall, and it seemed so dull and void of incident, that the very contrast served but to heighten her desire to return, that, at least, she might enjoy with them, once more, the coming festivities. (*NarBk*, 64)

Isabella, dwelling among "the excellent [white] people of Wahkendall," experiences the loneliness of exile. Her longing for the company of the black celebrants of the Pinkster festival prefigures an emotional reality of her life to come, which would be lived more and more among excellent alien people.

Harriet Beecher Stowe framed the encounter with Dumont differently. She remembered Truth saying that the meeting took place after "the slaves in New York were all set free" and that Dumont had come to the Van Wagenens to visit and had asked her if she wanted to go back and see the people on the old place.[39] Stowe's frame allows the event a different significance. In her retelling, the great Pinkster festival took on the excitement of its free celebrants. This reframing casts into relief Gilbert's insistence, using the authority of Frederick Douglass's *Narrative*, on keeping Truth's story in the slave narrative form. If the Pinkster holiday was being celebrated in the freed black community, Isabella's participation would have been part of the natural evolution of that community with its own customs and traditions into its place in the national life. Like most abolitionists, Gilbert had no imaginative conception of the ongoing life of the black community after slavery and no real political conception either.

At some point of Truth's trajectory from the white space of the Van Wagenens toward the black space of her old community, which was still subordinated to Dumont, she entered a liminal state in which a new identity of special selection was forged. On her way to Dumont's dearborn, she saw Jesus. At the point of convergence of the slave narrative and the conversion narrative, Truth's own visionary experience liberated her into a community of equals, in which Jesus functioned like an umbrella to protect her from the workday sun of the field. Even in the midst of her ecstatic vision the memory of that other field where white people abused you and beat you and abused your people was intense enough to stop the flow of "love to all creatures"; but the flow came on stronger, she said, until at last the white people were just white people to her. Before that, she explained later in a vivid image from the field, "She used to say she wished God would kill all the white people and not leave one for seed."[40] Now she found she could even love them.[41]

Notes

1. Stanton, et al., *History of Woman Suffrage*, 2:224.
2. Stowe, "Sojourner Truth, the Libyan Sibyl," 474.
3. Ibid., 473.
4. Sojourner Truth to James Redpath, written from Battle Creek, 17 June 1863, published in *The Commonwealth*, 3 July 1863.
5. Frances Titus included a notice, the source of which is unknown, that "Mrs. Stowe was mistaken in regard to Sojourner's ancestry. Her mother's parents came from the Coast of Guinea, but her paternal grandmother was a Mohawk squaw. The 'whoop' Sojourner gave in the horse-car at Washington was probably a legacy from her Mohawk ancestor" (*NarBk*, 308).

6. [Truth with Gilbert], *Narrative of Sojourner Truth* (1850), 2. Titus replaced this with "Sojourner does not know in what year she was born, but knows she was liberated under the act of 1817, which freed all slaves who were forty years old and upward" (*NarBk*, 13).

7. Gilbert Vale, *Fanaticism; Its Source and Influence, Illustrated by the Simple Narrative of Isabella, in the case of Matthias, Mr. and Mrs. B. Folger, Mr. Pierson, Mr. Mills, Catherine, Isabella, &c. &c* (New York: Published by G. Vale, 1835), part 1, 11. Defending Isabella against slanderous charges brought during her New York City residency, the journalist Gilbert Vale included in his book nine testimonies from Isabella's former owners and from several employers attesting to her veracity, trustworthiness, industriousness, honesty, good conduct, and "regular habits of great fidelity." The testimonials by Isaac Van Wagenen (the "Van Wagener" of *Narrative*) and John Dumont are reprinted at the back of the 1850 edition of *Narrative* with the Dumont passage abridged ([Truth with Gilbert], *Narrative of Sojourner Truth* [1850], 144).

8. Alphonso T. Clearwater, *The History of Ulster County, New York* (New York: W. J. Van Deusen, 1967), 61 and 262-63.

9. Frances Smith Foster, "Adding Color and Contour to Early American Self-Portraitures: Autobiographical Writings of Afro-American Women," in *Conjuring: Black Women, Fiction, and Literary Tradition*, edited by Marjorie Pryse and Hortense J. Spillers (Bloomington: Indiana University Press, 1985), 31.

10. See Terry Alford, "Islam," in *Dictionary of Afro-American Slavery*, edited by Randall M. Miller and John D. Smith (Westport: Greenwood Press, 1988), 371.

11. Levine, *Black Culture and Black Consciousness*, 33. Levine quotes the anthropologist Paul Radin: "The ante-bellum Negro was not converted to God. He converted God to himself."

12. See Clearwater, *The History of Ulster County, New York* for a notice composed by a slavemaster in the Hurley area in 1785 that confirms this practice of giving the occasional slave an opportunity to find a willing master:

> The bearer, Sym, his wife, a young healthy wench and a negro boy of about two years old, are for sale. The negro man has permission to look a master for himself and his wife and child. The Terms of payment will be made to the Purchaser. Whoever is inclined to purchase is desired to apply to Coenradt Elmendorph, Hurley, March 12, 1785. (266)

13. Truth's childhood relationship with her father can be contextualized usefully by the discussion in Willie Lee Rose, "Childhood in Bondage," in *Slavery and Freedom*, edited by William W. Freehling (New York: Oxford University Press, 1982), 37-48.

14. See Effie J. Squier, "Sojourner Truth," *Christian at Work* (28 September 1882): 17-18; and Mabee and Newhouse, *Sojourner Truth*, 219 and 228.

15. See *Anti-Slavery Bugle*, 8 November 1856. Truth told a New York City audience that "she had been twice married, and had five children, the oldest [Diana] being forty years of age" (*Tribune*, 16 September 1853).
16. Convincing evidence for this view is assembled by Mabee and Newhouse; they identify the brutal owner of Bob as the English painter, Charles Catton (*Sojourner Truth*, 5-7).
17. *Tribune*, 7 September 1853. See appendix 2 for the text of this speech.
18. William D. Piersen, *Black Yankees: The Development of an Afro-American Subculture in Eighteenth-Century New England* (Amherst: The University of Massachusetts Press, 1988), 89-90. For whites' preoccupation with the morality of the domestic system in the enslaved family, see Willie Lee Rose, "The Domestication of Domestic Slavery," in *Slavery and Freedom*, edited by William W. Freehling (New York: Oxford University Press, 1982), 18-36.

    In 1835 the journalist Gilbert Vale had recorded Isabella's statement in more straightforward prose:

    > During her residence with J. Dumont, she had five children, without a legal marriage, according to the custom of slaves; but during the greater part of the time she lived with a black man, on the farm, as her husband, to whom she was joined by a coloured man of the name of King, who frequently performed this office. (Vale, *Fanaticism*, part 1, 17)

19. See Mabee and Newhouse, *Sojourner Truth*, 248n.22. Truth sometimes spoke of her children as having been "sold away"; it is clear here that she meant they were taken from her by being enslaved at birth. Of the five, James died as a child; Peter was illegally sold out of state and then freed by a court; Truth took Sophia when she escaped, and the baby was purchased and set free by the Van Wagenens. These last two children Truth freed from slavery by her own actions. By the gradualist New York law that required those under the age of twenty-five at the time of the 1827 emancipation to continue serving their masters until they reached that age, Truth's daughters Diana and Elizabeth did not become legally free until around 1841 and 1850. The printed reference to "Hannah" in Peter's letter to Truth of 17 October 1840 is probably a misreading of "Diana" (*NarBk*, 77).
20. In the 1870s, when Truth was in her seventies, she helped to support herself by selling blackberries around Battle Creek, from "a tray loaded with boxes of berries which she carried 'on her head,'" retaining a most useful African carry-over into old age. See Berenice Lowe, "Michigan Days of Sojourner Truth," *New York Folklore Quarterly* 12 (Summer 1956): 128.
21. Frances Anne Kemble, *Journal of a Residence on a Georgian Plantation in 1838-1839* (London: Longman, Green, 1863), 60. This passage is discussed in Jacqueline Jones, *Labor of Love, Labor of Sorrow: Black Women, Work, and the Family from Slavery to the Present* (New York: Basic Books, 1985), 15.
22. *Anti-Slavery Bugle*, 8 November 1856.

23. See Minrose C. Gwin, "Green-eyed Monsters of the Slavocracy: Jealous Mistresses in Two Slave Narratives," in *Conjuring: Black Women, Fiction, and Literary Tradition*, edited by Marjorie Pryse and Hortense J. Spillers (Bloomington: Indiana University Press, 1985), 39-52, for an analysis of the mistress-slave relationship in the autobiographical narratives of Harriet Jacobs and Elizabeth Keckley.

24. For Jacobs's relationships to white mistresses see Hazel V. Carby, *Reconstructing Womanhood: The Emergence of the Afro-American Woman Novelist* (New York: Oxford University Press, 1987), 48-61.

25. In her version of Truth's "Aint I a Woman" speech, Frances Gage quoted Truth as saying "I have borne thirteen chilern and seen 'em mos' all sold off into slavery, and when I cried out with a mother's grief, none but Jesus heard—and ar'n't I a woman?" (*NarBk*, 134). If she said this, she may have been enacting for rhetorical purposes her mother's experience as more representative than her own: her mother had indeed had some thirteen children, all, including Sojourner herself, sold away from her, and may have wet-nursed white ones as well.

26. Stanton, et al., *History of Woman Suffrage*, 2:898.

27. Ibid., 2:224.

28. For the essential female economic activity of homespun production see Ann Douglas, *The Feminization of American Culture* (New York: Avon Books, 1977), 55-58.

29. Hurston, *Their Eyes Were Watching God*, 85.

30. For a detailed account of the legal aspects of the case, see Mabee and Newhouse, *Sojourner Truth*, 16-24.

31. Truth is known to have gone to court two other times in her life, successfully defending herself against slander in New York City in the 1830s and winning a judgment against a Washington, D.C. streetcar conductor after the Civil War. She thus joined a tradition of black women suing for their rights, begun as early as Lucy Terry (1730-1821), the first black woman poet to be recognized in this country. See Erlene Stetson, ed., *Black Sister: Poetry by Black American Women, 1746-1980* (Bloomington: Indiana University Press, 1981), 3 and 12.

32. See Franchot, "The Punishment of Esther," 141-65.

33. Jacobs, *Incidents in the Life of a Slave Girl*, 200.

34. Julia A. J. Foote, *A Brand Plucked from the Fire: An Autobiographical Sketch by Mrs. Julia A. J. Foote*, in *Sisters of the Spirit: Three Black Women's Autobiographies of the Nineteenth Century*, edited by William L. Andrews (Bloomington: Indiana University Press, 1986), 167.

35. William L. Andrews discusses post-War reunions with former masters in "Reunion in the Postbellum Slave Narrative: Frederick Douglass and Elizabeth Keckley," *Black American Literature Forum* 23, no. 1 (Spring 1989): 15-16. Truth had kept up a nearly continuous contact with Dumont because her daughters had remained with him for many years.

36. See Sterling Stuckey, "The Skies of Consciousness: African Dance at Pinkster in New York, 1750-1840," in *Going Through the Storm: The Influence of African American Art in History* (New York: Oxford University Press, 1994), 53-80.

37. James Fenimore Cooper, *Satanstoe* (Lincoln: University of Nebraska Press, 1962), 55. In her fascinating sketch of life in Albany before the Revolution, *Memoirs of An American Lady*, Anne MacVicar Grant describes periods of holiday misrule when a "savage liberty" was enjoyed:

> Indeed, there were three stated periods in the year when, for a few days, young and old, masters and slaves, were abandoned to unruly enjoyment, and neglected every serious occupation for pursuits of this nature. (92)

38. Stuckey, "The Skies of Consciousness," 56. See also A. J. Williams-Myers, "Pinkster Carnival: Africanisms in the Hudson River Valley," *Afro-Americans in New York Life and History* 9 (January 1985): 7-17; Williams-Myers relates Pinkster to Carnival in New Orleans and Rio de Janeiro.

39. Stowe, "Sojourner Truth, the Libyan Sibyl," 475. Vale wrote that Isabella left Dumont "one year before the state made her free, because he had promised her this favour, and lived with Van Wagenen, whose name she takes; but she returned to J. Dumont at his request" (Vale, *Fanaticism*, part 1, 17).

40. *Tribune*, 7 September 1853.

41. Stowe, "Sojourner Truth, the Libyan Sibyl," 476.

Three

The Claims of Human Brotherhood

We meet the monster prejudice everywhere.
Clarissa C. Lawrence,
Proceedings of the Anti-Slavery Convention, 1839[1]

*He try to make you think he everywhere. Soon
as you think he everywhere, you think he God*
Alice Walker,
The Color Purple[2]

It was in the social and religious turmoil and political ferment of New York City in the 1830s that Sojourner Truth matured the responses that made her a powerful antislavery speaker, a radical critic of racial prejudice, including racism in the woman's rights movement, and, in her seventies, a crusader for the resettlement of freedpeople on government land, not in Liberia, but in the United States that they had helped to build.

Truth's entry into the free black community in New York City in 1829 and her departure in 1843 coincided with two turning points in its history, which were in turn reflected in her own.[3] In 1827, during the great parade down Broadway celebrating the New York Emancipation Act, waves of marchers under painted banners led by the New York African Society for Mutual Relief, the Clarkson Benevolent Society, and the Wilberforce Benevolent Society were cheered from the sidewalks by black women from "every state in the Union," from West India, and by "hundreds who had survived the middle passage." Freed people marched through the city under banners lettered with the word *African.* "The people of those days," it was remembered, "rejoiced in their nationality and hesitated not to call each other Africans or descendants of Africa."[4]

Antislavery feeling was the constitutive element of free black consciousness. A newly-granted freedom to some of its members served to further impress upon the black community the injustice of enslavement. The status of the ten percent of blacks who were free was inextricably linked to the status of the ninety percent of blacks who were enslaved. This linkage was vividly reflected in the white-led colonization movement, widely backed by white antislavery activists, which proposed to remove and resettle the free black population into West Africa. Resistance to the intensifying activities of the American Colonization Society shaped organized black abolitionism. *Freedom's Journal*, the first black newspaper in the country, connected New York abolitionists with those up and down the coast (David Walker served as Boston correspondent). By 1830, black abolitionists, abetted by the valorization of individual responsibility preached in the revivals of the Second Great Awakening and by the mounting political successes of British abolitionism, which would succeed in abolishing slavery in the Empire in 1833, had begun to urge immediate, not gradual abolition.

Under the influence of James E. Forten and other black leaders, William Lloyd Garrison, a formerly committed colonizationist, was converted to the cause of immediatist abolitionism. Black leaders raised subscriptions to finance the printing costs of Garrison's new antislavery journal, the *Liberator*, in 1830; from its early subscription list of five hundred or so black readers, the *Liberator* had reached 2300 subscribers by 1834, three-fourths of them black. Many of them would have read, or had read to them, several of Phillis Wheatley's poems, which the *Liberator* reprinted between February and December 1832; they would have seen advertised in its pages in 1833 the epoch-making public speaking appearances of Maria Stewart. Encouraged by William Watkins and other black leaders, Garrison attempted to explain to a white audience the black rejection of colonization in an 1832 pamphlet, *Thoughts on Colonization*, which was partly subsidized and distributed in New York City by the white businessman Arthur Tappan.

The interlocking fate of enslaved and free blacks was evident in the growing numbers of fugitives and the increase in kidnappings of blacks in the city. The city hid many fugitives, as it had hidden Truth's husband Thomas for a year or two before he was found and forced to return by Dumont. All blacks in the city lived under the constant threat of kidnapping by slave catchers who abducted free blacks as well as fugitives. Blackbirds, a city gang of poor whites, which included many immigrants, abducted blacks for money. Slave masters employed the Blackbirds to attack the family of Henry Highland Garnet, which had escaped from slavery in Maryland and lived safely in New York City for five years. Garnet's parents escaped but his sister Eliza was abducted; she was freed only after abolitionist friends were able to intervene in court to establish her identity as a New York resident.[5]

From 1835 to 1839 David Ruggles led the New York Vigilance Committee, channeling hundreds of fugitives into the black underground and disclosing the clandestine operations of illegal slavers in the port and in the city. Suspicion of whites and the fear of betrayal by blacks overcame Frederick Douglass when he reached the city in 1838:

> There I was in the midst of thousands, and yet a perfect stranger; without home and without friends, in the midst of thousands of my own brethren—children of a common Father, and yet I dared not to unfold to any one of them my sad condition. I was afraid to speak to any one for fear of speaking to the wrong one, and thereby falling into the hands of money-loving kidnappers, whose business it was to lie in wait for the panting fugitive, as the ferocious beasts of the forest lie in wait for their prey.

Ruggles took Douglass to a boarding-house on Church Street, and later stood witness when the Reverend J. C. W. Pennington officiated at Douglass's marriage to Anna Murray. Engaged in the rescues of several fugitives at once, Ruggles was "watched and hemmed in on almost every side," Douglass remembered.[6]

After redirecting the American antislavery movement away from colonization, blacks entered a decade of relative cooperation with white abolitionists, which resulted in the muting of some of the more militant calls for forcible resistance to slavery. During the 1830s, black abolitionists aligned themselves with the principles of white moral reformers, committing themselves to ideals of individual self-improvement and exemplary action as a means of combating racism and influencing whites toward the abandonment of slavery. But some New York City blacks continued to lay the groundwork for independent political action unmediated by whites. In 1836 Ruggles wrote in the *Liberator* that "Self-defense is the first law of nature." He told a New York protest meeting in 1841: "Strike for freedom or die slaves."[7]

At the end of the 1830s, the black abolitionist movement was assessing the damage from a decade of moral suasion in growing economic discrimination and racial violence. The success of individual blacks had not so much served to destroy negative stereotypes as to increase white antagonism and violence. During the 1840s moral reform would yield to new strategies of political action. At the Buffalo meeting of the National Negro

Convention in 1843, Henry Highland Garnet clashed with Frederick Douglass and Charles Lenox Remond over his radical call for forcible resistance. A decade later, as an antislavery speaker in Ohio, Sojourner Truth, holding to the Garrisonian pacifist position, would clash with a Douglass who had long since abandoned nonresistance.

Most of what we know about Truth during this period comes from a book she helped to shape, written by the English radical journalist Gilbert Vale, who interviewed Truth and a number of people she associated with. His book *Fanaticism; Its Source and Influence, Illustrated by the Simple Narrative of Isabella* was published in 1835, fifteen years before the *Narrative*. The stories Truth told to Olive Gilbert in 1850 were shaped by a complex double consciousness as Truth created Isabella's life retrospectively for an abolitionist pen. Vale's "Narrative of Isabella" is a richly textured contemporary rendering of the younger Isabella's trial in the spiritual fires of New York's Burned-over District in the 1830s.[8] Describing her antislavery lecturing during the Civil War, Truth looked back: "Years ago, when I lived in the city of New York, my occupation was scouring brass door knobs; but *now* I go about scouring copperheads" (*NarBk*, 311).

Isabella must have welcomed the complexity and diversity of the city. In leaving rural New York for the city, she undoubtedly sought economic opportunity, and she saw in the post-emancipation city the largest number of black people she had ever seen around her. From Canal Street to Broadway and the Bowery Isabella would have seen blacks, who did most of the menial work of the town, everywhere: domestics carrying heavy burdens on their heads, workers in the fields, on the streets, bringing water from wells, cisterns, or springs, marketing, serving, herding, toting and fetching. In the city Isabella worked as a domestic and housekeeper and sometimes as a laundress, living with white employers on Fourth Street, Third Street, and later on Canal Street, joining the concentration of black women in the center of the city who served its wealthy residents.

Isabella could have been a proto-character in Rudolph Fisher's *City of Refuge*, written a century after her stay, craning her neck in wonder at the teeming city. The sturdy, competent country woman who told Harriet Beecher Stowe "I grew up pretty lively an' strong, an' could row a boat, or ride a horse, or work round, an' do 'most anything,"[9] must have reveled in the smells, the sounds, the size of the growing city, then approaching a population of 150,000 people, which nearly doubled in the fourteen years she lived there.

Perhaps Isabella felt the loosening of the structure of oversight and control that was at the heart of enslavement, when she had felt surveillance everywhere, and a relaxation of the constraining effect of living in a small town. She later described her sense of liberation of movement in the city: "As a slave she had never been allowed to go anywhere, but then she went round with the lady who brought her here, and she was determined if she was despised she would go among the white people and learn all she could."[10]

New York was a black and white city, in the churches, in the court-rooms, in the schools, in the horse cars, in the hospitals, in the prisons, in the burial grounds, in its pleasures. The African Grove theater, which had entertained the black community since 1821, was closed in 1829, the year Truth entered the city, because the city fathers feared "civil discord." The African Grove had segregated whites in the back of the theater because "whites do not know how to conduct themselves at entertainments of ladies and gentlemen of color."[11] Ira Aldridge, who became one of the great Shakespearean actors of the century, was at this time a student at the African Free School.

In the Vauxhall Gardens, extending from Broadway to the Bowery, a band played on summer nights and white New Yorkers came for fireworks displays. White vendors sold ice cream in the confectionery shops and in the public gardens during summer evenings, though it was noted that "some who are not particular as to the *quality* of this article, are supplied by colored men who take it round the city in covered pails." Certain streets and sidewalks where Isabella walked daily were among the few unsegre-gated spaces in the city, and these resounded with the sounds and sights of a lively black commerce. Lime-kilners could be seen everywhere. Black men sold bundles of straw for filling beds and door mats made of tarred rope alongside enterprising sellers of "tea water" at two cents a pail, from springs in the upper part of the island. Black street vendors sold baked pears drowning in molasses and Rockaway sand from two-wheeled carts, to be "put on newly scrubbed floors, to preserve them clean and pleasant." According to Mahlon Day's book of street cries of the period, "in warm weather, one may see large churns, mounted on a wheelbarrow, pushed along by colored men, mostly from Bergen, on the Jersey shore, crying BUTTER MEELECK!" From midsummer to late autumn New Yorkers could buy corn boiled in the husk and "sold for a penny an ear, principally by colored women, one of whom cries 'You who have money, (alas! I have none,) / Come buy my lilly white corn, and let me go home.'" Black chim-ney sweeps dominated that miserable work ("In this city the business of sweeping chimneys is confined to colored men and boys, although in London white men and boys are thus employed").[12] The enterprising self-marketing habits Truth exhibited later in her life on the road and in Battle

Creek, Michigan, must have been stimulated in New York City, where, amid the extremes of poverty and surfeit, she witnessed the perseverance of vendors and domestics who acted on the adage that heaven helps those who help themselves.

The multicultural streets of New York City in the 1820s and 1830s produced a comfortable Babel of sound to which Isabella added the supple and arresting patterns of her Dutch-English-African speech—"her inimitable patois." Speaking ten years after she had moved on from the city to become an itinerant evangelist, Truth recalled that when she had come to New York she had been "ignorant, and could not speak English very well."[13] The city became her education. The diversity of race, ethnic origin, and class enabled Truth to become conscious of the economic roots of racism. She told a largely black audience in New York City in 1853 that she had come to understand that the positive value of whiteness was that it signified "food and clothes":

> She used to say, "why was I black, when if I was white I could have plenty of food and clothes!" But now she gloried in her color. She rejoiced in the color that God had been pleased to give her, and she was well satisfied with it."[14]

The exclusion of blacks from political rights, against which Truth would become a tireless agitator, was apparent everywhere. Law as well as custom segregated the city. The political process was largely closed. Free black men could still vote in New York, which had not withdrawn the right as had some other Northern states during this period, but they suffered increasing restrictions; in 1826 a constitutional amendment abolished the property qualification for all (male) voters except blacks. Even for those blacks who owned property valued at $250, legal access to the polls did not mean actual access. "There is danger of their life sometimes," Truth told the Equal Rights Association in 1867; "I guess many have seen it in this city."[15]

All associational societies, churches, mutual aid and relief societies, literary societies, in the free black community dealt constantly with the realities of slavery. When Joseph Cinqué and the thirty-eight other blacks who mutinied on the slaver *Amistad* in 1839 were being held for trial, two of the most prominent male societies, the Philomathean and the Phoenix Society, sponsored a fund-raising event in support of the prisoners.[16] Black churches were often at the center of the associational networks, housing women's groups like the Female Mite Society and the Juvenile Daughters of Ruth, which met at the Zion Church on the corner of Leonard and

Church Street. The African Dorcas Society provided clothing to students at the African Free School.[17]

Excluded from the segregated public schools, future abolitionists training at the New York African Free School in the 1820s included Samuel Ringgold Ward, his cousin James McCune Smith, Alexander Crummell, George T. Downing, and Henry Highland Garnet. We are likelier to know what men were doing than what women were doing, although the city was filled with history-making black women. The lack of educational opportunities for most black women was noted in a proprietary voice by the *Colored American* in 1839: "We expect our females to be educated and refined; to possess all the attributes which constitute the lady, yet we fail to provide the means whereby they can acquire an education which shall fit them to become the wives of an enlightened mechanic, a storekeeper or clerk."[18]

Half of the black male abolitionists in New York were ministers, one of the few professions open to black men.[19] It is possible that the concentration of clergy among the New York City abolitionists contributed to limiting information we have about the political activities of black women during this period. Men who were radical in their support of abolitionism were often still, as churchmen, relatively conservative in their attitudes toward women. When some black women physically intervened to try to help fugitives in 1837, the *Colored American* fulminated "everlasting shame" and begged "their husbands to keep them at home and find some better occupation for them."[20]

Even so, in the 1840s when Mary Ann Shadd Cary was teaching at New York's Colored Grammar School No. 4, she had "such an air of impressive command" that she was able to stop a horse car on Broadway "at a time when colored women scarcely dared to think of riding in the stages."[21] Elizabeth Jennings told the New York Female Literary Society, which sent some of its members to the First Anti-Slavery Convention of American Women held in the city in 1837, that their minds were the greatest of the powers required by the times; in the 1850s she filed a successful suit to desegregate the New York City horse car system.

In 1834 when Maria Stewart arrived in New York City from Boston as a young widow "full of the greed for literature and letters," she joined the Female Literary Society. Alexander Crummell heard her read some of her work. Although Stewart had delivered her now-famous lectures (the first public lectures on politics ever given by an American woman) and had been published in the *Liberator*, she was not known as a lecturer in New York City in these important years. Educated black men in the city may have put up a resistance more urbane but just as disabling as she had discovered in her Boston audiences. Many years later Alexander Crummell remembered his "great surprise" at "finding in New York a young woman of my own people full of literary aspiration and ambitious authorship." Crummell believed that "in those days, that is at the commencement of the antislavery enterprise, the desire for learning was almost exclusively confined to colored young men."[22] The effect of a growing movement for woman's rights, in which Truth would eventually have a commanding voice, would make itself felt in the 1840 split in the American Anti-Slavery Society, when many of the New York abolitionist ministers, including Samuel Cornish, walked out over the participation of women in the organization.[23]

In her 1853 speech to John T. Raymond's congregation in the Abyssinian Baptist Church on Anthony Street, Truth made an interesting departure from her customary presentation of herself as the typical oppressed working woman speaking out for her class. She argued instead that her individual achievement in being accepted by white audiences constituted progress for the race.

> She asked the audience to review the history of the past fifty years, and although the course was slow, the colored race had vastly improved, and that menial position to which nature seemed to have consigned them was rapidly being changed for the better. How long ago was it that a colored woman could address a white audience of a thousand people, and be listened to with respectful attention. These things were signs of the times.[24]

Remembering Alexander Crummell's condescending reaction to Maria Stewart ("a person who had received but six weeks' schooling, who could not even pen her own thoughts, who had to get a little girl of ten years to write every word of this book—that such a person could compose essays of this kind and give expression to such thoughts and be the author of such a work!"), we can take some womanist pleasure in Truth's glorying words.

The white Methodist Church had taken an early position against slavery and had welcomed blacks as members, but even the most tolerant white Christians were capable of pigeon-holing blacks in strictly segregated areas ("martin-holes," and "human menageries," some called them). Even the Society of Friends practiced segregation in some of its meetings. In 1837, when Grace Douglass of Philadelphia was a delegate to the Anti-Slavery Convention of American Women in New York City (about a tenth of the members were black, and Douglass was elected vice-president), she had

had a difficult encounter at a Quaker meeting. Her daughter Sarah wrote of the experience:

> After she had been in Mtg. sometime a Friend came in & sat by her, & asked her who she lived with. Mother said she did not live with any one. The Fd. then said that the colored people sat up stairs "as Fds. do not like to sit by thy color" & added she had no objection herself to sit by her, but that when she came again she had better sit up stairs. She did not go to Mtg. again; she was attending the Women's Convention in N. Y. 1837 & was a stranger there, it was the first time she attempted to go to Fds. Mtg there.[25]

Although Gabriel Prosser had urged his followers in 1800 to "spare the Methodists and the Quakers," even by that early date their exclusionary practices had led to the disenchantment and disengagement of many blacks. The egalitarian promise held out by Methodism had wavered as the numbers of blacks entering the church had risen. The ordination of black preachers had never been permitted, and of course, neither white Methodists nor the African Zion Methodists allowed women to be ordained to the ministry.[26]

When Isabella left Kingston for New York City in the company of a white teacher, Miss Gear, she had a letter of introduction from the Kingston congregation to the Methodist Church in John Street, the mother-church of the American denomination. During 1828 and 1829, Isabella lived with white employers on Nassau Street and Duane Street, and "while in these situations she was a zealous and consistent member of the Methodist church, in John Street, joining the coloured class, and attending the meetings with the knowledge of her employers."[27]

Isabella left "the coloured class" of the white Methodists to join the African Methodist Episcopal Zion Church in Church Street. It was there, as an active member, that Isabella "exchanged the speaking pressure of the hand" denoting "spiritual sisterhood" with her sister Nancy without recognizing her (*NarBk*, 80). But neither the experience of organized religion in the white Methodist nor in the male-dominated African Methodist Episcopal churches satisfied Isabella, who shared that dissatisfaction with many imaginative enquiring women of the period who were straining against the obsolescent status relationships and rigid gender roles that were legitimated by male church authority. Within the church a hierarchical deference to male ministers made the efforts of an unauthorized woman who "wanted to be doing" unwelcome. Isabella had arrived in New York City at a time when many people felt as she did. They had anarchic dreams.

While still a member of the Zion Church, Isabella was frequently drawn to meetings conducted by one of her employers, the white fur merchant James Latourette, who had left the Methodist Church in 1828 to try to produce a more perfect version of Wesleyan religion. Offshoots from Latourette's group influenced holiness cults near Albany.[28] Isabella then became "well known among the Methodists" in the city, attended many camp meetings, and "became the means of *converting* some by her zeal," which was evidenced in her "long and loud preaching and praying, remarkable for their influence in converting."

> Mr. Latourette assured us the influence of her speaking was miraculous, that even learned and respectable people were running after her, and she even commanded a larger audience than the celebrated Maffet, when both were preaching on the same ground at the same time.[29]

Through Latourette, Isabella was drawn into an intense circle of reform-minded white women in the Bowery, who were turning the activist impulse within evangelicalism toward social reform, "establishing prayer-meetings in several places, where such a thing might least have been expected." There is a comic portrait of their prayer meetings in *Narrative:*

> But these meetings soon became the most noisy, shouting, ranting, and boisterous of gatherings; where they became delirious with excitement, and then exhausted from overaction. Such meetings Isabel had not much sympathy with, at best. But one evening she attended one of them, where the members of it, in a fit of ecstasy, jumped upon her cloak in such a manner as to drag her to the floor—and then, thinking she had fallen in a spiritual trance, they increased their glorifications on her account,—jumping, shouting, stamping, and clapping of hands; rejoicing so much over her spirit, and so entirely overlooking her body, that she suffered much, both from fear and bruises; and ever after refused to attend any more such meetings, doubting much whether God had any thing to do with such worship. (*NarBk*, 87)

Isabella had contacted a sisterhood imbued with a sense of proselytism, which was moving toward a preliminary redefinition of female identity:

> At that time, the "moral reform" movement was awakening the attention of the benevolent in that city. Many women, among whom were Mrs. Latourette and Miss Grear [sic], became deeply interested in making an attempt to reform their fallen sisters, even the most degraded of them;

and in this enterprise of labor and danger, they enlisted Isabella and others, who for a time put forth their most zealous efforts, and performed the work of missionaries with much apparent success. (*NarBk*, 86)

Soon Isabella was accompanying these women "to the most wretched abodes of vice and misery, and sometimes she went where they dared not follow" (*NarBk*, 86-87). This would have included innumerable houses in Five Points, where few outsiders indeed dared to go (when an inquiring Charles Dickens went there in 1842, he asked two policemen to accompany him).

At a meeting in 1832, Isabella received an invitation "to instruct the girls at the Magdalene Asylum, Bowery Hill," a much-publicized reformist boarding house for prostitutes under the direction of a wealthy reformer, Elijah Pierson. The Magdalene Asylum was supported by Arthur Tappan, the social reformer and antislavery advocate, an evangelical activist from Northampton, Massachusetts. Tappan and other evangelical reformers helped to establish the Asylum after the Canadian seminary student John R. McDowall published his *Magdalene Report* in 1831, exposing the conditions among a prostitute population he estimated at ten thousand. Isabella therefore joined a pioneering undertaking in urban social control, the first anti-prostitution campaign in the country. Although the Asylum was a short-lived experiment, it was an important entry-point for Isabella into a larger movement.

Some of the reform efforts that had originated in moral fervor came to recognize the prostitute's condition as an indictment of the inequality of a male ordered society that made prostitution an economic necessity for some women, a view voiced in Margaret Fuller's profiles of prostitutes published in the New York *Tribune* and also articulated by antislavery activist Wendell Phillips.[30] Carroll Smith-Rosenberg has argued that the moral reform crusade, with its ideal of reshaping male sexual behavior, was an important early manifestation of feminism. In the millennial New York of the 1830s, middle-class white women were using moral reform to gain control of their own sex-roles; grievances originating in discontent with gender roles resonated with their piety. Their pragmatic attempts to aid the city's prostitutes involved them in frank evaluations of sexuality and gender privilege, and their work had consequences for later feminists trying to break out of the sphere of domesticity and armchair religion.[31]

It was at the Magdalene Asylum in Five Points that Isabella formed her relationship with Elijah Pierson and ventured into the risky and revelatory association that occupied her in the years 1832-1834. When Pierson asked Isabella if she had been baptized, she answered "by the Holy Ghost."[32] They had much in common.

"In the vividness of his imagination," Gilbert Vale observed of Pierson, "he thought that God spoke to him." Attempting to understand the development of Isabella's religious faith, Vale thought that her earliest experience of Methodism in Kingston had been emotionally (and physically) liberating without challenging her understanding: "her strong body and mind had room for exertion; she out-prayed and preached her compeers, and received without doubting what was taught." Vale thought that Isabella's faith had made an "easy transition" to the style of James Latourette which "was merely Methodism in the extreme, and exactly suited her excited and active state of mind and body." Elijah Pierson was different:

> But when she went to Mr. Pierson, and found in him a close student of the Bible, and ready to give an answer to every one, in a free but gentle manner; and when she heard him advance other doctrines than those of Methodists, her faith and confidence left her; and, perhaps for the first time, she doubted that men could be sincerely in the wrong. Mr. Pierson was a man superior to any she had met with, and she readily received his interpretations, and became an inquirer.[33]

In a sense, Pierson was to Isabella as the white Shaker was to Rebecca Cox Jackson in her visions of this same period: "And often, when I would be in meditation and looking into things which was hard to understand, I would find him by me, teaching and giving me understanding."[34] Isabella left the African Zion Church and joined Pierson's group, where she was received as a spiritual equal, praying and exhorting; she also ate at the same table. In May 1832 she was working as Pierson's housekeeper on Fourth Street when she opened the door to an itinerant white prophet with a long flowing beard and hair and "her early impressions of seeing Jesus in the flesh, rushed into her mind." Matthias had revived in Isabella the image from her conversion experience, which she knew to be influenced "by the pictures in the large family Bibles she had seen." Vale himself had heard Matthias lecture, and agreed that "his aspect was certainly much like the engravings of Jesus Christ in the family bibles."[35]

Later, when Truth described her arrival in New York City in 1829, she said "She had known nothing of religion a few months before—not even that Jesus Christ was the Son of God."[36] In a sense she was entering religious life as a Christian without history, just as the primitive Christians had, and in that state she accepted the appearance of Matthias as another avatar of God with equanimity. Truth's innocence of Christian history paralleled the intention of the other members of the commune to separate themselves from it.[37] Isabella's immediate acceptance of a Christ-like embodiment might be consistent with African patterns of belief, which traditionally could accommodate new deities when necessary.[38]

Elijah Pierson's belief system was also constructed through parallels with primitive Christianity, and he accepted Matthias as the greater figure for whom he, as a latter day John the Baptist, had prepared the way. Matthias moved in, took over the household and ministry, and Isabella became devoted to him. During part of this period the commune moved to the estate of Benjamin and Ann Folger in Sing Sing, which Matthias named Zion Hill. Pierson and the Folgers were wealthy and prominent members of the New York business community. Their involvement as much as Matthias's eccentricity assured that the commune would eventually excite the public's curiosity.

For a time sensational copy about this tiny millennial cult filled New York newspapers and spilled over into pamphlets, fed by rumors surrounding Elijah Pierson's death at Zion Hill after a series of epileptic seizures.[39] In a dramatic court case Pierson's distraught family tried (unsuccessfully) to get Matthias convicted of poisoning Pierson. The Folgers regretted their participation in the cult's activities and tried to salvage their reputations by making even more sensational accusations that Isabella had tried to poison their breakfast coffee. Isabella in turn filed a libel suit against the Folgers who paid for their absurd charge with a huge settlement for the time, $125 and costs.

The publicity surrounding Pierson's death and the Folgers' charges underscored Isabella's vulnerability as the only black among a group of whites whose questionable religious practices were undergoing public scrutiny. William Stone's inflammatory indictment of Isabella, written as an apology for the Folgers' involvement in the commune, drew upon the association of conjuring practices with poisoning to label Isabella a "black witch," placing her "among the most wicked of the wicked."[40] In response Isabella, in what was probably her first dramatic interaction with the humming world of print supposedly closed to the illiterate, managed to get her own story into a book. In his radical newspaper, *Citizen of the World*, Gilbert Vale, an advocate of the rights of working people and an antislavery advocate, disputed Stone's account of events. Vale's public criticism "led to the application of a gentleman on the part of Isabella," who told Vale that she "was desirous of telling the whole truth." Vale's reply was a request that the man "bring her here immediately."[41] The appearance of this "gentleman" indicates that Isabella already had in 1835 a staunch group of defenders who would not abandon her even in the most unpropitious times and that she understood the power of the press for vindication as well as blame. That Vale's book was written based on her stories and circulated against the "white evidence" of the Folgers is as remarkable as the $125 award.[42] Both the act of initiating the book and the book itself provide us with invaluable insight into Isabella's New York City years.

The account of Isabella's years in the Matthias cult, including the period in which she believed that Matthias was a god, is usually used to establish the fraudulent character of the claims of Matthias, which is then used as evidence of Isabella's gullibility and victimization. To look at it this way is to be trapped in the unenviable position of the district attorney prosecuting Matthias for fraud in an indictment that alleged "that Matthias was in fact, not God" and had none of the powers he claimed. "Could it be proved that he was not God the Father?" the district attorney asked querulously; "Could it be proved he was not the Spirit of Truth?"[43] We are interested instead in what it was that attracted Isabella. It is instructive to note that the trial Judge Charles H. Ruggles thought Matthias was insane, as did three doctors, but other witnesses believed that he was "sane on all subjects except religion."[44] The judgment of these witnesses provides more than a little insight into the state of religious belief in New York in the 1830s.

The Mormon prophet Joseph Smith saw the prophet Matthias in Kirtland, Ohio in 1835, when Matthias was on his way west after his acquittal. Their meeting gives a context to the workings of the failed commune. Eight years earlier, Smith had received the golden plates from the angel Moroni on Hill Cumorah in New York State. The *Book of Mormon* had been published in 1830, while Isabella was still working with outcast women and Matthias was marching around Albany with a white banner "Rally Round the Standard of Truth." At this time Smith was planning the building of Zion in Independence, Missouri.[45] Always willing to talk doctrine, Smith was initially impressed by Matthias:

> His appearance was something singular, having a beard about three inches in length, quite grey; also his hair was long and considerably silvered with age; I thought him about fifty or fifty-five years old; tall, straight, slender built, of thin visage, blue eyes, and fair complexion; wore a sea-green frock coat and pantaloons, black fur hat with narrow brim; and, while speaking, frequently shut his eyes, with a scowl on his countenance. I made some inquiry after his name, but received no definite answer.

"He made some very excellent remarks," Joseph Smith observed, "but his mind was evidently filled with darkness."

Joseph Smith drew out Matthias on "his views respecting the resurrection":

He said that he possessed the spirit of his fathers, that he was a literal descendant of Matthias, the Apostle, who was chosen in the place of Judas that fell; that his spirit was resurrected in him; and that this was the way or scheme of eternal life—this transmigration of soul or spirit from father to son.[46]

The doctrine of the transmigration of spirits that Matthias expounded to Joseph Smith may have been one of the compelling elements of his belief system for Isabella. She explained to Gilbert Vale that Matthias "did not believe in the resurrection of the body, but that the spirits of the former saints would enter the bodies of the present generation, and thus begin heaven upon earth" and that he "did not believe in going to the sky."

> "Paradise," she observed, "was formerly on the earth, and it would be so now if the wicked were not here; the wicked then will be driven from the earth into the sky, and the earth made a paradise again for the good."[47]

Like the Second Adventists and other millennial sects of the time, the Matthias commune had designated a period (between 1831 and 1850) for the coming of the judgment described in the biblical book of Revelation. While the world lasted, the commune's property was to be held in common; Isabella had contributed her savings (which she lost), her furniture, and she worked without wages. She was meant to be a working equal, performing domestic work while the other members contributed whatever unlikely labor they could perform. Matthias expected women to be still and subservient, although Isabella does not seem to have conformed particularly. In the end, it was not so much her rights as a woman but her rights as a laborer that she invoked. She began to withdraw emotionally when Matthias ignored her complaint that she was doing other people's work, including his.

Vale himself was puzzled by the apparently complete acceptance of Isabella's presence by Pierson and Matthias and could only explain it by reverting to a racist stereotype: Isabella was allowed to be present at critical moments because, as in the South, "colored people, and especially slaves" are "scarcely regarded as being present." It is likelier that the acceptance of her physical presence secured Isabella to the group. Perhaps she tolerated Matthias's misogyny in exchange for this interracial acceptance.

All the members at Zion Hill were preoccupied with good and evil spirits, believing, for example, that sickness was a possession by an evil spirit. It was probably this belief, in which Pierson concurred, that resulted in his dying without medical attention. Once, when Isabella felt ill, Matthias struck her with a rawhide, apparently to drive out the evil spirit. Unlike Julia Foote, who when unjustly whipped "carried the rawhide out to the wood pile, took the axe, and cut it up into small pieces," Isabella's response to the rawhide was to recover her energy as if she had been liberated from the evil spirit's grasp.[48] When the jury at Matthias's trial asked her "what had become of Pierson's devil, or evil spirit," Isabella replied, "tartly," that "it might have entered into one of them."[49] The casting out of devils remained a favorite topic for Truth in her lecturing career. When she confronted the hissing audience at the Mob Convention in New York City in 1853, she twitted them with this: "Is it not good for me to come and draw forth a spirit, to see what kind of spirit people are of?"[50]

At the Asylum, Pierson had instituted a ritual of humility related to the story of Mary Magdalene's washing Christ's feet, in which the matron and Isabella had washed each other's feet.[51] In Matthias's commune Isabella again participated in a weekly rite of purification:

> This washing was performed in a perfect state of nudity; sometimes in
> a large tub; and at others, in a shower bath; both generally in the same
> room: the men ordinarily assisted the men, and the women the women.[52]

Matthias preached that shame itself was sin: the purest person experienced the least shame. Like many other sects rebelling against established forms of religion in the period, the Kingdom experimented with sexual arrangements. Even in the days of Pierson's authority, the group disavowed Christian marriage. Matthias introduced sexual relations between "match spirits"; Matthias and Ann Folger were "matched," Folger's husband was matched first with Matthias's daughter and then with the white servant Catherine Calloway. One of the communards, a Mr. Thompson, succinctly captured the scene as he was departing it: "There is too much changing of wives here; I have a nice little woman, and I should not much like to lose her."[53] Gilbert Vale believed that Isabella had not participated in the sexual matching because she was not attractive enough to obtain a "match spirit" ("she is near forty, not handsome, and coloured"); but he does not suppress her own remarkable statement that this was "circumstances, as much as any thing": "for at one time the spirit which affected the head, was infectious, and threatened the whole body."[54] Such a candid recognition of desire was in itself radical.

Vale's shrewdly composed account of what happened in the commune was balanced between two schools of evidence: the unimpeachable testimony of Isabella, which Vale respected, and the "white evidence," as he called it, with which he filled the second half of his book. At one point when Matthias was on trial for the death of Pierson (he was immediately acquitted by the Westchester Court system) his lawyer asked Isabella to testify for Matthias in the courtroom, so she had to supply character references, many of which she obtained from her slave masters in Ulster County. This was necessary not to save herself (the court had immediately thrown out any charges against her), but so that her testimony *as a black* would be accepted. Many state constitutions forbade blacks to testify in cases that involved whites.

There is unsubtle irony in the enthusiastic endorsement of Isabella by John J. Dumont and the other slave masters that Vale printed in his book: in 1834 in New York State people who had bought and sold other people could give character references to those they had marketed like farm animals without their own characters being called into question. These were the people who were credible in this country: the providers of the "white evidence" that Vale often referred to in his book. In this way, distinguished Bostonians had attested to the rational powers of Phillis Wheatley, without the self examination that would have challenged their use of reason in abetting her enslavement.

What Isabella's "fixed religious opinions now are," Vale admitted in his conclusion, "we know not":

> Her ancient faith is shaken; she is not a believer in the supernatural character of Matthias, but still regards most of his interpretations as more rational, and probably true, than that of any other teacher of religion; she compares him too with the clergy, with a tact not to be overcome, and draws a conclusion in his favour.[55]

Perhaps Isabella was comparing Matthias to the white Christian clergy who believed that African slavery was a God-ordained means of saving the African soul. At this time she was among the ten percent of blacks in the country who were not owned by nominal Christians. In the commune, Isabella had always seemed less deluded and less helpless than any of the other participants. In the end, she just packed the few pieces of furniture she had left and went back to work as a domestic on Canal Street, where, from her wages, she loaned money to the most destitute of the former cultists, the white servant Catherine Calloway. Vale retained a healthy respect for Isabella's boldness and her inscrutability.

> From our listening to this coloured female, questioning her frequently, and often recurring to very curious and doubtful subjects, we

have discovered that she too, like Mrs. B. Folger, is not exactly what she seems. Though born in this state, she has African features, and no apparent mixture of blood; she is not exactly bad looking, but there is nothing prepossessing or very observant or intelligent in her looks yet throughout we find her reflecting, "she had her own or private opinion on every thing;" and these opinions of her *own* we have frequently found very correct; yet she is not communicative, and if circumstances did not prompt her to tell all she knows, it would be difficult to get at it.[56]

Isabella's stay at the Zion Hill commune in the summer of 1834 when Elijah Pierson was tragically dying kept her out of the city during the worst anti-black violence prior to the Civil War. During the fourteen years of Truth's residence in the city, the rise of abolitionist agitation converged with the rising anti-black prejudice created by economic competition with the white immigrant working class. The commitment of the free black community to antislavery and the struggle of free black labor to survive in the lowest circle of economic activity made blacks a double target of white violence.

The "July Days" of 1834, in which violent mobs of as many as twenty thousand persons formed on anti-abolitionist, anti-black lines, began with the harassment of an integrated meeting at Chatham-street Chapel, where a black minister delivered an abolitionist sermon to a largely black audience. Inflammatory newspaper reports, charging that abolitionists were promoting "amalgamation" (interracial marriage), drew hostile crowds, which were dispersed only by the mayor's order. The English had abolished slavery in 1833, and the mere presence of an English stage manager at the Bowery Theatre drew the mob there. The Rose Street house of merchant-abolitionist Arthur Tappan was sacked and its furniture tossed into a bonfire. On succeeding nights, the crowds resumed the attacks, targeting, among others, the abolitionist-minister Samuel H. Cox. James Watson Webb's *Courier and Enquirer* applauded, writing "that these abolitionists and amalgamators should know the ground on which they stand." The Presbyterian Church on Spring Street, where abolition was preached from the pulpit, was the scene of a pitched battle between the militia and the mob.

But what had begun as an attack on abolitionist activity in support of blacks quickly became an attack on blacks themselves. The mob ransacked the St. Phillip's African Episcopal Church on Center Street, where the Reverend Peter Williams was rumored to have performed an interracial marriage. Rioting was at its worst in the Five Points area, where the rioters singled out black dwellings for attack. City control was regained by stationing the militia in Five Points as well as in St. John's Park and calling in a cavalry regiment.

In her study of the riots, Linda K. Kerber has argued that the egalitarian rhetoric of abolitionism represented an economic threat as much as a social one, and that the racial hatred expressed by the white mob was a cover for fears born of economic displacement. A contemporary newspaper interpreted the riots in just this way: "It is impossible to conceal the fact, that in consequence of the competition between free white labor and the black labor of the North, there is a feeling of bitter hatred already existing." Kerber notes other competitors with "free, white, skilled labor" were attacked along with blacks, including unskilled Irish immigrants, who were not noticeably active in this riot. In 1834, a year of economic recession in the city, the white immigrants who had come earlier and were better established feared the movement of everything below them, white or black.[57]

In 1832, the year Isabella met Pierson and Matthias, Maria Stewart delivered her powerful indictment of the dead-end racist economy for blacks in urban America:

> Do you ask, why are you wretched and miserable? I reply, look at many of the most worthy and most interesting of us doomed to spend our lives in gentlemen's kitchens. Look at our young men, smart, active and energetic, with souls filled with ambitious fire; if they look forward, alas! What are their prospects? They can be nothing but the humblest laborers, on account of their dark complexions; hence many of them lose their ambition, and become worthless. Look at our middle-aged men, clad in their rusty plaids and coats; in winter, every cent they earn goes to buy their wood and pay their rents; the poor wives also toil beyond their strength, to help support their families. Look at our aged sires, whose heads are whitened with the frosts of seventy winters, with their old wood-saws on their backs. Alas, what keeps us so? Prejudice, ignorance and poverty.[58]

Racism resulted in a ruthless constriction of job opportunities for black people. Only menial work was available, and the expectation that blacks would engage in it was universal. As a teacher in New York City, Sarah Douglass had been reduced to tears by the "first salutation" she had received at a Quaker meeting: "Does thee go out a house cleaning."[59]

Although the completion of the Erie Canal in 1825 transformed the city's trade, living conditions for poor people, white or black, were very

hard. In the 1820s and 1830s immigrant assaults on black communities in
the city were common, and resentment of free black workers was strong.
Artisan work and the more lucrative work of carters and draymen were
precluded. In 1837, the *Colored American* reported that under pressure
from white cartmen, black cartmen had been denied licenses to sell. Skilled
black workers all over the north faced the exclusion that Frederick
Douglass, a skilled caulker, had found on the wharves of New Bedford,
that "every white man would leave the ship, in her unfinished condition, if
I struck a blow at my trade."[60]

Friction between free blacks and the Irish, the two lowest groups on the
urban socio-economic ladder, increased as the rate of Irish immigration
escalated during the 1840s, although economic competition between
immigrant and free black workers created hostility throughout the white
immigrant working class. When Charles Dickens visited the Five Points
district, he saw William Henry Lane "spinning about on his toes and heels
like nothing but the man's fingers on the tambourine."[61] The street competition between William Henry Lane, the city's finest black dancer and
John Diamond, the greatest of the Irish jig dancers would be played out in
more violent ways, culminating in the disastrous anti-black Draft Riots
during the Civil War. Dorothy Sterling has pointed out that when
Elizabeth Jennings brought suit against the Third Avenue Railroad
Company, winning $225 and the right for blacks to ride public transporta-
tion, she told the Irish-born conductor who threw her off the Third
Avenue horse car that although she was "a respectable person, born and
raised in New York," she "did not know where he was born."[62]

In her 1853 speech to John T. Raymond's congregation at the
Abyssinian Church in Anthony Street, Truth compared the city she had
known in the years 1829-43 to the city she saw before her. She saw her
people pushed further to the margins, even, through the colonization
movement, pushed entirely out. She concentrated on the competition
between blacks and immigrant whites that had altered the city:

> She went on to talk of the colored people and their prospects. They
> were gradually being thrust out from every menial occupation by their
> white brethren; but she believed this was ominous of a better future.
> They were being prepared for some great change that would take place
> ere long. She was decidedly opposed to the colonization project; they
> must stay, and a short time would show that that was the best course.

Truth displayed her anti-immigrant bias in a satire of the work habits of
the whites whom she saw as taking away black jobs:

When the colored people were waiters, and did all the common and lower kinds of work the streets were clean; the servants scraped the dirt from the corners, swept out the gutters and half-way across the streets. Now, white folk clean boots, wait at table, lie about lazy, and beg cold victuals. The colored people did that sometimes too—but not to keep boarders on it! [Laughter.] . . . Not long ago nobody but colored people were coachmen and barbers, but now they have white Pompeys, with the livery coats on, and poor black Pompey goes to the wall.

In this speech, Truth observed that "The papers rarely recorded crimes committed by her race, though they often teemed with those committed against them."[63] Whether the papers recorded it or not, in the 1820s in New York City, the percentage of blacks in the population of the city jail and penitentiary sometimes reached two-thirds, when blacks represented only one twelfth of the city population. In the year that Isabella arrived in the city with her son Peter, 145 black children were committed to the city penitentiary, often for minor infractions that would not have led to the arrest of whites; they were sent to adult prisons because the juvenile facilities were strictly segregated.[64] Peter came to bitter knowledge of this discrepancy in the meting out of justice. In framing Peter's troubles with the law in *Narrative*, Olive Gilbert made the city itself the breeder of crime and vice. She did not count racist injustice among "the baneful influences going up from such a city" (*NarBk*, 73).

Perhaps never fully recovered from the traumas of his childhood, Isabella's son Peter was always in trouble in the city. "It was indeed hard," Truth told a black audience in 1853, "that their oppressors should bind them hand and foot, and ask them why did they not run."[65] With the help of a white benefactor, Peter had been enrolled in a navigation school, but he never attended classes. He had worked for a time for another white benefactor as a coachman in livery, a "black Pompey," as Truth referred to the vanishing black coachmen of the city. ("Some southern republican that, who puts his blacks in uniform, and swells with Sultan pomp and power," Charles Dickens wrote contemptuously of the wealthy New Yorkers who dressed their coachmen in livery.[66]) Peter rebelled from this masquerade and sold his livery. Isabella had "urged his going to sea, and would have shipped him on board a man-of-war," one of the few occupational paths open for black men, but Peter refused.[67] He was nevertheless helped by a support system that guided young men into careers at sea. When Peter was jailed in the Tombs after a series of misdemeanors in the summer of 1839, he was helped by a man in the black community "who sometimes helped young culprits out of their troubles, and sent them from city dangers, by shipping them on board of whaling vessels" (*NarBk*, 75-76).[68] A young black man thrown into the Tombs for misdemeanors would have needed help. In 1842 when Dickens expressed his revulsion at the rows of cells at the bottom of the Tombs, the jailer defended them: "Why, we *do* only put colored people in 'em. That's the truth."[69]

Peter got a place on the whaler *Zone*, which sailed from Nantucket under Captain Hiller in 1839. Truth preserved three of his letters as a kind of memorial to him by having them inserted in her *Narrative*. The letters suggest Peter's affectionate acquaintance with an extended family, including his sisters Sophia, Elizabeth, and Diana, and the children of Truth's siblings: "I would like to know how my sisters are. Does my cousins live in New York yet?"

> I am your only son, that is so far from your home, in the wide, briny ocean. I have seen more of the world than ever I expected, and if I ever should return home safe, I will tell you all my troubles and hardships. Mother, I hope you do not forget me, your dear and only son. I should like to know how Sophia, and Betsey, and Hannah [i. e., Diana], come on. I hope you all will forgive me for all that I have done. (*NarBk*, 77)

In the last letter published in the *Narrative* written in September 1841, Peter asked Truth to "tell me how all the people is about the neighborhood." He also especially asked "if you have been up home since I left or not. I want to know what sort of a time is at home." He had never been at home in the city; he meant by "home" the Dumont farm, to which his family had had such a protracted and tormented connection.

Sidney Kaplan has shown that the *Zone* returned from the Pacific in 1843 heavily laden with oil. Peter is not known to have returned with it.[70] We know that Truth never stopped thinking about Peter from a touching reference in the letter Olive Gilbert wrote to her in 1870:

> Was very glad your mind was set at rest about your son Peter. How strange are the events of our lives. How little we know of the world we live in, especially of the spiritual world by which we are surrounded. (*NarBk*, 276)

Truth had apparently contacted Peter through spiritualism.

Isabella entered New York as a primitive Christian. With Latourette, Pierson, and Matthias she was immersed in the phantasmagoric visions of perfectionism. She was trained in a social gospel that was interracial, and in the case of her moral reform work with the Magdalene Asylum, slanted toward woman's needs. Perhaps her experience of interracial acceptance in reform work and in the religious commune contributed to her becoming a Garrisonian in the 1830s when Garrisonian nonresistance was coming more and more under attack by black abolitionists. Isabella was developing a broad vision of social reform, in which evangelism went hand in hand with agitation for her race. Truth told the Chicago *Daily Inter-Ocean* in 1879 that in her itinerant evangelist period, after leaving New York City and before arriving among the antislavery activists at the utopian settlement at Northampton, she had preached "religion and abolition all the way."[71]

What *Narrative* records of Isabella's thoughts on the eve of her departure in 1843 suggests that the communal experiment had had a profound and lasting effect in the maturing of her social vision. In a despairing moment when she thought "that everything she had undertaken in the city of New York had finally proved a failure," she seems to have reached a point of enlightenment that shed light on everything in her future. The pivotal passage in the *Narrative* outlines the change in Isabella's thinking about the distribution of the twin goods of human labor and of property. Having lost her savings when the commune failed, Isabella had begun again as a wage earner, trying "to accumulate a sufficiency" to buy a home, "turning her hand to almost any thing that promised good pay" (*NarBk*, 98). Why poor working people are seldom able to succeed at accumulating and whether accumulation of a store is a proper goal become the objects of Isabella's analysis. Her New York City experiments in social reform and communal living combined with her sustained experience as a wage laborer texture her vision of the roiling struggle of rich against poor, and poor against poor.

Ownership had been at the heart of Truth's life experience. As a slave, she had never owned the product of her labor; not even her body had been her own. *She* had been owned. Now she "began to look upon money and property with great indifference, if not contempt."

> After turning it in her mind for some time, she came to the conclusion, that she had been taking part in a great drama, which was, in itself, but one great system of robbery and wrong. "Yes," she said, "the rich rob the poor, and the poor rob one another." True, she had not received the labor from others, and stinted their pay, as she felt had been practised against her; but she had taken their work from them, which was their only means to get money, and was the same to them in the end. For instance—a gentleman

where she lived would give her a half dollar to hire a poor man to clear the new-fallen snow from the steps and sidewalks. She would arise early, and perform the labor herself, putting the money into her own pocket. A poor man would come along, saying she ought to have let him have the job; he was poor, and needed the pay for his family. She would harden her heart against him, and answer—"I am poor, too, and I need it for mine." But, in her retrospection, she thought of all the misery she might have been adding to, in her selfish grasping, and it troubled her conscience sorely; and this insensibility to the claims of human brotherhood, and the wants of the destitute and wretched poor, she now saw, as she never had done before, to be unfeeling, selfish and wicked." (*NarBk*, 98-99)

These views, so starkly cast in terms of privilege and privation, elitist indifference and simple need, had been fostered in the streets of the city itself during one of its most critical periods. Isabella had achieved a hard-won political vision of the worth of work as arising from its function in a shared community built upon the real "claims of human brotherhood." Belittled by Gilbert as a naive failure to discern between miserly grasping and "a true use of the good things of this life for one's own comfort," Isabella's social revelation signaled her coming to full maturity. When Isabella achieved this vision of social responsibility, she became Sojourner. It was only left to say so:

Her next decision was, that she must leave the city; it was no place for her; yea, she felt called in spirit to leave it, and to travel east and lecture. She had never been further east than the city, neither had she any friends there of whom she had particular reason to expect any thing; yet to her it was plain that her mission lay in the east, and that she would find friends there. (*NarBk*, 100)

The woman who had once verified her good name by submitting to a court of law letters from some eight former employers and masters, determined to walk on without that name.

Having made what preparations for leaving she deemed necessary,—which was, to put a few articles of clothing in a pillow-case, all else being deemed an unnecessary incumbrance,—about an hour before she left, she informed Mrs. Whiting, the woman of the house where she was stopping, that her name was no longer Isabella, but SOJOURNER; and that she was going east. And to her inquiry, "What are you going east for?" her answer was, "The Spirit calls me there, and I must go." (*NarBk*, 100)

Notes

1. Dorothy Sterling, ed., *We Are Your Sisters: Black Women in the Nineteenth Century* (New York: W. W. Norton, 1984), 116.
2. Alice Walker, *The Color Purple* (New York: Pocket Books, 1982), 204.
3. This discussion is drawn from the introductory essay, "Colonization, Immediatism, and Moral Reform," in C. Peter Ripley, et al., eds., *The Black Abolitionist Papers* (Chapel Hill: University of North Carolina Press, 1985), 3:3-20.
4. Quoted from James McCune Smith, *Introduction to a Memorial Discourse; by Rev. Henry Highland Garnet* (Philadelphia: Joseph M. Wilson, 1865), 17-18. The significance of the parade is discussed in Sterling Stuckey, *Slave Culture: Nationalist Theory and the Foundations of Black America* (New York: Oxford University Press, 1987), 143-44.
5. James Oliver Horton, *Free People of Color: Inside the African American Community* (Washington, D.C.: Smithsonian Institution Press, 1993), 63-65.
6. Frederick Douglass, *Narrative of the Life of Frederick Douglass, an African Slave, Written by Himself*, edited by Houston A. Baker, Jr. (New York: Penguin Books, 1982), 143-45.
7. *The Liberator*, 6 August 1836 and 13 August 1841, quoted in Horton, *Free People of Color*, 88.
8. See the well-known description of this New York state locus of "habitual revivalism" in Whitney R. Cross, *The Burned-over District: The Social and Intellectual History of Enthusiastic Religion in Western New York, 1800-1850* (New York: Cornell University Press, 1950), 3.
9. Stowe, "Sojourner Truth, the Libyan Sibyl," 475.
10. *Tribune*, 7 September 1853.
11. Roi Ottley and William J. Weatherby, eds., *The Negro in New York: An Informal Social History* (Dobbs Ferry, New York: Oceana Publications, 1967), 72-73.
12. See *The Cries of New-York, with Fifteen Illustrations, Drawn from Life by a Distinguished Artist;[with] the Poetry by Frances S. Osgood* (New York: John Doggett, Jr., 1846), 5, 29; *The New York Street Cries, in Rhyme* (New York: Mahlon Day, ca. 1840), 10, 16.
13. She told the *National Anti-Slavery Standard*, 10 September 1853, that "I could not speak English until I was ten years old."
14. *Tribune*, 7 September 1853.
15. Stanton, et al., *History of Woman Suffrage*, 2:225; Leonard P. Curry, *The Free Black in Urban America 1800-1850: The Shadow of the Dream* (Chicago: University of Chicago Press, 1981), 88, 217-18.
16. Daniel Perlman, "Organizations of the Free Negro in New York City, 1800-1860," *Journal of Negro History* 56 (July 1971): 194-95.
17. Perlman, "Organizations of the Free Negro in New York City," 187.

18. *Colored American*, 23 November 1839.

19. Jane H. Pease and William H. Pease, *They Who Would Be Free: Blacks' Search for Freedom, 1830-1861* (New York: Atheneum, 1974), 289-90. In 1840 when the free black community numbered 16,358 people, there were ten prominent black churches according to Charles B. Ray, "Colored Churches in This City," *Colored American*, 28 March 1840; Ripley, et al., *The Black Abolitionist Papers*, 3:213.

20. *Colored American*, 13 April 1837.

21. *Frederick Douglass' Paper*, 9 November 1855.

22. See Maria W. Stewart, *America's First Black Woman Political Writer: Essays and Speeches*, edited by Marilyn Richardson (Bloomington: Indiana University Press, 1987), xvi, 93-94. Alexander Crummell's letter was included in a preface to the enlarged edition of Maria Stewart's *Meditations* (1879). Richardson writes that Stewart did lecture in New York (27 and 125n.51), although Crummell makes no reference to it.

23. For a description of the split see Gerda Lerner, *The Grimké Sisters from South Carolina: Pioneers for Woman's Rights and Abolition* (New York: Schocken Books, 1971), 282-86. See also Ripley, et al., *The Black Abolitionist Papers*, 1:83-84.

24. *Tribune*, 8 November 1853.

25. Sterling, *We Are Your Sisters*, 114, 130-31.

26. C. Eric Lincoln and Lawrence H. Mamiya, *The Black Church in the African American Experience* (Durham: Duke University Press, 1990), 50, 56-58; Curry, *The Free Black in Urban America*, 182. The A.M.E. Zion Church would eventually become the first among all Methodist denominations to give women the vote in church matters and to ordain them to the ministry.

27. Vale, *Fanaticism*, part 1, 19.

28. See Cross, *The Burned-over District*, 240-41.

29. Vale, *Fanaticism*, part 2, 18-21.

30. See Helen Beal Woodward, *The Bold Women* (New York: Farrar, Straus and Young, 1953), 253-58.

31. Carroll Smith-Rosenberg, "Beauty, the Beast and the Militant Woman: A Case Study in Sex Roles and Social Stress in Jacksonian America," *American Quarterly* 23 (October 1971): 563-84.

32. Vale, *Fanaticism*, part 1, 19.

33. Ibid., part 2, 125-26.

34. Jackson, *Gifts of Power*, 147. Jean McMahon Humez identifies the "white man" who influenced Cox as a Shaker by his appearance.

35. Vale, *Fanaticism*, part 1, 18 and 40.

36. *Tribune*, 7 September 1853.

37. Jan Shipps describes the "huge hiatus" created by the early Mormon "rejection of the institutional history of Christianity," which identified the period between the founding of the church and the days of the ancient Christian Apostles as a "Great Apostasy" (*Mormonism: The Story of a New Religious Tradition* [Chicago: University of Illinois Press, 1985], 51-52).

38. Piersen, *Black Yankees*, 71.

39. See William L. Stone, *Matthias and His Impostures; or the Progress of Fanaticism* (New York, 1835). Other sources include an anonymous pamphlet, *A Chapter in The History of Robert Matthews, Otherwise Known as Matthias, The Prophet, Together with His Trial for The Murder of Mr. Pierson* (Utica: 1835). Eye-witness versions by the protagonist and his wife may be found in Robert Matthews, *Memoirs of Matthias the Prophet* (New York, 1835); Margaret Matthews, *Matthias, by His Wife: With Notes on the Book of Mr. Stone on Matthias* (New York, 1835). For a modern account see Thomas McDade, "Matthias, Prophet without Honor," *New York Historical Society Quarterly* 62 (October 1978): 311-34.

40. Vale, *Fanaticism*, part 1, 8.

41. Ibid., part 1, 5-6.

42. For Vale's frequent references to "white evidence" see, for example, *Fanaticism*, part 2, 4, 9, 14.

43. McDade, "Matthias, Prophet Without Honor," 328-29.

44. Ibid., 332. Vale identified Judge Ruggles as one of the Kingston lawyers who had helped Isabella recover Peter.

45. McDade identifies some ideas Matthias may have borrowed from early Mormonism, including "invoking the name of Melchizedek, the aversion to baptism by sprinkling, the designation of Christians as gentiles, his denigration of women, and even his naming of Zion Hill" ("Matthias, Prophet Without Honor," 334).

46. [Joseph Smith], *History of the Church of Jesus Christ of Latter-Day Saints* (Salt Lake City: Published by the Church, 1904), 2:304-7. When Smith learned that his visitor was "the noted Matthias of New York," he told him that "his doctrine was of the devil, that he was in reality in possession of a wicked and depraved spirit."

47. Vale, *Fanaticism*, part 1, 52-53.

48. Andrews, *Sisters of the Spirit*, 176.

49. Vale, *Fanaticism*, part 2, 82.

50. See Stanton, et al., *History of Woman Suffrage*, 1:567.

51. Vale, *Fanaticism*, part 1, 22.

52. Ibid., part 2, 10.

53. Ibid., part 1, 39, 82.

54. Ibid., part 2, 39.

55. Ibid., part 2, 125-26.

56. Ibid., part 1, 62-63.

57. See Linda K. Kerber, "Abolitionists and Amalgamators: The New York City Race Riots of 1834," *New York History* 48 (January 1967): 28-39. Arguing that "the Irishman's rival for jobs in New York City in 1834 was not so much the free Negro as it was the white immigrant of older stock," Kerber notes that "only a very few of the names of those brought to trial are Irish, and that a large number of Irishmen volunteered to help put down the negroes' enemies." Things had changed by 1863, when the Irish

initiated the New York City draft riots. See also Curry, *The Free Black in Urban America*, 101.

58. Stewart, *Maria W. Stewart*, 48-49.

59. Sterling, *We Are Your Sisters*, 131.

60. Frederick Douglass, "My Escape to Freedom," *Century Magazine* 23 (November 1881), quoted in Horton, *Free People of Color*, 106. See also Curry, *The Free Black in Urban America*, 18. By 1837, the *Colored American* began collecting names, residences, and occupations of the black community in New York City, as well as a list of black churches, and of the Benevolent and Literary Institutions. See Daniel Perlman, "Organizations of the Free Negro in New York City," 181.

61. Charles Dickens, *American Notes* (Gloucester, Massachusetts: Peter Smith, 1968), 112. The great black dancers of the period were often present at Pinkster celebrations according to Sterling Stuckey, "The Skies of Consciousness," 72.

62. See Sterling, *We Are Your Sisters*, 223-24.

63. *Tribune*, 8 November 1853.

64. Curry, *The Free Black in Urban America*, 112-16.

65. *Tribune*, 7 September 1853.

66. Dickens, *American Notes*, 100.

67. Seafaring was an upwardly mobile occupation of many black men. Until the 1840s, black seamen could get "regular, even tolerant employment" (W. Jeffrey Bolster, "'To Feel Like a Man': Black Seamen in the Northern States, 1800-1860," *Journal of American History* 76 [March 1990]: 1192-93). In 1839 the Colored Seamen's Home in Dover Street began to provide services to the two thousand black sailors who lodged in the city between voyages. The Home was looted in the New York City Draft Riot during the Civil War.

68. It is of great interest that the man who intervened and was able to obtain the release of Isabella's son was named Peter Williams. Apparently, in his own act of self-naming, young Peter had for some time been calling himself "Peter Williams," perhaps in emulation of the community activist and abolitionist minister of St. Phillip's African Church. Isabella could hardly believe Peter's rescue "till she found herself in the presence of Mr. Williams, and heard him saying to her, 'I am very glad I have assisted your son; he stood in great need of sympathy and assistance; but I could not think he had such a mother here, although he assured me he had'" (*NarBk*, 75-76). Was this "respectable colored barber" (barbering was a dignified profession with high status in the black community), whose name Peter "had been wearing" the Reverend Peter Williams, Jr., known especially for his interventions with young black men? It is a frustrating convention of Truth's scribes to give little attention to the black characters in her story; we learn that Truth spoke "to a friend" about Lincoln (*NarBk*, 174), but we are not told that the friend is *Harriet Tubman*. Much of Truth's New

York history remains to be written, and the Peter Williams episode is only a small indication of this.

69. Dickens, *American Notes*, 103.
70. Sidney Kaplan, "Sojourner Truth's Son Peter," *The Negro History Bulletin* 19 (November 1955): 34.
71. *Daily Inter-Ocean*, 13 August 1879.

Four

Sojourners

*Hear my prayer, O Lord, and give ear
unto my cry; hold not thy peace at my tears:
for I am a stranger with thee,
and a sojourner, as all my fathers were.*

Psalm 39:12

*I think some people would understand
the quintessence of sanctifying grace if
they could be black about twenty-four hours.*

Amanda Berry Smith,
Autobiography, 1893[1]

The woman who boarded the Fulton Street ferry early in the morning on the first day of June 1843 had chosen for herself a name that resonated with the pain of an oppressed people dwelling for many generations in a strange land. Within the Old Testament context the sojourner was the non-Hebrew stranger who lived among the Hebrews. During part of their own history, the Hebrews had lived as sojourners among the Egyptians, with some rights and duties; afterward they had been enslaved: "My people went down aforetime into Egypt to sojourn there; and the Assyrians oppressed them without cause"(Isaiah 53:4).[2]

Harriet Beecher Stowe told Truth's story of naming:

My name was Isabella; but when I left the house of bondage, I left everything behind. I wa'n't goin' to keep nothin' of Egypt on me, an' so I went to the Lord an' asked him to give me a new name. And the Lord gave me Sojourner, because I was to travel up an' down the land, showin' the people their sins, an' bein' a sign unto them. Afterwards I told the Lord I wanted another name, 'cause everybody else had two names; and the Lord gave me Truth, because I was to declare the truth to the people.[3]

Truth's bold intention to strike out as an itinerant evangelist had formed in a climate of luxuriant enthusiasm. The emotionally charged revival style of preaching of the Great Awakening of the 1730s and 1740s appealed to African captives and their African American descendants. In her elegy for George Whitefield, the great Awakening preacher, Phillis Wheatley repeated the words that offered such emotional succor to the oppressed:

"Take him, ye *Africans*, he longs for you,
Impartial Saviour is his title due:
Wash'd in the fountain of redeeming blood,
You shall be sons, and kings, and priests to God."[4]

The ecstatic spirituality and inclusive message of revivalist Methodism and other evangelizing denominations appealed to blacks in the Second Great Awakening in the early part of the nineteenth century and was influenced by the shaping vitality of black oral traditions. A style of preaching that accommodated audience response had been shaped in black congregations and amounted to a partial Africanization of religious style. The roots of Truth's performance style, whether singing or speaking, lie in an aesthetics of participation that defined African religious practice spilled over into Christian revivalism.[5]

Christian hymns exerted a powerful attraction for the enslaved black community and black voices influenced the style of the great camp meeting songs. At a Methodist camp meeting in 1828, Truth heard the revival hymn, "There is a Holy City," with its vision of those who "came from tribulation / To everlasting day," to claim their "bright temple / and crowns above the sky." The message for those still caught up in tribulation was not different from Jupiter Hammon's consolation to his New York city audience in 1786: "Our slavery will be at an end, and though ever so mean, low and despised in this world, we shall sit with God in his Kingdom, as Kings and Priests, and rejoice for ever and ever."[6] Truth made songs of day to day tribulation resonant with protest. Like the songs sung by Fannie Lou Hamer and Bernice Johnson Reagon they became a weapon in a liberationist struggle for people in the here and now.

I am pleading for my people—
A poor, downtrodden race,
Who dwell in freedom's boasted land,
With no abiding place. (*NarBk*, 302)

Truth's use of song to concentrate the attention of her audience on a
concrete political and social reality differed from the revivalist use of song
to involve the crowd emotionally. When Truth sang a song that evoked
the experience shared only among black people, she sang it into an ironic
space that opened up between the song and her many white listeners.
"Unlike sacred music," Sherley Anne Williams has written, "the blues
deals with a world where the inability to solve a problem does not necessarily mean that one can, or ought to, transcend it."[7] Truth's performances demonstrated the dialectical relation between the gospel and the
blues.

When Truth stayed with Harriet Beecher Stowe at Stone Cottage in
Andover in the summer of 1853, Stowe often observed Truth "singing and
fervently keeping time with her head"; Truth loved "hymns whose burden
was, 'O glory, glory, glory, / Won't you come along with me?'" and "when
left to herself, she would often hum these with great delight, nodding her
head." Stowe was struck by the immediacy of the world the singer conjured
into being, mistaking Truth's lyric intensity for naiveté. Truth sang "Away
to Canada," black poet Joshua McCarter Simpson's reappropriation of
Stephen Foster's blackface anthem "Oh! Susanna." Truth would have heard
Simpson's song in Ohio, and it had been published in *The Liberator* 10
December 1852, only a few months before Truth's visit to Stowe. Simpson
frequently used Queen Victoria and Canada to personify the promise and
attainment of liberty in his poetry. Hearing Truth sing "Away to Canada,"
Stowe believed, as Sarah Bradford did when she heard Harriet Tubman
sing it, that it expressed "simple faith" in a literal event:

The queen comes down unto the shore,
With arms extended wide,
To welcome the poor fugitive
Safe onto freedom's side.[8]

When Truth sang "There is a Holy City" she transformed the city's
location from the vague "starry regions" to a place "above the stairs and
regions," making it somewhere a person could get to. Stowe described the
powerful effect of Truth's performance:

She sang with the strong barbaric accent of the native African, and with those indescribable upward turns and those deep gutturals which give such a wild, peculiar power to the negro singing—but above all, with such an overwhelming energy of personal appropriation that the hymn seemed to be fused in the furnace of her feelings and come out recrystallized as a production of her own.[9]

Truth's song was a harbinger of the "great song" that W. E. B. Du Bois heard rising at the advent of freedom for the enslaved, which came neither from Africa nor from white America, music "improvised and born anew out of an age long past, and weaving into its texture the old and new melodies in word and in thought."[10] What Stowe heard as Truth's "barbaric accent" was a more stirring analog to Whitman's "barbaric yawp" of the same period: the voiced aspiration of a people.

Opposition to "heathenish" forms of spirituality was growing among black intellectuals as the churches underwent class stratification during the 1830s. Daniel Payne saw in the exuberant song-singing ("I would not let them sing their 'spiritual songs'") a manifestation of ignorance and superstition that contributed to racist reactions toward the black community.[11] Some black intellectuals deplored the formidable influence wielded by male ministers with no theological training who relied on conversion experiences for their authority. Mary Ann Shadd Cary protested that their lack of moral leadership on social and political issues corrupted the black community itself. In *The North Star* in 1849, Shadd Cary denounced a "corrupt clergy" as "hanging like millstones about our necks," deploring their "gross ignorance and insolent bearing" and "a character for mystery they assume."[12]

The preaching women who were challenging societal prohibitions on so many fronts were much less liable to Shadd Cary's charge. Their very existence constituted a powerful challenge to forms of oppression that affected both blacks and women. Truth did not disguise her feelings about "the fashionable so-called *religious* world," declaring in the words of the parable that "it is empty as the barren fig-tree, possessing nothing but leaves" (*NarBk*, xii). She complained to a New York City audience in 1853 that costly church buildings towered over the urban poor who were "living in low dens and sky-lighted churches" while "the parsons went away into Egypt among the bones of dead Pharaohs and mummies, and talked about what happened thousands of years ago." "Big, Greek-crammed mouthing men," Truth called them.[13]

For these laboring women who came to literacy in the conventional sense late and painfully or not at all, the rich texture of their thought was woven from the sounds and sights of the Bible. Although Rebecca Cox Jackson may have read Jarena Lee's writings after she was taught to read by divine intervention, she claimed that she had been ordered by God to read no other book but the Bible.[14] Jarena Lee had "never had more than three months schooling"; she "therefore watched the more closely the operations of the Spirit." Julia Foote was "a poor reader and a poor writer," and had lost the sight of one eye; but she felt the Spirit "quickening" her "mental faculties."[15]

The domestic labors that gave structure to Rebecca Cox Jackson's visionary experience—cooking griddle cakes, washing quilts, sweeping the garret with a "half-worn broom"—were also for Truth a setting for the divine: "She found her religion as she was at her work, as she washed her dishes, and all she could say or think was Jesus." But she found her outreach in New York City hindered by her low status:

> She wanted to get among her own colored people and teach them this, but they repulsed and shoved her off, yet she felt she wanted to be doing.
>
> She used to go and hold prayer meetings at the houses of the people in the Five Points, then Chapel st, but she found they were always more inclined to hear great people, and she instanced the case of one colored woman who declining her prayers, said she had two or three ministers about. She (the Speaker) went off weeping while her dying sister was looked upon as a "glory of Zion."[16]

Elizabeth, a black evangelist who started preaching in 1808, was also made to feel "despised" and "unfit to assemble with the congregation with whom I had gathered"; she felt she "was looked upon as a speckled bird by the ministers."[17] Zilpha Elaw had a powerful answer to critics who gave a pretense of comparing the relative moral worth of the less- and the more-educated believers when they were really discussing the admixture of class elements; she argued that "the illiterate coloured Christian" would have sufficed for "the apostolic era," but that irrelevant standards of politeness and delicacy "have been superadded to the Christian precept, by the supererogative pride of high-toned sensibility and civilization."[18]

Some of the irate male clergy were well-educated, some ignorant; most simply condemned female lecturing and preaching as a challenge to their own traditional power. Clashes with the clergy, committed to their own version of Paul's proscription against women preaching, figured dramatically in the struggle for woman's rights. In the early 1840s, Julia Foote's ministry was opposed by Jehiel Beman, a prominent antislavery and temperance preacher and the pastor of the A.M.E. Zion Church of Boston.

Remembering his "sneering, indifferent way," Foote wrote later that "Even ministers of Christ did not feel that women had any rights which they were bound to respect," bitterly echoing the Supreme Court's Dred Scott decision.[19]

Truth's conversion experience, which took place around 1827, manifested visionary conventions that were familiar to other early nineteenth-century black Methodist women. As it can be reconstituted from the reports of Olive Gilbert and Harriet Beecher Stowe, Isabella was walking toward her former slave master Dumont, whom she had once invested with the absolute power to see and hear her wherever she was, when God revealed himself to her as being "*all over*," so that she understood "that there was no place where God was not." She was seized by a fear of retribution and feared God's "awful look," thinking that God could extinguish her as he might blow out a lamp. "Oh, God, I did not know you were so big," was her response, after which, in Gilbert's words, she went into the house "to resume her work." She wanted "to talk to God" but felt speechless, wishing for someone to speak to God for her. A fire so consuming that Isabella "could feel it burnin', burnin', burnin' all around me, an' goin' through me" made her cry for somebody to "stand between God an' me!" Just when she felt that God's incendiary presence would annihilate her, "a space seemed opening between her and God," which had the effect of shielding her from God's fire. She "felt as it were somethin' like an *amberill* [umbrella] that came between me an' the light, an' I felt it was *somebody*—somebody that stood between me an' God; an' it felt cool, like a shade." Truth apparently experienced her own flesh as bruised and putrefied: thinking the "somebody" might be a known friend, she was shocked by an image of this friend's flesh all "'bruises and putrifying sores,' like herself."

The "umbrella" effect issued from a bright distinct human form (afterward Truth always expected the spirit to assume "his bodily appearance"). The spirit was quiet when she affirmed it but moved "restlessly about, like agitated waters" when she said "I don't know you." Stowe wrote that Truth described this restless movement as being "like the sun shinin' in a pail o' water, when it moves up and down." To sustain the spirit's presence Truth repeated like a mantra "I know you," and at a point apparently near unconsciousness she heard the spirit "saying distinctly, 'It is Jesus.'" Both Gilbert and Stowe described Truth's vision of the world brightening; Gilbert says that the "air sparkled as with diamonds"; Stowe wrote that "every little bit o' stone on the ground shone like glass." Truth told Gilbert that she believed Jesus was the "pure spirit" that was created in Adam and Eve, which "fled to heaven" and returned "in the person of

Jesus" and that "previous to a personal union with him, man is but a brute, possessing only the spirit of an animal" (*NarBk*, 65-69).[20]

In 1878 when Truth was in her eighties, she spoke at Cooper Union accompanied by the eldest of the spirit-rapping Fox sisters. Truth recounted her experience of finding Jesus: "I felt Him come between God and me as sensibly as I ever felt an umbrella raised over my head."[21] The images of labor in Truth's conversion experience, the hot sun scorching the head of the field worker, the umbrella, which could be a kindly proffered makeshift shade or an unaccustomed proffering of a symbol of great dignity, the spirit dancing like the sun's rays in the house servant's pail of carried water, could be set beside the vision of the young Zilpha Elaw. Elaw was "milking the cow and singing," when a tall, long-haired figure robed in white to his feet opened his arms and smiled at her, the authenticating element in her vision being that the cow saw it too.[22]

It is possible that Truth's decision to leave New York City to preach "up and down the land" followed a second-stage spiritual awakening at least similar to sanctification. She experienced an extreme sense of guilt and worthlessness which was replaced by a coherent vision of the social world as "one great system of robbery and wrong," following which "she felt called in spirit" to travel and preach. Leaving New York City, Truth looked back with an overwrought sensibility as if to a Biblical scene of conflagration:

> She left the city on the morning of the 1st of June, 1843, crossing over to Brooklyn, L. I.; and taking the rising sun for her only compass and guide, she "remembered Lot's wife," and hoping to avoid her fate, she resolved not to look back till she felt sure the wicked city from which she was fleeing was left too far behind to be visible in the distance; and when she first ventured to look back, she could just discern the blue cloud of smoke that hung over it, and she thanked the Lord that she was thus far removed from what seemed to *her* a second Sodom. (*NarBk*, 100)

The black women evangelists who took to the road in the 1830s, those we know about, faced the hazards of racism to an extraordinary degree. The strain of solitary travel was increased by the rigid segregation of transportation as they traveled on foot through the countryside and by steamer, canal boat, or coach. On one trip Julia Foote contended with a fellow passenger in the stage out of Binghamton who showed "his dark, slave-holding principles" and an abusive man on the canal packet out of Oxford. On a boat heading from New York to Boston in 1845, Foote was "compelled to sit on deck all night, in the cold, damp air—prejudice not permitting one of my color to enter the cabin except in the capacity of a servant."[23] Segregated transportation presented dramatic problems for Truth; in her old age she told Elizabeth Cady Stanton that she had "been sent into the smoking-car so often she smoked in self-defense—she would rather swallow her own smoke than another's."[24]

Although, in the spiritual heat of a great camp meeting around 1820, Zilpha Elaw saw that "both high and low, rich and poor, white and coloured, were all melted like wax before the fire," she especially praised God's "ever-mindful care" in helping her to find a separate tent to house "a considerable number of coloured people." During her daring missions to the slave states, Elaw lived under constant danger "of being arrested and sold for a slave."[25] Jarena Lee preached to an old slaveholder on Cape May, who "did not believe the coloured people had any souls." Lee joined the American Antislavery Society in 1840, believing that the slave state kept the gospel from reaching "every nation."[26]

Lodging was a problem. When she preached in the North, Jarena Lee traveled the A.M.E. church circuit, and was often sheltered by its congregations. Resentful male clergy tried to close the homes of their Methodist flock to Rebecca Jackson in 1835 or 1836. One night in the center of Long Island, Truth was turned away from supposedly Christian lodgings "some twenty times" and spent the night in a dance hall with some kindly drunkards (*NarBk*, 102-5).

Bewildered parents, domineering brothers, hostile husbands, and over-anxious children questioned the itinerants' sanity. Julia Foote's mother resisted her association with the sanctified, telling her she was "half crazy now"; her husband threatened to send her "to the crazy-house."[27] When they heard Truth had left New York, her children's "imaginations painted her as a wandering maniac—and again they feared she had been left to commit suicide"; she wrote to them from Berlin, Connecticut assuring them "of her continued life and her love" (*NarBk*, 109).

Like that of Zilpha Elaw, Truth's early itinerant ministry was self-supported, reflecting no man's licensing and no denomination. She debated with a minister in Connecticut her strongly held view "against a paid ministry." Determined to take no more money than was essential, she went about "lecturing some, and working some, to get wherewith to pay tribute to Caesar," but "two or three York shillings at a time were all she allowed herself to take." Truth said that "she worked for the Lord; and if her wants were supplied, she received it as from the Lord" (*NarBk*, 102, 108, 114).

Beginning by attending other preachers' meetings wherever she came across them and speaking to anyone she could find, Truth soon began to find large audiences of her own (*NarBk*, 101). She traveled by boat to Connecticut and headed north-east, arriving in New Haven, where the meetings were many and "she was allowed to express her views freely, and without reservation" (*NarBk*, 105). Sometimes she advertised her meetings; sometimes she was helped from place to place by an expanding network of people who responded to her preaching. A "zealous sister" sent her on to Bristol; from Bristol she traveled to Hartford with a note from a writer who urged the "sister" to whom he wrote to send Truth on to other brothers and "where she can do the most good":

> Please receive her, and she will tell you some new things. Let her tell her story without interrupting her, and give close attention, and you will see she has got the lever of truth, that God helps her to pry where but few can. She cannot read or write, but the law is in her heart. (*NarBk*, 106)

The itinerant black women preachers ministered to black and white audiences. It was not customary for women of any race to speak in public, and more daunting for a black woman surrounded by whites. In the 1830s Zilpha Elaw attended a camp meeting on Cape Cod that was harassed by hundreds of young men "connected with the highest families" who were bent on "dispersing the camp-meeting altogether." They were mostly converted in the end, along with "many others both white and coloured," after insisting on hearing "the woman" preach.[28] Only months after her arrival in Northampton in 1844, Truth was present at a nearby camp meeting that was about to be addressed by a white woman preacher, when a hundred or so young men tried to break it up, "making the most frightful noises, and threatening to fire the tents." Truth "found herself quaking with fear":

> Under the impulse of this sudden emotion, she fled to the most retired corner of a tent, and secreted herself behind a trunk, saying to herself, "I am the only colored person here, and on me, probably, their wicked mischief will fall first, and perhaps fatally." (*NarBk*, 115)

As the white woman preacher stood "trembling on the preachers' stand," Truth took the night in hand:

> Sojourner left the tent alone and unaided, and walking some thirty rods to the top of a small rise of ground, commenced to sing, in her most

fervid manner, with all the strength of her most powerful voice, the hymn
on the resurrection of Christ—

It was early in the morning—it was early in the morning,
Just at the break of day—
When he rose—when he rose—when he rose,
And went to heaven on a cloud.

All who have ever heard her sing this hymn will probably remember it
as long as they remember her. The hymn, the tune, the style, are each too
closely associated with to be easily separated from herself, and when sung
in one of her most animated moods, in the open air, with the utmost
strength of her most powerful voice, must have been truly thrilling.
(*NarBk*, 116-17)

There were "two congregations on this ground," Truth said—"The
other preachers have the sheep, *I* have the goats."

As she commenced to sing, the young men made a rush towards her,
and she was immediately encircled by a dense body of the rioters, many of
them armed with sticks or clubs as their weapons of defence, if not of
attack. As the circle narrowed around her, she ceased singing, and after a
short pause, inquired, in a gentle but firm tone, "Why do you come about
me with clubs and sticks? I am not doing harm to any one." "We ar'n't a
going to hurt you, old woman; we came to hear you sing," cried many
voices simultaneously. (*NarBk*, 117)

The story of Truth's triumph at the camp meeting demonstrated the
power she could wield over a crowd even in this early stage of her public
speaking career. But evidence of the power over wild beasts is also evidence of the existence of the beasts. The empathy that arose between the
audience of wild young white men and the mesmerizing black singer could
only temporarily conceal the volatile incoherence of the social body of the
1840s, so starkly embodied in the image of a peaceful black woman in her
fifties ("I am the only colored person here") hiding in a tent from a band of
marauding whites, even if it was the Lord's tent.

In her "home-made" songs, Truth built on old revival hymns; she also
appropriated the language and rhythm of black spirituals and folk songs, as
she did in her Civil War praise songs and glory shouts.[29] In her performances the chanting rhythms of the black sisters of the evangelists' circuit
modulated into the blues tradition of Billie Holiday, who had to let Artie

Shaw's white singer take the stand when they traveled down South. Escape from death—escape for the crucified Jesus, then escape for everyone through Jesus—is the theme of "It Was Early in the Morning"—and we cannot think of "When He rose, when He rose, when He rose" except as a fulfillment of that wildly expressive African belief that the people, crushed under slavery's weight, could nevertheless fly, not just to heaven, but back to Africa. Truth's musical invention was just right for her entrapped reality at the camp meeting. It looked back to Africa and forward to Bessie Smith, as Sherley Anne Williams imagined her, chasing the Klan away from the back of her tent.

> . . . and that
> night in Concord when
> she chased the Klan out
> from behind our tent.
> Just cussed them out while
> the mens stood shaking
> in their pants; she went
> on with her number
> like it was routine—
> cept she "never
> *heard* of such shit."[30]

In New York City, Truth had attended a meeting led by the prophet of the Second Advent of Christ, William Miller, "where she saw a great many enigmatical pictures hanging on the wall, which she could not understand, and which, being out of the reach of her understanding, failed to interest her" (*NarBk*, 109-10). In 1843, many Second Adventists read portents of the end of the world and of the coming of Christ in comets and meteor showers. Expectations of such events were "shaking the very foundations of the universe" in the minds of believers, filling them with "noisy terror." Truth calmed the incendiary imaginations of such a group in Connecticut:

> You seem to be expecting to go to some parlor *away up* somewhere, and when the wicked have been burnt, you are coming back to walk in triumph over their ashes—this is to be your New Jerusalem!! Now, *I* can't see any thing so very *nice* in that, coming back to such a *muss* as that will be, a world covered with the ashes of the wicked! Besides, if the Lord comes and burns—as you say he will—I am not going away; *I* am going to stay here and *stand the fire*, like Shadrach, Meshach, and Abednego! And Jesus will walk with me through the fire, and keep me from harm. Nothing belonging

to God can burn, any more than God himself; such shall have no need to go away to escape the fire! No, *I* shall remain. Do you tell me that God's children *can't stand fire?*" And her manner and tone spoke louder than words, saying, "It is *absurd* to think so!" (*NarBk*, 110-12)

Again among the Adventists in Springfield, a witness noted "her commanding figure and dignified manner" and her "remarkable talent for singing," and the particular "aptness and point of her remarks, frequently illustrated by figures the most original and expressive":

> As we were walking the other day, she said she had often thought what a beautiful world this would be, when we should see every thing right side up. Now, we see every thing topsy-turvy, and all is confusion. (*NarBk*, 114)

The network of heterogeneous believers that sent Truth criss-crossing Connecticut and Massachusetts included people for whom the social gospel mandated all sorts of reforms in the world. All kinds of people shared Truth's desire to find her beliefs embodied in a communal setting. In 1841 and 1842, Rebecca Cox Jackson was in the Syracuse area with the "Little Band" and in Albany with the Perfectionists; in 1843 she was visiting the Watervliet Shaker community near Albany, where she would live for some years after 1847. Shaker communities had practiced integration of black and white members since the Revolutionary War and while their abolitionist sentiments did not include political action, they were strongly held.[31] Near the same time that Jackson was visiting the Watervliet Shakers near Albany, Truth was thinking of finding a place with the Shakers at Enfield.

> She now began to think of finding a resting place, at least, for a season; for she had performed quite a long journey, considering she had walked most of the way; and she had a mind to look in upon the Shakers, and see how things were there, and whether there was any opening there for her. (*NarBk*, 113)

The enthusiasm of Second Adventist believers in Springfield, who took her in with admiration and affection, turned Truth aside from her investigation of Enfield, leaving in suspension the wonderful possibility of her response to the theological feminism of Shakerism so eloquently embraced by Jackson and Rebecca Perot. Truth apparently discussed Bronson

Alcott's utopian community at Fruitlands as a possible destination, but in the end, encouraged by her Second Adventist friends, she headed for Northampton.[32]

Truth's Second Adventist friends may have felt that the abolitionist reputation of the Northampton Association of Education and Industry would appeal to Truth. The Northampton area had been a center of antislavery activity for some years before the founding of the Association, unintimidated by the hostile feelings of many of its own citizens. In 1838, Lydia Maria Child, who was trying to help make a success of an antislavery sugar beet factory in Northampton, wrote to a friend:

> I have never been so discouraged about abolition since we came to this iron-bound Valley of the Connecticut. I have ceased to believe that public opinion will ever be sincerely reformed on that question til long after emancipation has taken place.[33]

In the same year, David Lee Child spoke on the Annexation of Texas to an antislavery convention in Northampton. In 1843, the Latimer Convention at Northampton sent delegates to the Massachusetts legislature to petition against slavery.

Austin Ross, Calvin Fairbanks and Samuel L. Hill kept stations of the Underground Railroad in the area. At Hill's station, his son reported, some passengers stopped only "five minutes for refreshments" or to change conductors, but some, attracted by "the balmy anti-slavery climate," settled temporarily in the area. The refugees "became the talking centers for our neighbors and sympathizers to gather around." William Wilson stayed in Northampton long enough to earn money to return South and begin the long struggle to rescue his family. Josiah Henson, one of the models for Stowe's "Uncle Tom," traveled this line on one of his trips to Canada.

The great activist from New York City, David Ruggles, who had helped Frederick Douglass to escape (and witnessed Douglass's marriage to Anna Murray), had been brought to Northampton, in failing health and nearly blind, to settle. Ruggles and Seth Hunt tried to rescue an enslaved girl whose master had brought her to Northampton, inducing the local sheriff and a judge to explain to her that her coming into a free state had left her free; but the girl was too frightened of her master to leave him. Ruggles had also aided Basil Dorsey after his escape from Maryland in 1836. In January 1844, Dorsey settled in Northampton, a few months before Truth's arrival.[34]

Giles Stebbins, who became Truth's life-long friend and delivered her funeral sermon, spent a year in Northampton when he was twenty-five; he remembered the Sunday meetings in the factory dining room, "always provocative of thought, usually interesting, sometimes crude." William Lloyd Garrison, who was married to the sister of George Benson, one of the founders of the Association, would speak "under the shade of a great pine in the grove on the hilltop." In April 1844 the Hutchinson Family singers sang in the communal dining room, where Frederick Douglass, "then so recently 'chattel personal,'" spoke along with Hill and others. The same night Douglass talked for three hours at an antislavery meeting in the town hall. John Hutchinson carried away a strong impression of Dr. James Boyle "in his quaint Continental costume."[35]

It was James Boyle who made Truth a gift of the old stereotype plates of her 1850 *Narrative* in the 1870s, making it possible for her to begin the expanded version with Frances Titus. In 1870 in New York City, Boyle wrote to Truth, his "dear old friend of more than thirty years' acquaintance," adding as a postscript:

> All the years during which we have known each other, we were co-laborers in the anti-slavery movement, and now we see our wishes accomplished in the overthrow of that horrid wall of crimes and cruelties which Church and State combined to perpetuate. The great God is leading the bondmen and bondwomen through a Red Sea to their freedom, and writing their deed of enfranchisement with the point of the sword, in the blood of their oppressors North and South. (*NarBk*, 264)

This was vintage Boyle. The reforms of both Church and State had been his specialty as one of the most influential itinerant revivalists in the Burned-over District. In 1834 Boyle and John Humphrey Noyes published the *Perfectionist* magazine, which had served as the principal written contact among the many far-flung perfectionist cults in New York state. Boyle abandoned the holiness movement by 1836 and became active in Garrisonian abolitionism, spending some years as an agent for the Ohio Antislavery Society before joining the Northampton community in 1842.[36]

Garrison spent many weeks at a time in Northampton, and he and Boyle were striking companions on the lecture stage. "Mr. Garrison and Mr. Boyle held forth on abolition," Sylvester Judd noted in his diary in July 1843. "These men are too vituperative and denunciatory of almost everybody to do the greatest good."[37] In late 1843, Boyle was canvassing middle and eastern Massachusetts, soliciting money for the financially-troubled Northampton Association from "the friends of social reform throughout New England and New York State." James Boyle as much as anyone may have been in the minds of the Springfield reformist friends who advised Truth to go to Northampton.

Frederick Douglass, who as a fugitive saw the Association "almost at its beginning," described the Northampton Association as "from the first a protest against sectism and bigotry and an assertion of the paramount importance of human brotherhood." It was part of the "great mental wave of reform that passed over New England," giving rise to other utopian socialist experiments at Brook Farm and the Hopedale Community:

> It struck me at once that the reformers had a tremendous task before them. I knew that many of them were people well to do in the world, and I naturally wondered how they could content themselves to leave the smooth and pleasant paths of life to which they were accustomed, for the rough and thorny ways they were now compelled to tread. The site of the Community was decidedly unpromising. The soil was poor and had little or nothing upon it but stubby oaks and stunted pines. The most hopeful thing I saw there was a narrow stream meandering through an entangled valley of brush and brier, and a brick building which the communists had now converted into a dwelling and factory. The place and the people struck me as the most democratic I had ever met. It was a place to extinguish all aristocratic pretensions. There was no high, no low, no masters, no servants, no white, no black.[38]

Truth did not like the look of Northampton at first sight, perhaps because, being organized around a factory, it was unlike her ideal of a utopian community. She was won over by the members' commitment to hard work:

> But she thought she would make an effort to tarry with them one night, though that seemed to her no desirable affair. But as soon as she saw that accomplished, literary and refined persons were living in that plain and simple manner, and submitting to the labors and privations incident to such an infant institution, she said, "Well, if these can live here, *I* can." (*NarBk*, 120)

There is no record of the historic meeting of Sojourner Truth and Frederick Douglass from Truth's point of view, but Douglass included a portrait of Truth in "What I Found at the Northampton Association," written toward the end of his life, and saturated with grievances.

> David Ruggles was not the only colored person who found refuge in this Community. I met here for the first time that strange compound of wit and wisdom, of wild enthusiasm and flint-like common sense, who

seemed to feel it her duty to trip me up in my speeches and to ridicule my efforts to speak and act like a person of cultivation and refinement. I allude to Sojourner Truth. She was a genuine specimen of the uncultured negro. She cared very little for elegance of speech or refinement of manners. She seemed to please herself and others best when she put her ideas in the oddest forms. She was much respected at Florence, for she was honest, industrious, and amiable. Her quaint speeches easily gave her an audience, and she was one of the most useful members of the Community in its day of small things.[39]

This fascinating passage betrays a world of frustration. In Douglass's construction, Truth's "strange compound" seems to separate into opposing elements: "wit" and "wild enthusiasm" are lined up on one side, "wisdom" and "common sense" on another; Douglass's regard for "cultivation and refinement" are opposed to Truth's disdain "for elegance of speech or refinement of manners." While he himself makes "efforts" (literally, gestures of force, of power), Truth misapprehends her "duty" (literally, the conduct due to a superior): turning her submission upside down, she instead tries "to trip me up in my speeches" and "to ridicule my efforts to speak and act like a person of cultivation and refinement."

Douglass's resentment brims over in his description of Truth's "quaint speeches" that "easily gave her an audience." Perhaps there was a deliberate pandering to her audience, Douglass implies, since there was cunning in Truth's quaintness, and she "seemed to please herself and others best when she put her ideas in the oddest forms." In accusing Truth of a kind of dishonesty in self-representation, Douglass must also implicitly acknowledge Truth's mastery. Some splinter of self-awareness pricks at his resentment, evident in his curiously painful articulation "my efforts to speak and act like a person of cultivation and refinement." Douglass cannot *not* acknowledge to himself the baneful truth that from the public platform he too is only "act[ing] like a person." Professional abolitionism was a tragic profession.

Truth was not *genuine* in her self-representation, Douglass seems to argue, and taking on the aspect of the most clinical of Darwinians, as if to examine a breed apart, he locates what *was* genuine: her biology; "She was a genuine specimen of the uncultured negro." In an extraordinary reversion to the language found in certain kinds of testimonials, Douglass identifies Truth's qualities as "honest, industrious, and amiable." He cannot *not* draw the appropriate stereotype: she was "useful" in the daily life of Northampton ("in its day of small things"), that is, she was *a good domestic.*

Well, she *was* a good domestic, and such were in demand at Northampton. When Elihu Burritt visited the community he was struck by "how utterly impractical, unnatural, visionary and absurd was this chimerical species or Association":

> Accomplished ladies who had left good homes and the luxuries of refined life, were here surrounded by their half-abandoned children, trying to learn the trade of some factory operative.[40]

"In 1847, I was at home in Zion," Rebecca Cox Jackson wrote, "and my lot was to mend and put in good order the Brethren's clothes that came in the wash every week." Just as Jackson, an experienced seamstress, mended clothing for the Watervliet Shakers, Truth washed clothes in the Northampton community.[41] A sketch by Charles Burleigh, Jr. shows "Sojourner Truth at a Wash Tub" in the laundry in the basement of the silk factory. Charles Sheffield reports that Truth "was chief laundress of week days, and Mr. [James] Atkins says he used to help her wring out the clothes on Mondays when work in his department was dull."[42] "When we first saw her," Olive Gilbert wrote, "she was working with a hearty good will; saying she would not be induced to take regular wages" (*NarBk*, 121).

Although the communal experiment was dissolved in 1846, Truth stayed on in Northampton. When the bad faith of the affluent managers of the Matthias commune resulted in the loss of Truth's savings, she simply went back to work as a valued servant in New York City. When the Northampton Association failed, in large part because of business errors on the part of its educated middle-class founders, Truth continued to work to support herself as a housekeeper for George Benson in Northampton, doing the kind of work that was always in demand.

In April 1850, attempting to recoup some of the losses of George Benson's business failure, Samuel L. Hill sold property to many former Associationists, including Basil Dorsey and "Isabella Vanwagner sometimes called Sojourner Truth." Almost immediately after this Truth was joined by her daughters, Sophia, Elizabeth, and Diana. Truth kept her house in Northampton until the fall of 1857, when she moved to another associationist community in Harmonia, Michigan, a center of spiritualism. Later she settled in Battle Creek, where Truth again gathered her family around her, now including her grandchildren.[43]

The period from the dissolution of the Association to the publication of the *Narrative* would have been crucial for Truth. After 1846, according to antislavery editor William L. Chaplin, Truth "commenced her advocacy of the rights of her race during our war with Mexico" (*NarBk*, 269). The years leading up to the passage of the Fugitive Slave Act (1850) produced growing anxiety among black women everywhere. In 1849, Rebecca Cox Jackson "was brought into deep tribulation of soul about my people"; in 1850, she dreamed that in Philadelphia "the men had killed all the women and children, and were dragging them like dogs through the street."[44] In July 1851 a diarist recorded that "Rebecca Jackson and the other colored woman that came with her, have started out, in their own gift, some time, last week, on a mission to convert her nation."[45] Women were shifting around on the antislavery stage. In 1848, Ellen Craft dressed in men's clothing to escape with her husband from Georgia; arriving in Boston with William Wells Brown, she traveled around the state, lecturing with her husband, until the new dangers created by the Fugitive Slave Act forced them to escape to England. In 1849, learning that she was to be sold into the South, Harriet Tubman walked away from slavery in Maryland to Pennsylvania. By 1850 she had saved enough money from her work as a cook and laundress to begin her forays back into the South to rescue her family. In 1851 Frances Watkins Harper "left Baltimore to seek a home in a Free State," settling for a time in Ohio. In the same year twenty-eight-year-old Mary Ann Shadd Cary emigrated to Canada, where she became the first black woman newspaper editor, working, even if inharmoniously, with activist Mary Miles Bibb in settlements where the black population was rising rapidly.[46] At the end of the decade that saw the publication of Douglass's great autobiography and that of William Wells Brown (these must have been much talked of at Northampton), Nancy Gardner Prince published her *Narrative of the Life and Travels of Mrs. Nancy Prince* and Truth published her own *Narrative*.

The conclusion to Truth's 1850 *Narrative* gives no hint of either her present or future activism. So coextensive did Truth's life and the recording of it in *Narrative* seem to Gilbert, that in its last pages Gilbert was naively describing the onset of Truth's pacific old age, in support of which the audience of the *Narrative* was invited to provide charitable financial aid. Gilbert was so absorbed in her portrait of Truth as an aging "child of nature" that though she was present at the inception of one of the most extraordinary public speaking careers of the century, she apparently did not see it coming.

With her *Narrative* in print, Truth entered on a path of public oratory, financed by the dissemination of the book, in an activist career that would both accommodate itself to the static requirements of the printed narrative and make strategic use of it in expanding and overturning some of its most constricting stereotypes. When Olive Gilbert wrote to Truth after the Civil War in a plaintive attempt to reincarcerate Truth in her image ("I did not think you were laying the foundation of such an almost world-wide reputation when I wrote that little book for you, but I rejoice and am proud that you can make your power felt with so little book-education" [*NarBk*, 277]), Truth had long since modeled an aggressive new form of black womanhood that had grown from its roots without denying them.

Unified by a dream of equality more than by any agreement as to the precise path by which this could be achieved, many black women worked in traditional community groups or independently in their ministrations to blacks or to whites. Although black women activists lacked the resources for the kind of close-knit community across geographical boundaries available to white abolitionists, their pioneering work helped to shape a movement toward freedom for blacks and for blacks as women. The black women activists had tried to include white women; the Female Anti-Slavery Society of Salem, Massachusetts, organized by black women in 1832, had been the first such woman's organization in the country, and in 1834 it had reorganized to admit white women. Clarissa Lawrence held important positions both before and after the reorganization. Charlotte Forten and Grace Douglass were founding members, and Margaretta Forten was recording secretary of the interracial Philadelphia Female Anti-Slavery Society formed in 1833. Susan Paul, Martha and Lucy Ball, and Julia Williams belonged to the interracial Boston Female Anti-Slavery Society. Although the Ladies' New York City Anti-Slavery Society, organized in 1835, effectively excluded black women and less affluent white women by setting a membership fee of twenty-five dollars, the predominantly black female Manhattan Anti-Slavery Society had at least one white woman member. At the Anti-Slavery Convention of American Women in New York City in 1837, Grace Douglass served as a vice-president and the convention printed Sarah Forten's poem, "We Are thy Sisters."

By 1848, when Truth was cementing her relationships with white women abolitionists, Sarah Douglass was organizing black women in the Women's Association of Philadelphia, answering Frederick Douglass's call for the help of "*colored* Anti-Slavery ladies."[47] In 1848 black women achieved a significant breakthrough, with the support of Douglass and Martin Delany, when the National Convention of Colored Freedmen meeting in Cleveland, Ohio redesignated voters as "persons," giving women the right to participate equally with men.[48]

At the Northampton Association women voted in decision-making. Among abolitionist white women there was a reaching outward to gather in the voices of black women. Olive Gilbert was part of an urgent contingent of white women, including Amy Post and Lydia Maria Child, who were actively interested in producing the stories of black women as overt protests against the slaveholding patriarchy, but who also served themselves by speaking through the voices of black women.[49] As a black woman Truth was implicated in both causes at the same time, whether she wanted to be or not, whether she agitated or not; she thus moved naturally toward the convergence, doubly despised in the popular imagination, of abolitionism and feminism.

Gilbert writes of Truth's attachment to Northampton that "it must have been no small thing to have found a home in a 'Community composed of some of the choicest spirits of the age,' where all was characterized by an equality of feeling, a liberty of thought and speech, and a largeness of soul, she could not have before met with, to the same extent, in any of her wanderings" (*NarBk*, 120). This does not fully state the reality.

What Truth had found at Northampton was an entry into the organized network of middle-class antislavery agitation, with its access to lecture halls, churches, private homes, and publicity. Just past fifty years old, Truth was already a remarkable speaker; her wit, her energetic intelligence, her personal presence, and the story of her life made her an invaluable asset to the antislavery cause. The cause would have found her soon enough; by coming to Northampton she saved everyone that trouble. G. W. Putnam wrote to the *Liberator* after hearing her speak that the audience "saw in her proof of the natural equality (to say the least) of the negro and the white." To demonstrate this to an audience was the great purpose to which the abolitionists dedicated their black speakers. "It is devoutly to be wished," Putnam acknowledged, "that all whites were her equals."[50]

In October 1850, only two years after the first woman's rights convention at Seneca Falls, Truth is first documented as a reform speaker among abolitionists and feminists, on the platform of the woman's rights convention in Worcester, Massachusetts. The idea of a world turned upside down that Truth had expressed to her Springfield friends on a quiet walk before her move to Northampton was now developed for her wider audience at Worcester: "Woman set the world wrong by eating the forbidden fruit, and now she was going to set it right."[51] Truth resumed this attack on the Christian patriarchy's justification of the subordination of women with obstinate eloquence at the famous Akron convention in 1851. Woman is an agent. Woman is *the* agent. "What if I am a woman?" asked Maria Stewart; God had raised up the reformed Magdalene to preach the resurrection, both Stewart and Jarena Lee proclaimed.[52] Strategically recuperating Eve, the original fallen woman, Truth concurred. In her other memorable utterance at this important speaking debut, Truth said that "Goodness never had any beginning; it was from everlasting, and could never die. But Evil had a beginning, and must have an end." Lucretia Mott repeated Truth's words in her closing address.[53]

Much remains to be recovered about interchanges between black and white women in these years, since the presence of black women is little acknowledged in official proceedings; but a contemptuous report of the Worcester Convention in the New York *Herald* notes that "Frederick Douglass was also in the meeting, and quite a lion, and several dark colored sisters were visible in the corners."[54] Truth's presence with other black women may explain the Convention's passing a resolution acknowledging the special plight of enslaved women.

The theme of the newspaper coverage of the Worcester Convention in the hostile New York *Herald* was "Awful Combination." It was described as a "motley mingling of abolitionists, socialists, and infidels, of all sexes and colors," and the report carried an epigraph from Thomas Middleton's *The Witch of Edmonton*: "Black spirits and white, / Blue spirits and gray, / Mingle, mingle, mingle, mingle, / You that mingle may."[55] Wendell Phillips, Lucy Stone, Abby Kelley Foster, Lucretia Mott, Frederick Douglass and Sojourner Truth were named as making up a pack of "fanatical mongrels."[56] Truth's appearance on the platform led the scandalized reporter to call her "Dinah": "And why not? In a convention where sex and color are mingled together in the common rights of humanity, Dinah, and Burleigh and Lucretia, and Frederick Douglass, are all spiritually of one color and one sex, and all on a perfect footing of reciprocity."[57]

The hostile coverage of the Worcester Convention, with its charge that the participants desired an "amalgamation of sexes and colors," used the public fear of the antislavery movement to intensify public anxiety about the woman's rights movement. Concern that feelings against the one campaign could be manipulated to destroy the other caused some agitators for woman's rights to try to distance themselves from antislavery issues, or at least to emphasize the distinctness of their own issues at their public meetings, just as male abolitionists, white and black, had tried to distance themselves from negative public response to the woman's movement.

One month after the Worcester Woman's Rights Convention, Truth made her first documented antislavery speech at the Fifteenth Annual Meeting of the Rhode Island Anti-Slavery Society, held in Mechanics' Hall in Providence in November 1850. Both Truth and Frederick Douglass spoke about the "new Law for Man-hunting":

Sojourner Truth said, she had been a slave, and was not now entirely free. She did not know anything about politics—could not read the newspapers—but thanked God that the law was made—that the worst had come to worst; now the best must come to best.[58]

Truth was expressing a Garrisonian view that slavery was essentially a moral issue and that its evil would be put down by good when people were persuaded of its existence. By its very extremity, the Fugitive Slave Law would make the evil completely clear to Northern people who had not fully understood how slavery reached into their own lives. Many black abolitionists, however, had by this time repudiated Garrisonian moral suasion. At the Providence meeting, Frederick Douglass, who had opposed Henry Highland Garnet's fiery call for slave resistance at the 1843 black convention in Buffalo, was now joined by Charles Lenox Remond in advocating forcible resistance. "There are some things for which men deserve to die," Douglass said. The Rhode Island Anti-Slavery Society did not endorse this view, noting hopefully that a "spirit of generous toleration of each other's conscientious convictions of duty" prevailed. This could not last long.[59]

By the time of the passage of the Fugitive Slave Law, black abolitionists like Douglass, Martin Delany, and Mary Ann Shadd Cary were urging separatist organizations in order to free their movement from the racism and unacceptable tactics of white abolitionism. Because Truth was joining the forces of Garrisonian abolitionism at a time when major black abolitionists had separated themselves in disillusionment, her usefulness to the Garrisonians was exploited, putting her at something of a distance from other black abolitionists. The Garrisonian stance on woman's rights would hold her in their ranks.

In December Truth spoke to the Old Colony Anti-Slavery Society in Plymouth, Massachusetts, which was celebrating the 230th anniversary of the landing of the Pilgrims at Plymouth Rock. Truth denounced Daniel Webster and the Fugitive Slave Law, sharing the platform with Garrison and British abolitionist George Thompson, famous for his efforts to end West Indian slavery.[60] Garrison had planned an extended speaking tour for which he had promised to pay Truth's expenses. In February and March 1851, when Garrison was too ill to make the trip, George Thompson invited Truth to travel with him and he covered her expenses. In 1835 Sarah Forten had written excitedly to Elizabeth Whittier about Thompson's lecture to the Philadelphia Female Anti-Slavery Society; later in the year, Thompson's appearance before the Boston Female Anti-Slavery Society caused a riot.[61] Zilpha Elaw was ministering in Boston "when Mr. George Thompson was lecturing there on the abominations of slavery," and she found that "much light was diffused by his zealous exertions in the cause of emancipation."[62]

A more equivocal report of Thompson came from Sarah Remond, who had lectured to large audiences in England for the Ladies and Young Men's Anti-Slavery societies, and had found herself "received here as a sister by white women." In 1859 she wrote in anger to Maria W. Chapman of the Boston Female Anti-Slavery Society that George Thompson had stopped Remond and Ellen Craft from addressing a London antislavery meeting, apparently because they were women. She had been wrong, she wrote, to place him among "reliable" men like Garrison, Phillips, and Jackson: "I am satisfied he is not of them."[63] Truth, however, retained her respect for Thompson. Writing to Garrison in 1864, Truth honored Thompson for his egalitarianism, remarking his indifference to the fact that she was "poor and a black woman."[64]

Truth headed into Western New York with Thompson and G. W. Putnam to a number of antislavery conventions. Sometimes Frederick Douglass appeared with them. Truth spoke "in her peculiar manner" on this trip, and Putnam noted her public speaking ability "which surprises the educated and refined" and her "mind of rare power."[65] In March of 1851 Anna Murray Douglass dictated a letter indicating that George Thompson was lecturing in Rochester, where Frederick Douglass had been publishing the *North Star* since 1847 in the basement of a black Methodist church.[66] In Rochester, Truth began her long friendship with antislavery activist and feminist Amy Post, who had been one of the leaders at the Seneca Falls and Rochester woman's rights conventions in 1848. By the time Truth arrived in Rochester, Amy Post had already established a close friendship with Harriet Jacobs, who had lived with the Posts for several months after her move to Rochester. Jacobs was part of an antislavery group, and was working in the reading room at the abolitionists' library located over the headquarters of *The North Star*; she was already encountering the white feminist rhetoric that identified the oppression of women with chattel slavery.[67]

Harriet Jacobs was among many of the Post circle in Rochester who participated in spiritualist experiments. Isaac and Amy Post were near the fountainhead of the waves of spiritualism that inundated the northeast after the young Fox sisters, to whom the Posts acted as mentors, heard spirit "knockings" in 1848. Spiritualism was a rebellious new religious movement that evidenced the soul's immortality by communicating with the spirits of the dead. Within the movement the accepted relations between the sexes and their religious and cultural roles were being constantly reexamined. As Ann Braude has demonstrated, spiritualism held

special attractions for people with radical social views, including many abolitionists, William Lloyd Garrison and William Cooper Nell among them,
and many feminists. During this period, Rebecca Cox Jackson and Rebecca
Perot, who had left the Shakers in Watervliet to take the word of Christ's
Second Appearing to the black community in Philadelphia, were partici-
pating in séance spiritualism.[68] Truth shared the interest in spirit manifes-
tations, which may not have been antithetical to African traditions of
contact with the spirit world.[69] While staying with the Posts in the spring
of 1851 Truth took part in a séance at their home.[70]

In May of 1851 Truth left Rochester alone to begin a series of antislavery appearances in Ohio, where readers of the Salem, Ohio *Anti-Slavery
Bugle* had already learned that a formidable abolitionist speaker had
emerged in the East, "springing upon the arena of this great conflict with
an energy and overwhelming power."[71] At the end of the month Truth
wrote back to Amy Post:

> I have arrived safe in Ohio. I got to Buffaloe on the evening of the
> same day I left you. I left Buffalo Friday night and arrived in Cleaveland
> on Saturday. Had a beautiful passage up the lake. Stopped among the col-
> ored friends and was treated with great kindness until Tuesday. Attended
> a meeting and sold three dollars worth of books.[72]

The eyes of abolitionists were on Ohio in 1851. A border state, separated from slave territory by the great river over which fugitive blacks
crossed to safety, Ohio had passed stringent laws to discourage blacks from
entering or settling in the state. After the passage of the Fugitive Slave
Law in 1850, the slavery issue more than ever dominated public debate.
The Garrisonians were especially active in northeastern Ohio, and Abby
Kelley Foster denounced "the black laws of Ohio" in speaking engagements all over the state.

White activist Sallie Holley was in school at Oberlin, the first such institution to admit both black men and black and white women. In late May
1851 Holley and "two other 'ultras,' aspired to the best horse and buggy at
Oberlin for three days, at fifty cents a day," and drove to Akron to a
Woman's Rights convention, where they heard "Aunt Fanny Gage,
Sojourner Truth, Caroline M. Severance, and other champions of the faith,
and were vastly entertained, especially by Sojourner's discomfiture and rout
of a young preacher who had the temerity to come up against her."[73] In
Akron the ongoing resistance of black women evangelists to the black clergy

and the ongoing resistance of middle-class white women to the white clergy converged. After Akron, woman's resistance had a different face. This was the convention at which Truth gave her historic "Ain't I a Woman" speech, pretty much giving a new definition to the whole idea of womanhood.

Antislavery conventions in Ohio as elsewhere became "the school in which woman's rights found its ready-made disciples." The "exhaustive arguments on human rights" of the antislavery activists fed activism among Ohio women, and the convening of the Ohio Constitutional Convention in 1850 caused them to focus on state laws discriminating against women.[74] In 1850 Emily Rakestraw Robinson had called and conducted the first woman's rights convention in Ohio at Salem. Robinson's husband Marius was a passionate abolitionist who had been injured by proslavery mob violence during the 1830s. He had just taken over the editorship of the Salem *Anti-Slavery Bugle* from Oliver Johnson who had resigned at the end of April.[75] The Salem convention, at which "Josephine S. Griffing uttered her first brave words for woman's emancipation, though her voice had long been heard in pathetic pleading for the black man's rights," had taken the practical decision to exclude men from speaking, the only woman's rights convention to have done so.[76] It was still so unusual for women to speak in public that the women wanted to work out their ideas without the stress of facing a mixed audience; Emily Robinson explained that "they were not yet quite ready to stand afresh face to face with that mighty force prejudice."[77]

Men were allowed into the Convention at the Unitarian Church in Akron in 1851, and Marius Robinson was an official recording secretary. There was some anxiety, not just about speaking before men but about facing hostile newspaper coverage of the kind that antislavery agitation received. Frances Gage described Truth's entry into the Unitarian Church at Akron as provoking anxiety among the women that the newspapers might use Truth's presence to submerge the woman's rights cause in abolitionism:

> Again and again timorous and trembling ones came to me and said with earnestness, "Don't let her speak, Mrs. G. It will ruin us. Every newspaper in the land will have our cause mixed with abolition and niggers, and we shall be utterly denounced." My only answer was, "We shall see when the time comes."[78]

In fact, news reports in sympathetic journals, such as Horace Greeley's *Tribune*, Garrison's *Liberator*, and the Salem *Anti-Slavery Bugle*, all of which were more antislavery than profeminist and more interested in defusing hostility toward an antislavery speaker than perpetuating it, did not report on the atmosphere. But the women were not wrong to be anxious that the focus might shift, with Truth's presence, from their kind of feminism to an abolition affair: Truth's performance was a historic joining of abolitionism and feminism bodied forth in her own person.

Although Ohio antislavery activist and feminist Frances Gage often heard Truth speak afterward, her description of Truth's part in the Akron Convention has been attacked by some historians.[79] The official record of Truth's performance at Akron in *History of Woman Suffrage* is based on an essay published twelve years after the event. Gage's essay in the *National Anti-Slavery Standard* in early-May 1863 was written in response to Harriet Beecher Stowe's popular essay on Truth, the "Libyan Sibyl," which had appeared in April in the *Atlantic*.[80] Both essays described encounters with Truth that had taken place a decade or more earlier. But unlike Gage, Stowe had not maintained contact with Truth after her one visit to Andover in 1853. Both the essays were written at a point when Truth had been ill and Stowe at least believed her to be dead, hence their elegiac character.

Frances Gage followed Stowe in modeling Truth's idiom on a conception of Southern black plantation speech to which readers of *Uncle Tom's Cabin* had become accustomed.[81] In representing Truth's speech, both Stowe and Gage produced framed stories, subordinating her "inimitable *patois*" to their standard English, creating an effect of exoticism and simplicity that could be interpreted as inferiority.[82] No one who tried it was capable of transcribing Truth's speech patterns, which she seems to have shaped strategically for each public performance; in her constant sarcastic tug of war with her listeners, she actually may have adopted some of these stereotyped dialect features at times. But no one attempting an orthographic transcription of her sound tried to account for black speech patterns in the Ulster County area, the Dutch language she spoke until she was ten or eleven, and the New York and New England speech patterns that surrounded her afterward. Except for a few fragments that seem somehow uncannily authentic we do not know how Truth sounded. Stowe and Gage used colonialist transcription techniques that emphasized what they heard as the deviant aspects of Truth's speech without conveying any very good sense of its autonomy, and stereotypical assumptions doubtless lie behind many of their distortions of Truth's speech."[83]

But once this is said, something else must be said as well. The white male newspaper reporters who composed third-person standardized English accounts of the substance of Truth's speech at Akron also had their own agendas, dominated by their determination to employ Truth in their campaign to elevate the antislavery cause. Although they did not subordinate her in dialect within a standard English account, it is not necessarily easier to see Truth evolving out of the frame they did supply, which suppressed the radical intent of her challenge to the white patriarchy.

These men were not trying to be Truth. Frances Gage and Harriet Beecher Stowe, for the moment, were. We do not know how many times Frances Gage dramatized the day at Akron to listeners, but we know that Harriet Beecher Stowe had performed her dialect rendition of Truth at least once. In 1857 Mary Beecher Perkins wrote th..c Stowe had regaled William Wetmore Story and Elizabeth Gaskell with a dialect representation of Truth at Story's breakfast table in Rome.[84] The complex psychological reasons why a gifted white woman like Gage and a white woman of genius like Stowe desired to try on the identity of a black woman like Truth probably resist simple analysis. In reading their essays we must imagine we are at a séance at which a complex composite spirit is called up, some part Sojourner Truth and many parts Gilbert, Gage, and Stowe; the Spirit is their Truth.

Story relied on Stowe's portrait of Truth as the inspiration for his 1861 sculpture, "Libyan Sibyl." Stowe described Truth's characteristic demeanor to Story; Story made the statue, which was exhibited in London in 1862.[85] Stowe then incorporated the description of the statue by the critic for the London *Athenaeum* into her 1863 essay:

> Her forward elbow is propped upon one knee; and to keep her secrets closer, for this Libyan woman is the closest of all the Sibyls, she rests her shut mouth upon one closed palm, as if holding the African mystery deep in the brooding brain that looks out through mournful, warning eyes, seen under the wide shade of the strange horned (ammonite) crest, that bears the mystery of the Tetragrammaton upon its upturned front.[86]

Gage may have seen Truth in this habitual posture at Akron, but she was probably also influenced by the description of the statue when she wrote that "old Sojourner, quiet and reticent as the 'Libyan Statue,' sat crouched against the wall on a corner of the pulpit stairs, her sun-bonnet shading her eyes, her elbow on her knees, and her chin resting on her broad, hard palm."[87]

Stowe had imagined Truth's speech dressed in the eloquence of "the African Saint Augustine or Tertullian," and her body made "queenly":

> How grand and queenly a woman she might have been, with her wonderful physical vigor, her great heaving sea of emotion, her power of spiritual conception, her quick penetration, and her boundless energy![88]

Gage, evoking Stowe's "queenly image," saw "a tall, gaunt black woman in a gray dress and white turban, surmounted by an uncouth sun-bonnet, march deliberately into the church, walk with the air of a queen up the aisle, and take her seat upon the pulpit steps."[89]

On the second day of the Akron Convention, during which Jane Swisshelm and Emma Coe gave significant speeches, the anxieties of the women shifted from the reporters to the clergymen who presented opposition statements to the resolutions.[90] "There were few women in those days that dared to 'speak in meeting,'" Gage wrote, referring somewhat bitterly to the broad-based representation of Methodist, Baptist, Episcopal, Presbyterian, and Universalist ministers in attendance as "the august teachers of the people."

Truth's speech was divided into sections, each attacking a spurious definition of what woman is. It seems clear that what drew Truth to her feet was some argument grounding woman's inequality in biology. Gage's description of a slow, solemn, and visionary Truth ("eye piercing the upper air, like one in a dream") recalls the *Athenaeum* critic's view of the statue's "brooding brain that looks out through mournful, warning eyes."[91] But her image of "this almost Amazon form, which stood nearly six feet high, head erect" captures the direction of Truth's argument.[92]

Since Truth's Akron speech, which came to be known as "Ain't I a Woman,"[93] lives in a series of intertextual elaborations, we consider three accounts: contemporary reports in the New York *Tribune*, 6 June 1851, in the Salem *Anti-Slavery Bugle*, 21 June 1851, and Frances Gage's later account in the *National Anti-Slavery Standard*, 2 May 1863. Parallel passages from the three accounts are grouped, so that the reader can compare the substance and style of the transcripts.

> She said she was a woman, and had done as much work in the field as any man here. She had heard much about equality of the sexes, but would not argue that question. (*Tribune*)

> I am a woman's rights. I have as much muscle as any man, and can do as much work as any man. I have plowed and reaped and husked and chopped and mowed, and can any man do more than that? I have heard much about the sexes being equal. I can carry as much as any man, and can eat as much too, if I can get it. I am as strong as any man that is now. (*Anti-Slavery Bugle*)

I have plowed and planted and gathered into barns, and no man could head me—and ar'n't I a woman? I could work as much and eat as much as a man (when I could get it), and bear de lash as well—and ar'n't I a woman? (*National Anti-Slavery Standard*)[94]

This radical argument collapsed two racially specific constructions of womanhood. One was that of true (white) womanhood, which was stereotyped as physically weak, vulnerable, with a moral strength that emanated from the purity of a neutral (neutered) female body. The other was that of untrue (black) womanhood, which was stereotyped as physically strong, incapable of fine sentiment, with an immorality that emanated from the impurity of an animalistic sexual body. Truth threw the whole weight of her prestige as an asset to the abolitionist cause behind her dramatic self-portrait as an enslaved field worker, then she radically turned this self-portrait in a new direction to attack true womanhood. To the pathos of the underfed slave woman's enforced labor, Truth added an exultation in the laboring female body as an efficient working organism, hearty, hungry, and competitive. In an assertively sexualized gesture, baring the muscular flesh of her working arm, she replaced the scene of the baring of black woman's flesh on the auction block or in the master's bed by an Amazonian scene of power in which the black body reveals itself as the instrument of the autonomous black spirit. Maria Stewart had argued that the black woman's body would be as valuable in the sight of others as the white woman's body if their laboring and living conditions were equal: "And why are not our forms as delicate, and our constitutions as slender, as yours? Is not the workmanship as curious and complete?"[95] Truth rejected the onlooker's gaze. Shaking off the ghostly white incubus of femininity used to manipulate the bodies of all women, Truth recolonized her body as the site of her own pleasure.

Gage wrote that one of the clergy "claimed superior rights and privileges for man because of superior intellect."[96] This view of difference had been upheld by some of the women present. In her response, Truth may have given an uneasy moment to Jane Swisshelm, who disliked Truth's extremism, by addressing the contention in Swisshelm's earlier speech "that there is a difference in [men's and women's] physical organization, and therefore in their intellectual."[97]

All she could say was, that if she had a pint of intellect and man a quart, what reason was there why she should not have her pint *full*. [Roars of laughter.] (*Tribune*)

As for intellect, all I can say is, if woman have a pint, and man a quart—why can't she have her little pint full? You need not be afraid to give us our rights for fear we will take too much,—for we can't take more than our pint'll hold. (*Anti-Slavery Bugle*)

"Den dey talks 'bout dis ting in de head. What dis dey call it?" "Intellect," whispered some one near. "Dat's it, honey. What's dat got to do with woman's rights or niggers' rights? If my cup won't hold but a pint and yourn holds a quart wouldn't ye be mean not to let me have my little half-measure full?" (*National Anti-Slavery Standard*)

"Another [clergyman] gave us a theological view of the awful sin of our first mother," Gage wrote.[98]

She said she could not read, but she could hear. She had heard the Bible read, and was told that Eve caused the fall of man. Well, if woman upset the world, do give her a chance to set it right side up again. (*Tribune*)

I can't read, but I can hear. I have heard the bible and have learned that Eve caused man to sin. Well, if woman upset the world, do give her a chance to set it right side up again. (*Anti-Slavery Bugle*)

Turning again to another objector, she took up the defense of Mother Eve. . . . and she ended by asserting "that if de fust woman God ever made was strong enough to turn de world upside down all her one lone, all dese togeder," and she glanced her eye over us, "ought to be able to turn it back and git it right side up again, and now dey is asking to, de men better let 'em." (*National Anti-Slavery Standard*)

Yet another minister had refuted woman's claim to equality "because of the manhood of Christ," arguing that "if God had desired the equality of woman, He would have given some token of His will through the birth, life and death of the Saviour."[99] This was a popular argument with both white and black clergy; a year later, in denying the requests of black women to be licensed preachers, the A.M.E. *Christian Recorder* asked editorially, "When the Messiah's grand mission was to be executed, was the male or female form assumed?"[100] Truth responded that

She learned also from the new Gospel that man had nothing to do with bringing Jesus into the world, for God was his father, but woman was his mother. Jesus respected woman, and never turned her away. By woman's influence the dead was raised, for when Lazarus died Mary and Martha, full of faith and love, came to Jesus and besought him to raise their brother to life. He did not turn them away, but "Jesus wept," and Lazarus came forth. (*Tribune*)

The Lady has spoken about Jesus, how he never spurned woman from him, and she was right. When Lazarus died, Mary and Martha came to him with faith and love and besought him to raise their brother. And Jesus wept and Lazarus came forth. And how came Jesus into the world: Through God who created him and a woman who bore him. Man, where is your part? (*Anti-Slavery Bugle*)

"Den dat little man in black dar, he say woman can't have as much right as man, 'cause Christ wa'n't a woman. *Whar did your Christ come from?*" . . . Raising her voice still louder, she repeated, "Whar did your Christ come from? From God and a woman. Man had not'ing to do with him." (*National Anti-Slavery Standard*)

If fear of unfavorable newspaper coverage motivated some of the women at the convention, fear of the clergy motivated others. Gage saw these two issues as central to Truth's performance; for her, Truth's speech was significant because it rescued women from the attacks of hostile men. But what has made Truth's speech a defining moment in the history of the woman's rights movement was another issue entirely, and one that the women in the convention, including Sallie Holley and her friends who came away talking about Truth's clash with a clergyman, may have only imperfectly grasped.

In one electrifying statement, which Gage placed at the opening of the speech and the two male reporters employed as Truth's climactic conclusion, Truth forced a potentially troubling and certainly divisive vision. She redrew the triangle of white woman-black slave-white man to reposition some *blacks* as *women*, a hard position, which would in the end have separated these white women from many of the white male abolitionists on whom they depended, who were working for the emancipation of *slaves*, not slaves as *women*. For all the differences in wording among the reports of the speech, it is the substance of only this passage that can really be disputed, and the different handling in the three sources is revealing.

But the women are coming up, blessed be God, and a few of the men are coming up with them; but they have a heavy burden to bear, for the slaves and the women look to them for redemption. (*Tribune*)

But the women are coming up blessed be God and a few of the men are coming up with them. But man is in a tight place, the poor slave is on him, woman is coming on him, he is surely between a hawk and a buzzard. (*Anti-Slavery Bugle*)

I tink dat 'twixt de niggers of de Souf and de women at de Norf all a talkin' 'bout rights, de white men will be in a fix pretty soon. (*National Anti-Slavery Standard*)

Both Frances Gage and the *Bugle* reporter wrote that Truth said that the white man was caught between the black slave and the white woman; but the *Bugle* reporter chose a neutral nonracial expression to show the white man's predicament, "between a hawk and a buzzard," in preference to the more specific and more threatening position "between the negroes of the South and the women at the North all talking about rights" (Gage's "niggers of de Souf and de women at de Norf"). The *Tribune*, however, reported something entirely different. Unlike the *Anti-Slavery Bugle* and the *National Anti-Slavery Standard*, which were abolitionist organs, the *Tribune* was a major metropolitan newspaper with a sympathetic but less focused audience. The *Tribune* reporter did not report *anything* precarious about the white man's position: in the *Tribune* account, Truth said that enlightened sympathetic men had a heavy burden to bear, "for the slaves and the women look to them for redemption."

It has been argued that Truth never said "Ain't I a woman." This is a surprising argument, since both the *Tribune*'s phrase "She said she was a woman" and the more awkward "She said I am a woman's rights" reported by the *Bugle* can be reasonably understood as affirmative restatements of this question, and "What is a woman" was certainly the speech's theme. Whether Truth said "Ain't I a Woman" can be most easily answered from internal evidence. Truth's entire speech was a transformation worked on the old abolitionist slogan "Am I not a man and a brother," which had already been recast in the women's movement as "Am I not a woman and a sister?" The phrase was so integral to the thinking of women antislavery activists that the ladies of Ashtabula County, Ohio gave Truth a white satin banner that pictured the "Kneeling figure of a woman with uplifted hands" under the phrase, "Am I not a Woman and a Sister?" Truth asked "Am *I* not a woman?"

Jean Fagin Yellin has traced the image of the kneeling black slave figure as it evolved from the Wedgewood cameo, "Am I not a man and a brother?" in the 1780s in England into the slave woman supplicant, "Am I not a woman and a sister?" that was imported from England to America in

1830 to decorate a woman's feature of *The Genius of Universal Emancipation*. Antislavery white women were asked to put themselves in the position of the powerless black woman; the supplication, voiced in the motto "Am I not a woman and a sister" invited white women to also imagine themselves as liberators of the enslaved woman. Yellin shows the impetus toward feminism in the imaginative identification with the powerless (black) kneeling figure simultaneously overlaid by the self-image of (white) rescuing agent: "enacting these complex patterns of address and avoidance, they recoded and re-recoded the emblem of the female supplicant, picturing themselves as chain-breaking liberators and as enchained slaves pleading for their own liberty, then asserting it and freeing themselves."[101]

Yellin argues that Maria Stewart had acknowledged and reformulated the abolitionist slogan in 1833 in her eloquent assertion of woman's right to public speech: "What if I am a woman; is not the God of ancient times the God of these modern days?"[102] Truth's speech at Akron made "Am I not a woman and a sister/Ain't I a woman" a political question among women agitating for a political solution to the subjugation of women. Yellin interprets both Truth and Harriet Jacobs in *Incidents in the Life of a Slave Girl* as transforming the "Am I not" slogan into the more powerful text, "A'n't I a woman?" Yellin's reading of Gage's assertion that Truth "had taken us up in her strong arms" as simply a reversal of the racial roles of the icon figures of supplicant and rescuer[103] could be extended to account for what is undoubtedly Gage's source for this image, Harriet Beecher Stowe's image of Truth nursing a white woman invalid in Stowe's house: "One felt as if the dark, strange woman were quite able to take up the invalid in her bosom, and bear her as a lamb, both physically and spiritually."[104]

Experiencing Truth at Akron, the audience saw something more threatening than the invalid's nurse. Stowe wrote that she contemplated Truth sadly as one of those "noble minds and bodies, nobly and grandly formed human beings, that have come to us cramped, scarred, maimed, out of the prison-house of bondage."[105] What might have been, Stowe wondered, if such were "suffered to unfold and expand" under benevolent tutelage. She was not thinking of the unfolding at Akron, when the seated, bowed figure rose up to her full six feet of height, raised her muscular arm, and transformed the black female supplicant of the abolitionist icon into the free black woman, sovereign herself.

After this defining moment in Truth's career and in the history of black women in this country, Truth left Akron in a very good mood. Frances Gage had seen that "at intermissions she was busy selling the 'Life of Sojourner Truth,' a narrative of her own strange and adventurous life."[106]

Truth wrote to Amy Post, "I sold a good many books at the Convention and have thus far been greatly prospered." She was now part of another network through which she could disseminate her writing, locate audiences, and move from place to place. She told Post that at the Convention she had "found plenty of kind friends just like you & they gave me so many kind invitations I hardly knew which to accept of first."[107]

Truth's mission had expanded beyond the preaching of her sojourning sisters, who continued to carry the still radical message that they had been authorized by God to speak, to act, to change lives, working their changes on the power structure of Christian patriarchy. At Akron, Truth went a different way. While she never denied the power of the Spirit in sustaining her life work, at Akron Truth had drawn on a uniquely modern and secular source of authorization and empowerment: her own lived history of resilience, what she would famously come to call "the deeds of my body."

Notes

1. Amanda Berry Smith, *An Autobiography: The Story of the Lord's Dealings with Mrs. Amanda Smith the Colored Evangelist* (Chicago: Meyer & Brother, 1893), 116-17.

2. In the Old Testament the Sojourn is the period the Jacob tribes resided in Egypt, from the time they told Pharaoh "For to sojourn in the land are we come," to the Exodus. Relating "sojourn" to "Egypt" are Genesis 12:10; 47:4; Exodus 12:40; Deuteronomy 26:5; Isaiah 53:4; and Jeremiah 42:15, 17; 43:2; 44:12, 14.

3. Stowe, "Sojourner Truth, the Libyan Sibyl," 478.

4. Phillis Wheatley, "On the Death of the Rev. Mr. George Whitefield. 1770," *Poems on Various Subjects, Religious and Moral* (London: A. Bell, 1773), 23.

5. C. Eric Lincoln and Lawrence H. Mamiya, *The Black Church in the African American Experience*, 47-50 and 346-81; William D. Piersen, *Black Yankees*, 66-73.

6. Jupiter Hammon, *An Address to the Negroes in the State of New York, by Jupiter Hammon, Servant of John Lloyd, jun, Esq of the Manor of Queen's Village, Long Island* (New York: Carroll and Patterson, 1786), quoted in Milton C. Sernett, ed., *Afro-American Religious History: A Documentary Witness* (Chapel Hill: University of North Carolina Press, 1985), 37.

7. See Sherley A. Williams, "The Blues Roots of Contemporary Afro-American Poetry," in *Chant of Saints: A Gathering of Afro-American Literature, Art, and Scholarship*, edited by Michael S. Harper and Robert B. Stepto (Urbana: University of Illinois Press, 1979), 125-26.

8. Stowe, "Sojourner Truth, the Libyan Sibyl," 479. See Sarah Bradford, *Harriet Tubman: The Moses of Her People* (Secaucus, New Jersey: The

Citadel Press, 1974 [1886]) for Tubman's version, in which the fugitives hear Queen Victoria say "Dat she was standing on de shore, / Wid arms extended wide, / To give us all a peaceful home, / Beyond de rolling tide" (50). Joan R. Sherman, *Invisible Poets: Afro-Americans of the Nineteenth Century*, 2nd ed. (Chicago: University of Illinois Press, 1989), 35-41, discusses Simpson's sophisticated use of poetic language. Eric Lott, *Love and Theft: Blackface Minstrelry and the American Working Class* (New York: Oxford University Press, 1993), 203-7, analyzes the significance for white working class thought of the many variations on Foster's 1847 "Oh! Susanna, " which he calls "the summation of blackface song craft," but he does not discuss Simpson's extremely important black freedom version.

9. Stowe, "Sojourner Truth, the Libyan Sibyl," 476-77. Stowe compared Truth's performance to that of the renowned French actress Rachel, "who was wont to chant the 'Marseillaise' in a manner that made her seem . . . the very spirit and impersonation of the . . . avenging mob which rose against aristocratic oppression; . . . Sojourner, singing this hymn, seemed to impersonate the fervor of Ethiopia." Wendell Phillips also compared Truth's power over an audience to that of Rachel (480). For a description of Rachel, regarded as the greatest actress of the first part of the nineteenth century and the idol of Sarah Bernhardt, see Arthur Gold and Robert Fizdale, *The Divine Sarah: A Life of Sarah Bernhardt* (New York: Vintage Books, 1992), 36-38.

10. W. E. B. DuBois, *Black Reconstruction* (Millwood, New York: Kraus-Thomson, 1976), 124. See the discussion of Truth's and Tubman's religious songs, which incorporated "concrete historical conditions related to the slaves' desire to live free, human lives" in Angela Y. Davis, "Black Women and Music: A Historical Legacy of Struggle," in *Wild Women in the Whirlwind: Afra-American Culture and the Contemporary Literary Renaissance*, edited by Joanne M. Braxton and Andrée Nicola McLaughlin (New Brunswick: Rutgers University Press, 1990), 3-21.

11. See Daniel Payne, *Recollections of Seventy Years* (Nashville: A.M.E. Sunday School Union, 1888), 93; for a discussion of attitudes toward female preaching in the A.M.E. during this period, including the effort to curb singing and other participatory elements in the service, see Jean McMahon Humez's discussion in her edition of Rebecca Cox Jackson's autobiography, *Gifts of Power*, 311-16, especially 315 n11.

12. Ripley, et al., *The Black Abolitionist Papers*, 4:32

13. *Tribune*, 8 November 1853.

14. Humez's Introduction in Jackson, *Gifts of Power*, 43 n.41; 44.

15. Andrews, *Sisters of the Spirit*, 48, 182.

16. *Tribune*, 7 September 1853. For Jackson's domestic imagery see Jackson, *Gifts of Power*, 49-50, 99-102, 119.

17. [Elizabeth]. *Elizabeth: A Colored Minister of the Gospel Born in Slavery* (Philadelphia: Tract Association of Friends, 1889), quoted in Bert J. Loewenberg and Ruth Bogin, eds. *Black Women in Nineteenth-Century*

American Life (University Park: Pennsylvania State University Press, 1978), 132.

18. Andrews, *Sisters of the Spirit*, 117-18.
19. Ibid., 20, 204, 207.
20. Stowe, "Sojourner Truth, the Libyan Sibyl," 475-76.
21. *Tribune*, 7 December 1878.
22. Andrews, *Sisters of the Spirit*, 57.
23. Ibid., 215, 218. Compare this to the bitter experience of Harriet Jacobs who traveled in 1843 by steamboat to Albany as a nurse for a white family, in Jacobs, *Incidents in the Life of a Slave Girl*, 175.
24. Stanton, et al., *History of Woman Suffrage*, 2:928.
25. Andrews, *Sisters of the Spirit*, 80-81, 91.
26. Ibid., 46, 6.
27. Ibid., 185, 198.
28. Ibid., 111-12.
29. Truth created both songs she sang at this camp meeting, "It Was Early in the Morning" and the militant "I Bless the Lord I've Got My Seal," of which only a stanza remains:

> I bless the Lord I've got my seal—to-day and to-day—
> To slay Goliath in the field—to-day and to-day;
> The good old way is a righteous way,
> I mean to take the kingdom in the good old way.
> (*NarBk*, 119)

See Mabee and Newhouse, *Sojourner Truth*, 226-27.

30. Sherley Anne Williams, "The Empress Brand Trim: Ruby Reminisces." Copyright © 1982 by Sherley Anne Williams. As first appeared in *Some One Sweet Angel Chile* (William Morrow). Reprinted by permission of the author and The Sandra Dijkstra Literary Agency. See Erlene Stetson, *Black Sister*, for this early version.
31. Humez's Introduction in Jackson, *Gifts of Power*, 25-26.
32. It makes for cheerful imagining to think of the good Truth could have done at Fruitlands; in 1844 George Benson hoped to bring Bronson Alcott to Northampton to head the school there but nothing came of it. See Alice Eaton McBee, 2nd, *From Utopia to Florence: The Story of a Transcendentalist Community in Northampton, Mass., 1830-1852* (Northampton: Smith College Studies in History, 1947), 57.
33. *Letters of Lydia Maria Child* (Boston: Houghton Mifflin, 1883), 31, quoted in Dorothy B. Porter, "Anti-Slavery Movement in Northampton," *The Negro History Bulletin* 24, no. 2 (November 1960), 34.
34. Charles A. Sheffield, *The History of Florence, Massachusetts* (Florence: The Editor, 1895), 131 and 165-68. See also McBee, *From Utopia to Florence*, 48.
35. Sheffield, *The History of Florence, Massachusetts*, 127 and 134-35.
36. Cross, *The Burned-over District*, 189-91, 240, and 245; Cross ranked Boyle "next in influence after Finney, Nash, and Burchard." He speculates that

Boyle may have been influenced by the departure from Methodism into holiness by the New York City group led by Truth's associate James Latourette.

37. McBee, *From Utopia to Florence.*
38. Douglass's reminiscence, "What I Found at the Northampton Association," is included in Sheffield, *The History of Florence, Massachusetts,* 129-32.
39. Sheffield, *The History of Florence, Massachusetts,* 131-32.
40. See Elihu Burritt, *The Learned Blacksmith: The Letters and Journals of Elihu Burritt,* edited by Merle Curti (New York: Wilson-Erickson, 1937), 17. The factory, which Gilbert described as inelegant, made silk thread, as part of a pioneering venture in silk production (Sheffield, *The History of Florence, Massachusetts,* 55-64).
41. Jackson, *Gifts of Power,* 237-38.
42. Sheffield, *The History of Florence, Massachusetts,* 96. The various departments of the Community included agricultural, lumber, domestic, cutlery and blacksmithing, silk manufacture, silk growing, store, accounting and secretarial. Members were paid for their work on a graduated scale according to age—a penny an hour for children under twelve, between three and four and a half cents for teenagers, and six cents per hour for those twenty and older (Sheffield, *The History of Florence, Massachusetts,* 87-90).
43. McBee, *From Utopia to Florence,* 70; Hill gave Truth a mortgage for the total purchase price of $300, which she had paid in full by 1854. For the Harmonia settlement see Mabee and Newhouse, *Sojourner Truth,* 95-103.
44. Humez's Introduction in Jackson, *Gifts of Power,* 213, 223.
45. Ibid., 32.
46. William Still, *The Underground Railroad* (Philadelphia: Porter & Coates, 1872), 756; Sterling, *We Are Your Sisters,* 66-69; Shirley J. Yee, *Black Women Abolitionists: A Study in Activism, 1828-1860* (Knoxville: University of Tennessee Press, 1992), 66-73.
47. See Yee, *Black Women Abolitionists,* 86-111. Debra Gold Hansen argues that the black women in the Society were quickly marginalized (*Strained Sisterhood: Gender and Class in the Boston Female Anti-Slavery Society* [Amherst: University of Massachusetts, 1993]). See Sterling, *We Are Your Sisters,* 104-50 for black women's organizations, including abolitionist societies.
48. Yee, *Black Women Abolitionists,* 144-45.
49. See Erlene Stetson, "Studying Slavery," 69 and 71. For the complex relations of Amy Post and Lydia Maria Child to Harriet Jacobs, see Jean Fagan Yellin, "Texts and Contexts of Harriet Jacobs' Incidents in the Life of a Slave Girl: Written by Herself," in *The Slave's Narrative: Texts and Contexts,* edited by Charles T. Davis and Henry Louis Gates, Jr. (New York: Oxford University Press, 1985), 262-82; William L. Andrews, *To Tell A Free Story: The First Century of Afro-American Autobiography, 1760-1865* (Chicago: University of Illinois Press, 1988), 247-48.
50. *The Liberator,* 28 February 1851.

51. *Tribune*, 26 October 1850. Karma Lochrie quotes a medieval cleric who argued that Eve "spoke but once and threw the whole world into disorder" (Lochrie, *Margery Kempe and Translations of the Flesh*, 107).

52. Stewart, *Maria W. Stewart*, 68; Andrews, *Sisters of the Spirit*, 36.

53. *Tribune*, 26 October 1850.

54. *Herald*, 25 October 1850.

55. Ibid. The Middleton lines were also used as stage direction in Sir William Davenant's seventeenth-century version of *Macbeth*.

56. *Herald*, 28 October 1850.

57. Ibid.

58. *National Anti-Slavery Standard*, 28 November 1850.

59. Ibid. For Garnet's speech see Ripley, et al., *The Black Abolitionist Papers*, 3:403-12; for the growing independence of black abolitionists in the 1840s see the Introduction to this same volume, especially 19-35.

60. *The Liberator*, 3 January 1851.

61. Sterling, *We Are Your Sisters*, 121-22.

62. Andrews, *Sisters of the Spirit*, 134.

63. Sterling, *We Are Your Sisters*, 178-79.

64. Mabee and Newhouse, *Sojourner Truth*, 56. "We have received your 'shadow,'" Thompson wrote to Truth in 1864, acknowledging receipt of her photograph, and addressing her as "Dear Mother, Sojourner Truth" (*NarBk*, 295).

65. *The Liberator*, 4 April 1851.

66. Sterling, *We Are Your Sisters*, 135-36.

67. See Yellin's Introduction in Jacobs, *Incidents in the Life of a Slave Girl*, xvi and xxxii.

68. Ann Braude, *Radical Spirits: Spiritualism and Women's Rights in Nineteenth-Century America* (Boston: Beacon Press, 1989), 3, 11, 29. For Harriet Jacobs and spiritualism, see Jacobs, *Incidents in the Life of a Slave Girl*, 248-49; Nancy Hewitt, "Amy Kirby Post," *University of Rochester Library Bulletin* 37 (1984): 13. Mabee and Newhouse discuss Truth's spiritualist connections in Harmonia and Battle Creek (*Sojourner Truth*, 95-103).

69. In the waning days of the Matthias commune a distraught Ann Folger had taken shelter in Isabella's bed, declaring that "she could not lay alone, for that Pierson's spirit haunted her." Isabella had replied, "I wish to God he would appear to me, I would ask him what he wanted" (Vale, *Fanaticism*, part 2, 92).

70. *Anti-Slavery Bugle*, 3 May 1851.

71. *Anti-Slavery Bugle*, 17 May 1851.

72. Truth to Amy Post, no date, probably written just after the Akron Convention, which was held 28 and 29 May 1851, IAPFP, UR.

73. Sallie Holley, *A Life for Liberty: Anti-Slavery and Other Letters of Sallie Holley*, edited by John White Chadwick (New York: G.P. Putnam's Sons, 1899), 57.

74. For a description of the political climate of antislavery agitation in Ohio leading up to the Salem and Akron Conventions, see chapter six, "Ohio," in Stanton, et al., *History of Woman Suffrage*, 1:101-3.

75. *National Anti-Slavery Standard,* 8 May 1851.

76. Stanton, et al., *History of Woman Suffrage,* 1:110-11.

77. Quoted in Lerner, *The Female Experience,* 342; for a selection of letters between Marius and Emily Robinson detailing proslavery violence in Ohio during the 1830s, see 59-69.

78. *National Anti-Slavery Standard,* 2 May 1863.

79. Gage's version of Truth's speech has been attacked both for its use of dialect and, more recently, for its supposed inaccuracy. See Jeffrey C. Stewart's Introduction in [Sojourner Truth, Olive Gilbert and Frances Titus], *Narrative of Sojourner Truth; A Bondswoman of Olden Time, With a History of Her Labors and Correspondence Drawn from Her "Book of Life"* (New York: Oxford University Press, 1991), xxxiii-xxxv. Stewart reprinted Truth's Akron speech in the reporter's version given in the Salem, Ohio, *Anti-Slavery Bugle,* 21 June 1851, and he seems to argue that Gage's rendering of the speech "in a rather crude Southern dialect" dishonors Truth. In *Sojourner Truth,* Mabee and Newhouse also reprint the *Anti-Slavery Bugle* version (67-82); they dismiss Gage's account of the setting, the effect of the speech on the Convention, and its relative importance in the woman's rights movement. Margaret Washington also reprinted the *Anti-Slavery Bugle* version as an appendix to her 1850 edition of the *Narrative,* arguing that "The veracity of Gage's recall of Sojourner's speech is questionable" (117-18). As Sojourner Truth might have said, and probably did, "whar dar is so much racket dar must be something out o'kilter" (*National Anti-Slavery Standard,* 2 May 1863).

80. Frances Titus printed a modified version of Gage's account in *NarBk* (131-35). The editors of *History of Woman Suffrage* seem to have used the version Titus used in *NarBk,* prefacing it by identifying Truth not as one of the great figures in woman's rights history but as "Mrs. Stowe's 'Lybian [sic] Sibyl.'" (Stanton, et al., *History of Woman Suffrage,* 1:114-17). Compare Stowe, "Sojourner Truth, the Libyan Sibyl," 473-81 and *NarBk,* 151-72.

81. For a discussion of the influence of Stowe's essay in the creation of a nineteenth-century persona of Truth, identifying elements of racist caricature, see Nell Irvin Painter, "Sojourner Truth in Life and Memory: Writing the Biography of an American Exotic," *Gender and History* 2, no. 1 (Spring 1990): 8-11. For the essay's place in the context of the treatment of the exotic in American literature of the period, see Jane Crossthwaite, "Women and Wild Beasts: Versions of the Exotic in Nineteenth Century American Art," *Southern Humanities Review* 19 (1985): 97-114.

82. See John Wideman, "Frame and Dialect: The Evolution of the Black Voice," *The American Poetry Review* (September-October 1976) and the definition of "framed story" in Gayl Jones, *Liberating Voices: Oral Tradition in African American Literature* (New York: Penguin Books, 1991), 199.

83. See Gayl Jones, *Liberating Voices,* 203.

84. Joan D. Hedrick, *Harriet Beecher Stowe: A Life* (New York: Oxford University Press, 1994), 270.

85. "Some years ago, when visiting Rome, I related Sojourner's history to Mr. Story at a breakfast at his home. . . . A few days after, he told me that he had conceived the idea of a statue which he should call the Libyan Sibyl. Two years subsequently, I revisited Rome, and found the gorgeous Cleopatra finished. . . . Mr. Story requested me to come and repeat to him the history of Sojourner Truth, saying that the conception had never left him. I did so; and a day or two after, he showed me the clay model of the Libyan Sibyl" (Stowe, "Sojourner Truth, the Libyan Sibyl," 480-81).

86. Quoted by Stowe, "Sojourner Truth, the Libyan Sibyl," 481; see also *NarBk*, 171-72. Working from Stowe's description of Truth, Story represented the Sibyl with "legs crossed, leaning forward, her elbow on her knee and her chin pressed down upon her hand" (letter from Story, quoted in James, *William Wetmore Story and His Friends*, 2:71).

87. *National Anti-Slavery Standard*, 2 May 1863.

88. Stowe, "Sojourner Truth, the Libyan Sibyl," 480.

89. *National Anti-Slavery Standard*, 2 May 1863.

90. Stanton, et al., *History of Woman Suffrage*, 1:114. "The reports of this Convention are so meagre that we can not tell who were in the opposition; but from Sojourner Truth's speech, we fear that the clergy, as usual, were averse to enlarging the boundaries of freedom."

91. Stowe, "Sojourner Truth, the Libyan Sibyl," 481.

92. *National Anti-Slavery Standard*, 2 May 1863.

93. Titus transcribed the question "And ar'n't I a woman"; in *History of Woman Suffrage* it is transcribed "And a'n't I a woman" (1:116). Truth is recorded in other speeches as using "Aint," the more natural form.

94. This argument formed the whole of the impression taken away by the reporter for *The Liberator* who in a brief paragraph noted that "Sojourner Truth spoke in her own peculiar style, showing that she was a match for most men. She had ploughed, hoed, dug, and could eat as much, if she could get it. The power and wit of this remarkable woman convulsed the audience with laughter. I wish I could report every word she said, but I cannot" (13 June 1851).

95. Stewart, *Maria W. Stewart*, 48.

96. Gage, *National Anti-Slavery Standard*, 2 May 1863.

97. See the report in *The Liberator*, 13 June 1851. Truth nonetheless retained her ties with abolitionist-feminist Jane Grey Cannon Swisshelm, and in 1864, she stayed with Swisshelm for the first three weeks after she arrived in Washington, D.C.

98. Gage, *National Anti-Slavery Standard*, 2 May 1863.

99. Ibid.

100. Humez's Introduction in Jackson, *Gifts of Power*, 313 n7.

101. See Jean Fagan Yellin, *Women & Sisters: The Antislavery Feminists in American Culture* (New Haven: Yale University Press, 1989), 3-26.

102. Ibid., 46-47; see Stewart, *Maria Stewart*, 68.

103. Yellin, *Women & Sisters*, 79-82.

104. Stowe, "Sojourner Truth, the Libyan Sibyl," 479.
105. Ibid., 480.
106. *National Anti-Slavery Standard,* 3 May 1863.
107. Truth to Amy Post, undated, ca. 29 May 1851, IAPFP, UR.

Five

I Saw the Wheat Holding up Its Head

I never saw so clearly the nature and intent of the Constitution before. Oh, was it not strangely inconsistent that men fresh, so fresh, from the baptism of the Revolution should make such concessions to the foul spirit of Despotism! that, when fresh from gaining their own liberty, they could permit the African slave trade—could let their national flag hang a sign of death on Guinea's coast and Congo's shore! Twenty-one years the slave-ships of the new Republic could gorge the sea monsters with their prey; twenty-one years of mourning and desolation for the children of the tropics, to gratify the avarice and cupidity of men styling themselves free! And then the dark intent of the fugitive clause veiled under words so specious that a stranger unacquainted with our nefarious government would not know that such a thing was meant by it. Alas for these fatal concessions. They remind me of the fabulous teeth sown by Cadmus—they rise, armed men, to smite.

Frances Watkins Harper,
National Anti-Slavery Standard, 9 April 1859

Toward the end of her last year at Oberlin, Frederick Douglass invited Sallie Holley to write for the *North Star*, which he had launched in 1847 against the bitter opposition of the Garrisonians. In mid-1851 the title of his new venture, *Frederick Douglass' Paper*, would leave no doubt as to who controlled its editorial viewpoint. Holley refused; by the end of the summer of 1851 Abby Kelley Foster had already recruited her for the Garrisonian Ohio campaign to preach disunionism and nonresistance across the state, filtered through a growing Garrisonian-sanctioned feminist awareness. Sallie Holley made joking reference to having found her real "sphere." In the Western Anti-Slavery Society women held many of the leadership positions.

Holley, Truth, Parker Pillsbury, the offbeat Charles C. Burleigh, "allowing his hair to hang in curls about his neck," and the Ohio abolitionists, Josephine Griffing and her husband, and Marius and Emily Robinson, covered the Ohio circuit "in the days of outlawry for anti-slavery." If they found the churches, halls, and schoolhouses closed to them, they spoke in the groves. Once in an Ohio village a shoemaker asked them in, "taking off his apron, shoving back his bench," and they worked the crowd of passersby and onlookers. They put on a good show: Holley, the young white "lady pleading so earnestly for the slave-woman; her beautiful face full of the warm human sympathy of her plea," Pillsbury, the working-class bane of the pro-slavery churches ("Pillsbury is a very bitter devil"), and the dramatic Truth.

> Following Mr. Pillsbury, would rise, towering, the striking form and features of Sojourner Truth, in her turban, and with wit and pathos she would wring our hearts, and wreathe our faces with smiles, and even convulse us with laughter, at the story of her old slave life in New York, before the act of emancipation in the Empire State of 1828.[1]

Truth's performances often took this form of testimony, grounded in revivalist experience. In Ohio the constitutive elements of Truth's social vision—enthusiastic religion, antislavery, and woman's rights agitation—were all in full play. Truth mostly worked alone, Holley wrote:

> Miss Putnam, Mr. and Mrs. Griffing, Parker Pillsbury, and myself compose our travelling party, in one carriage. Every few days Sojourner Truth joins us and aids in our meetings. She travels in a buggy by herself. An anti-slavery friend loaned her a pony and buggy for the entire summer. She is quite a strong character and shows what a great intellect slavery has crushed. She talks like one who has not only *heard* of American slavery, but has *seen* and *felt* it. As she eloquently exclaimed last evening, "All the gold of California, all the wealth of this nation, could not restore to me that which the white people have wrested from me."[2]

Truth told Lucy Colman that during those weeks traveling around Ohio with the pony and buggy "whenever she came to a place where two roads met, she laid the lines down and said, 'God, you drive,' and he always drove her to some good place, where she had a successful meeting."

Colman thought Truth's success in gathering Ohio crowds was because "Her voice was very fine."

> She paid her way, and her horse was well taken care of, but I think she did not convert to *real* abolitionism many on that trip. The people were curious to hear her talk and sing.[3]

Truth told Harriet Beecher Stowe that her customary procedure was to go around to camp meetings, set up the white banner that she carried in her pocket (she pulled it out to show Stowe, who remembered that it had antislavery slogans but not which ones), and begin to sing; her singing would attract people, and then she would preach to them.[4] Parker Pillsbury pictured Truth lecturing in Ashtabula County: "Her tall, erect form, dressed in dark green, a white handkerchief crossed over her breast, a white turban on her head, with white teeth and still whiter eyes, she stood, a spectacle weird, fearful as an avenger."[5]

Truth's style was always interactive and responsive, lifting a complex argument into the light and exposing its hitherto unseen defect to the dazzle of her insight. What Ann Douglas has written of Margaret Fuller, "When she could, she walked toward what she sensed as the opening area of significance,"[6] applies equally well to Truth. She was the perfect platform speaker, thinking on her feet, collecting and refocusing the energy of her audience to be turned back against it like a laser beam. The *Anti-Slavery Bugle* wrote that Truth "would sometimes throw in the way of the politicians, a most ugly difficulty—a whole argument, with premise, conclusion and application, in a single question."[7]

In an encounter of which legend was made Truth clashed with Frederick Douglass at the anniversary meeting of the Western Anti-Slavery Society in Salem, Ohio in August 1852.[8] In the early 1850s radical abolitionists were embroiled in a critical debate over the role of the Constitution in legitimating slavery, which pitted Garrisonians against those who wished to use the political process to combat slavery. The staunchly Garrisonian Western Anti-Slavery Society was united on two principles: that the Constitution was a document that authorized slavery and that its members rejected political action (voting; office-holding), which implied consent to a government that sanctioned slavery. Their resolutions called for "a dissolution of the union" and a rejection of political activism in favor of the radical Christian position of moral suasion: "Resolved, That no political platform yet erected, has any virtue or merit, which should tempt us from our present impregnable position, as a strictly moral and religious anti-slavery movement."[9]

Truth elsewhere expressed her Garrisonian view of the Constitution in one of her most memorable articulations:

> Children, I talk to God and God talks to me. I go out and talk to God in the fields and the woods. This morning I was walking out, and I got over the fence. I saw the wheat holding up its head, looking very big. I go up and take hold of it. You believe it, there was *no* wheat there? I say, God, what *is* the matter with *this* wheat? and he says to me, "Sojourner, there is a little weevil in it." Now I hear talking about the Constitution and the rights of man. I come up and I take hold of this Constitution. It looks *mighty big*, and I feel for *my* rights, but there aint any there. Then I say, God, what *ails* this Constitution? He says to me, "Sojourner, there is a little weevil in it."[10]

Douglass had held such a view as a Garrisonian, but he had gradually abandoned the Garrisonian call for dissolving the union and had recently rejected their view that the Constitution was a slaveholding document. In *North Star* editorials in 1849 Douglass had acknowledged that the governing principles of the Constitution were antislavery even if the framers' intent had not been. He now advocated an active role in the political process.[11] The Salem *Anti-Slavery Bugle*, the official organ of the Western Anti-Slavery Society, reported that when the meeting rejected a resolution on political action, Douglass "made reply, with a view to show that we may innocently support the Government and hold office under it."[12] Holding these "views of the Constitution and of the voting question," Douglass's presence in Salem among the "Disunion abolitionists" generated high drama.[13]

But there was low drama as well. Oliver Johnson, the former editor of the *Anti-Slavery Bugle*, recorded a spectacular confrontation between Douglass and Truth for the Garrisonian weekly, the *Pennsylvania Freeman:* "Mr. Douglass, in the course of his speech, took occasion to glorify Violence as in some circumstances far more potent than Moral Suasion." According to Johnson, Douglass "ridiculed the idea that anything short of the shedding of the blood of tyrants could afford relief":

> When his argument on this point had reached its climax, and the audience had been wrought to a high pitch of excitement by his rhetoric—in answer to his exclamation, "What is the use of Moral Suasion to a people thus trampled in the dust?" was heard the voice of Sojourner Truth, who asked, with startling effect, "Is God gone?"[14]

Oliver Johnson later wrote that "no bullet ever went to its mark with greater accuracy than that with which this interrogatory pierced the very heart of the question, and Douglass stood demolished and silent."[15] More than half a century later, Douglass himself still thought of Truth's question as an act of vandalism:

> We were all for a moment brought to a stand-still, just as we should have been if someone had thrown a brick through the window.[16]

It is easy to see in the language of the white reporters why the incident left its mark on Douglass—a mark probably deeper than the one made by Truth's pointed question. Douglass would remember being humiliated on a public occasion by a black woman; but he probably remembered longer the use to which this public humiliation was put by white antislavery activists who opposed his call for resistance and seem to have gloried in the sight of Douglass "demolished and silent."

Writing for the *Liberator*, Parker Pillsbury used sexualized language to report Douglass's victimization by a "slave woman" (Truth had been free for 26 years, as Pillsbury well knew):

> In two or three instances, poor old Sojourner Truth, the slave woman, pierced him through and through with a single dart, sent with that fearful aim and precision for which she is so eminently distinguished.

To his *Liberator* audience Parker Pillsbury termed Douglass "our once faithful and powerful coadjutor," *formerly* among the "master spirits."[17] Pillsbury reduced Douglass's ideological shift to an issue of "manhood." Douglass had possessed his "manhood" when he was on the Garrisonian non-resistance side; he had lost it when he went over to the pro-resistance side; he regained it momentarily by his forceful oratory at the Western Anti-Slavery Meeting; and then he had been emasculated by the sharp wit of a castrating black woman. This is surely one of the costliest of the many battles Douglass fought on the treacherous ground of the nineteenth-century cult of manhood. Denied under slavery the white male-defined freedom of patriarchal manhood, many black men measured their progress as men against the illusory white norm.[18] Truth challenged Douglass's politics, not his manhood. The white abolitionists' accounts, if not the event, reverberate with the hidden anxieties of power, saturated as always with those of race and of gender.

Douglass had committed the ultimate sins against Garrison: he had adopted a political party, endorsed the Constitution, and challenged the pacifist principles of Christian radicalism. But in a sense these had only compounded his original sin: that of establishing an independent antislavery newspaper in the arena of the *Liberator* and the *Anti-Slavery Standard* and in direct competition with the Salem *Anti-Slavery Bugle*, whose editors particularly resented Douglass's encroachment on their small circulation.[19] The fireworks at the Salem meeting were really set off by newspapermen.

The "Is God dead?" exchange was not reported in the account of the Western Anti-Slavery Society meeting in the 3 September 1852 issue of *Frederick Douglass' Paper.* Douglass waited. In a sense, he had worded his way around Truth before. When Truth's *Narrative* appeared in 1850, Olive Gilbert had inserted into it some opinions critical of slave holidays taken fresh out of Douglass's 1845 *Narrative;* thus in the critical scene in which the impetuous Isabella, who liked to sing and dance, walked toward Dumont's dearborn with the vision of Pinkster revelry before her eyes, she was framed by the words of the austere Douglass. After Truth's death, in his reminiscence "What I Found at the Northampton Association," Douglass circumscribed Truth's easy convivial movement among the Northampton Association reformists to the circuit of "its day of small things." Douglass's silence in not reporting the 1852 encounter at Salem was a holding action. He saved the exchange for a revisionist passage in his final expanded autobiography, *My Life and Times*, and this time he was not left speechless:

> Speaking at an Anti-Slavery convention in Salem, Ohio, I expressed this apprehension that slavery could only be destroyed by blood-shed, when I was suddenly and sharply interrupted by my good old friend Sojourner Truth with the question, "Frederick, is God dead?" "No," I answered, "and because God is not dead slavery can only end in blood." My quaint old sister was of the Garrison school of non-resistants, and was shocked at my sanguinary doctrine, but she too became an advocate of the sword, when the war for the maintenance of the Union was declared.[20]

Some years would pass after the Salem confrontation before Truth would advocate the sword. By the end of the decade even the nonresistant Garrison, who had burned a copy of the Constitution at a public gathering in 1854, had begun to see a constitutional weapon against slavery in the use of the war power.[21] The Civil War took place. Douglass waited to compose the scene until he could revise it by recontextualizing Truth in her later altered state of mind (read: She Was Wrong at Salem). Truth spoke to the moment. Douglass spoke to the page. Not for the first time, Douglass had worded his way out.

But Truth's "Is God Dead?" question would not die. By reducing the historic exchange between two courageous black speakers on the most critical issue of their time to a personality conflict, self-interested white critics denigrated Douglass in a way that was also denigrating to Truth. Although, as Douglass belatedly pointed out, Truth had abandoned the path of Garrisonian nonresistance by the 1860s, Frances Titus had "Is God Dead?" (definitely not "Ain't I a Woman?") engraved on Truth's gravestone. In canonizing this phrase from an instance of black-on-black conflict, white people in the nineteenth century awarded transcendent value to the concept of black non-resistance. Truth's "Is God dead?" resonated in black history, but in a different way, invoking the idea of justice in an unjust world, without recalling its original context. Situated at the heart of the abolitionist wars of the 1850s, the notoriety generated by the exchange must be seen as part of the process by which images of black women and black men were repeatedly manipulated by white society for its own purposes. It is not that Truth did not mean what she said in that startling moment: but she meant it *then*, in *that moment*. On 2 January 1866, in the opening months of what would prove to be not the end of oppression but the beginning of another long era of it, Truth sent a message from Washington to Amy Post in Rochester: "Where's Frederick," she asked, wondering anxiously "that his voice is not heard in this trying hour." [22]

Like the cultural construction of manhood the white patriarchal construction of womanhood got in the way of cooperation between black and white women. Many women in the white feminist movement may not have grasped how much their own racism would affect the histories of both black women and men. Antoinette Brown probably said more than she realized when she protested the class of "genuine bigots" who approached woman's rights activists, absurdly, in her opinion, "with somewhat of the feeling with which Miss Ophelia regarded Topsy, the abhorrence that is experienced on drawing near a large black spider."[23]

The exclusive focus on the vote in the white feminist movement was a post-War development; the early movement had fought for rights on many fronts. An editorial opinion expressed in the early 1880s in *History of Woman Suffrage* regretfully confirmed that debates in the early Woman's Rights Conventions found "the speakers dwelling much more on the wrongs in the Church and the Home, than in the State":

> But few of the women saw clearly, and felt deeply that the one cause of their social and religious degradation was their disfranchisement, hence the discussions often turned on the surface-wrongs of society.[24]

Working with white feminists in this period, Sojourner Truth, Nancy Gardner Prince, Sarah Remond, Frances Watkins Harper, and other black women spoke continually on the "surface-wrongs" of society, which for them went far below the surface.

In September 1853 Truth spoke in New York City at the infamous Mob Convention, described in the official history as "the first overt exhibition of that public sentiment woman was then combating." Her appearance on the platform was said to embody "the two most hated elements of humanity": being black and being a woman.[25] Truth was greeted by an abusive crowd of men who had paid twenty-five cents each for admission to the Broadway Tabernacle.

With her genius for quickly grasping the fundamental aspects of an audience's discontent and turning it back upon itself, Truth attacked the resentment of woman's speech outside the domestic sphere; at the same time she undermined the "mother" argument employed by the women themselves. The hissing heckling men at the Mob Convention insisted on a maternal image of woman, not the image of the strong-minded independent woman represented by the speaker for woman's rights: "When she comes to demand 'em, don't you hear how sons hiss their mothers like snakes, because they ask for their rights; and can they ask for anything less?" In a parodic reversal of the bad mother scolded by her angry sons, Truth scolded her audience for being failed sons of improper mothers: "If they'd been brought up proper they'd have known better than hissing like snakes and geese." She was not looking to the mothers of these men for help.

Like Maria Stewart, Truth invoked Queen Esther, but not simply as a heroic representative of womanhood. When Esther came unauthorized into the king's presence, he offered her half a kingdom; she wanted both less and more: the rescue of the Jewish people, threatened by the king's men. Truth also wanted both less and more: "Now, women do not ask half of a kingdom, but their rights, and they don't get 'em." Truth identified the Persian king with the authority of the state, an authority greater than her male audience: "Should the king of the United States be greater, or more crueler, or more harder?" Carrying on her comparison, she placed the hissing audience in the place of Haman, the persecutor of the Jews, who was hanged by the king on the gallows he had built for a Jew (that is, the king found out his desire and turned it back on him):

> The king ordered Haman to be hung on the gallows which he prepared to hang others; but I do not want any man to be killed, but I am sorry to see them so short-minded. But we'll have our rights; see if we don't; and you can't stop us from them; see if you can.[26]

This was a threat of some substance, radically attacking the whole concept of "spheres." In invoking the power of the state to protect some of its citizens against others, Truth also arrogated to herself a position within statecraft: not an exemplary but a political position. In this she was also subtly moving away from Garrisonian moral suasion.

In building bridges between white and black women, activists of both groups were hindered by their own struggles with the prevailing mythology of "womanhood." White feminists might have tried to escape the constraining gender role assigned them, but they seldom admitted their complicity in producing the double-bind of the black woman's role. Angela Davis has traced the origin of disabling stereotypes of black women to the ideological apparatus of institutionalized slavery.[27] The purity of the white woman was a conceptual device used to reinforce the image of the black woman as seducer, shielding white mistresses from their complicity in the sexual exploitation of black women. By a further bizarre mystification, the black woman's ability to survive sexual attack was taken as a sign of her immorality.[28] The entrapping establishment of traditional white gender roles could seem a positive goal for people trying to break free from the pervasive negative images.[29]

The construction of motherhood was an important element in the white patriarchal construction of the black female body. Sexual exploitation made the maternal a contested ground for black women. Rarely was the issue forced into the public debate of white feminists in the manner that Nancy Gardner Prince presented it to the Fifth National Woman's Rights Convention in Philadelphia in 1854:

> Mrs. Prince, a colored woman, invoked the blessing of God upon the noble women engaged in this enterprise, and said she understood woman's wrongs better than woman's rights, and gave some of her own experiences to illustrate the degradation of her sex in slavery. On a voyage to the West Indies the vessel was wrecked, and she was picked up and taken to New Orleans. Going up the Mississippi she saw the terrible suffering of a cargo of slaves, among them a large number of young quadroon girls with infants in their arms as fair as any lady in this room.[30]

Prince presented an image of the maternal that implicated every white woman in the audience, graphically figuring in this image of suffering what Hazel Carby has called the "opposing definitions of motherhood and womanhood for white and black women which coalesce in the figures of the slave and the mistress."[31]

In 1858 from her home in Battle Creek, Truth accepted Josephine Griffing's urging to cross over into Indiana to lecture against the restrictions on the persons and movements of blacks enacted in the various Black Laws. Like Ohio, Illinois, Kentucky and Tennessee, Indiana had passed laws to keep blacks from settling within its borders. Since 1831, blacks wishing to settle in Indiana had had to register with county officials and give bond. The infamous Article XIII of the state constitution of 1851 prohibited blacks from coming into the state to live. Blacks were prohibited by Indiana law from voting and serving in the militia; they could not send their children to public schools and were barred from giving evidence in court cases involving white people. The state of Indiana dedicated some of its public funds to help finance the colonization of blacks in Liberia. Nevertheless, the 1860 census showed 11,428 blacks had migrated to the "free soil" of Indiana.[32]

In the fall of 1858, Truth held a series of antislavery meetings in Northern Indiana, which were reported on in the *Liberator*. In Silver Lake, in Kosciusko County, Truth was suspected of being "a mercenary hireling of the Republican party," and a large group of proslavery Democrats and their sympathizers attended. At this meeting, the deeply embedded gender politics of proslavery agitation were dramatically exposed.

The nature of the challenge to Truth at Silver Lake was explicit: "A rumor was immediately circulated that Sojourner was an imposter; that she was, indeed, a man disguised in women's clothing."

> At the close of the meeting, Dr. T. W. Strain, the mouthpiece of the slave Democracy, requested the large congregation to "hold on," and stated that a doubt existed in the minds of many persons present respecting the sex of the speaker, and that it was his impression that a majority of them believed the speaker to be a man. (*NarBk*, 138)

Strain "demanded that Sojourner submit her breast to the inspection of some of the ladies present, that the doubt might be removed by their testimony"; although these ladies "appeared to be ashamed and indignant at such a proposition," a presumably male voice vote ("a boisterous 'Aye'") approved the disrobing.

Two kinds of time are conflated in this one dramatic scene: the time-bound event itself in which the enslaved black woman is disrobed by the white master, and the seemingly timeless state of being in which the event is always about to repeat itself because the coercive control and sadistic exploitation of her body by white men are psychologically grounded in her own sense of being. Both the event and its prospective repetitions foreground the voyeuristic enjoyment of the black woman's body by the white owner who can bring it at any time before his eyes, as well as manipulate it, make it the object of his visual delight.

The stripping of the black woman's body is the sexualized prelude to the torture that lies at the heart of so many slave narratives. Truth said, from her own experience, that when she heard stories of "whipping women on the bare flesh, it makes *my* flesh crawl, and my very hair rise on my head!" (*NarBk*, 27). The disrobing is the sign that the black woman's body *is under the power of* the white man. A white school master, acting as a surrogate master, told Elizabeth Keckley "I am going to whip you, so take down your dress this instant."

> Recollect, I was eighteen years of age, was a woman fully developed, and yet this man coolly bade me take down my dress. I drew myself up proudly, firmly, and said: "No, Mr. Bingham, I shall not take down my dress before you. Moreover, you shall not whip me unless you prove the stronger. Nobody has a right to whip me but my own master, and nobody shall do so if I can prevent it."[33]

The resonating bitterness in the scene at Silver Lake is richly complicated by the contradictory avowed reason the white men give for wishing to see Truth's breasts:

> Confusion and uproar ensued, which was soon suppressed by Sojourner, who, immediately rising, asked them why they suspected her to be a man. The Democracy answered, "Your voice is not the voice of a woman, it is the voice of a man, and we believe you are a man." (*NarBk*, 138)

The "Democracy" challenged Truth's "voice," invoking the stereotype of the voiceless suffering woman. Frederick Douglass wrote that he could always remember his mother's profile, "but the image is mute, and I have no striking words of her's treasured up."[34] The deep-voiced powerful orator is declared *not* a woman because she *has* a voice: not just its timbre but its efficacy identifies it to her persecutors as a man's voice.

Truth turned the place upside down by resorting to a purely woman-identified voice expressing woman-identified experience. The men wished to evoke the spectacle of the black woman's body unclothed and vulnerable to them, a body that did not speak with a woman's voice. Truth offered this stunning reversal of their spectacle, substituting for the masculine spectacle of the body raped a woman's spectacle of the body enigmatically nurturing:

Sojourner told them that her breasts had suckled many a white babe, to the exclusion of her own offspring; that some of those white babies had grown to man's estate; that, although they had sucked her colored breasts, they were, in her estimation, far more manly than they (her persecutors) appeared to be; and she quietly asked them, as she disrobed her bosom, if they, too, wished to suck! (*NarBk*, 139)

Here is a dazzling play on white manhood and white womanhood and the matrices of gendered oppression. Truth challenges the manhood of those who question her sex: the white babies sucking her expropriated milk were "more manly than they." They have fantasized her as the vulnerable woman's body: now she forces them to imagine themselves as helpless white infants, malleable, defenseless, purely physical, and wholly in *her* power, dependent for their lives on the black woman's breasts. In her total reversal of taboo, she exposes her breasts and invites them to suck *now*. She uncolonized herself.

When the Civil War began in 1861, it was considered (by whites) to be a white man's war. Bitterly ingrained racial prejudice prevented Northerners from consenting to fight beside black troops. Moreover, white Northerners did not believe black men capable of being good soldiers. There were political considerations, Lincoln said in refusing two black regiments offered by the state of Indiana: "To arm the negroes would turn 50,000 bayonets from the loyal Border States against us that were for us." The stakes were indeed high, as Frederick Douglass argued: "Once let the black man get upon his person the brass letters, U.S., let him get an eagle on his button, and a musket on his shoulder and bullets in his pocket, and there is no power on earth which can deny that he has earned the right to citizenship in the United States."[35] Even so, in January 1863 the state of Massachusetts began to enlist black troops. Among those recruiting were Frederick Douglass, Charles Lenox Remond, William Wells Brown, and Martin Delany, joined by Josephine Ruffin, Harriet Jacobs, and Mary Ann Shadd Cary, the only woman to work as an officially commissioned recruiter.

When Massachusetts was unable to fill its Fifty-fourth from within the state, recruits came from all over, including Truth's grandson, James Caldwell, and two of Frederick Douglass's sons. The Fifty-fourth Massachusetts under Colonel Robert Shaw won fame and glory in the assault on Fort Wagner, near Charleston, in mid-July 1863. The battle, which the New York *Tribune* said "made Fort Wagner such a name to the colored race as Bunker Hill has been for ninety years to the white Yankees," was narrowly lost with huge black casualties.[36] Harriet Tubman described it as a dreadful harvest.

> And then we saw the lightning, and that was the guns; and then we heard the thunder, and that was the big guns; and then we heard the rain falling, and that was the drops of blood falling, and when we came to get in the crops, it was dead men that we reaped.[37]

In a letter written from Rochester in 1867 to the *Anti-Slavery Standard*, Truth expressed a vehement opposition to reconciliation with the defeated Southerners which stemmed from their brutal treatment of prisoners of war, including her grandson.

> I had a grandson who was a prisoner in South Carolina, with some of Massachusetts' darling sons, who suffered untold misery—Captains and other officers the same. I am ashamed to put on paper the horrible things they were obliged to submit to, under these rebel fiends.[38]

From the beginning, black enlistees knew that the Confederacy enslaved or brutalized blacks taken prisoner if it did not massacre them outright. Nevertheless, by the end of October the Union Army had fifty-eight black regiments numbering with their white officers over 37,000 men.[39]

Truth collected donations of food for the black enlistees from the area around her home in Battle Creek who were gathered at Camp Ward. Colonel Bennett "ordered the regiment into line 'in their best' for the presentation" (*NarBk*, 173), which was followed by a patriotic speech. For the First Michigan Regiment of Colored Soldiers, Truth composed the rousing, brashly defiant, irreverent and joyous "The Valiant Soldiers" ("We hear the proclamation, massa, hush it as you will; / The birds will sing it to us, hopping on the cotton hill"). This song is stirringly performed in our time by Sweet Honey in the Rock as "Sojourner's Battle Hymn" in Bernice Johnson Reagon's arrangement. Truth sang it in Detroit and Washington. A nineteenth century source reprinted Truth's song, describing the effect of a Civil War regiment singing:

> She composed this song for "her boys," the colored regiment from Battle Creek, Michigan, but it soon became a favorite with all the colored soldiers. An old veteran told the writer he once heard a black regiment sing it just before a battle and they made the welkin ring, and inspired all

who heard it. Imagine a thousand Negro soldiers singing the following lines to the tune of "John Brown's Body."[40]

Truth proclaimed in her battle hymn that

Father Abraham has spoken, and the message has been sent;
The prison doors have opened, and out the prisoners went
To join the sable army of African descent,
As we go marching on. (*NarBk*, 126)

"Father Abraham" spoke the Emancipation Proclamation in 1863, but only some of the "prison doors" opened: it freed only those slaves living in the Confederate states, and even the majority of those freedpeople stayed on the Southern plantations until the end of the war. But from the earliest months of the conflict some enslaved men and women had run away from plantations to reach Union camps; finally declared "contrabands of war" by the Union generals, thousands of them clustered in camps in the Washington area. Among the first war work performed by black women was aid to these refugees, organized by Harriet Jacobs, Elizabeth Keckley, and others. In August 1862, Harriet Jacobs wrote to the *Liberator* describing the Government headquarters for the hundreds of "contrabands":

> I found men, women and children all huddled together without any distinction or regard to age or sex. Some of them were in the most pitiable condition. Many were sick with measles, diptheria, scarlet and typhoid fever. Some had a few filthy rags to lie on, others had nothing but the bare floor for a couch. They were coming in at all times, often through the night and the Superintendent had enough to occupy his time in taking the names of those who came in and those who were sent out. His office was thronged through the day by persons who came to hire the poor creatures.[41]

Elizabeth Keckley was attending Mary Todd Lincoln in the White House as dressmaker and confidante. Keckley had lost a son in the war. In 1862, she organized The Contraband Relief Association, afterward the Freedmen and Soldiers' Relief Association of Washington. There were an estimated 40,000 blacks newly come to the District of Columbia by the end of the war, all under the nominal jurisdiction of the army.[42]

The work to aid these people, already begun by black women like Jacobs and Keckley, was joined by Truth in the fall of 1864. Coming to Washington by way of speaking engagements in Detroit, Boston, New

York and New Jersey, Truth had stayed with her Quaker friend Rowland Johnson in Orange, New Jersey. Truth's letter to Johnson from Washington gives a characteristic picture of her arrangements when she settled herself in a new location. She would be housed by people in the abolitionist network, would be organizing and generating support for her activities by publicizing her whereabouts in antislavery journals, and, by selling her *Narrative* and her photographs, she would make just enough money to allow her to carry on her work.

> Enclosed please find four shadows (carte de visites). The two dollars came safely. Anything in the way of nourishment you may feel like sending, send it along. The Captain sends to Washington every day. Give my love to all who inquire for me, and tell my friends to direct all things for me to the care of Capt. George B. Carse, Freedman's Village, Va.[43]

Truth traveled with her fourteen-year-old grandson, Elizabeth's son Sammy Banks, who had become a trusted companion and who accompanied her often through the next several years of her relief work with the freedpeople. Staying with Jane Swisshelm in her early weeks in Washington, Truth spoke at benefits for the Colored Soldiers' Aid Society held in Henry Highland Garnet's Presbyterian Church.

Rowland Johnson sent along to the same issue of the *Anti-Slavery Standard* part of a letter from Captain G. B. Carse, of the Commanding Department of the Veteran Reserve Corps, Government Farms, Virginia, who described Truth's work in Freedmen's Village; Carse wrote that "Sojourner is to have a house rent free, and a house to speak in that will hold upwards of two hundred persons. This place she can call her own, and need ask permission from no one, but go straight on and do what she thinks best; and although she came amongst us a stranger, she has found those who are willing to assist her in her good work."[44]

Truth's early faith that the Lincoln presidency would finally embrace full emancipation exceeded that of many other antislavery activists. In 1864, when Truth was actively campaigning for Lincoln's reelection, she met Harriet Tubman in Boston; Tubman distrusted Lincoln's commitment to blacks, noting the Union's initial refusal to enlist black troops and then, after admitting them, giving them unequal pay.[45] "It takes a great while to turn about this great ship of State," Truth replied (*NarBk*, 174).

Through the good offices of Elizabeth Keckley, Truth went to the White House on 29 October 1864 in the company of Lucy Colman, a white abolitionist also working with freedpeople.[46] Truth gave a masterful account intended for publication of her visit to Lincoln in her letter to

Rowland Johnson, versions of which were published in the *Liberator* and the *Standard*. As so often happened when she shaped a letter orally, Truth constructed the dialogue of power that was the common form of her interaction with her audience on the lecture stage. Writing from Freedmen's Village in Arlington, Virginia, Truth described Lincoln's "kindness and consideration to the colored persons as to the whites" in his reception area:

> The President was seated at his desk, Mrs. C— said to him, "This is Sojourner Truth, who has come all the way from Michigan to see you." He then arose, gave me his hand, made a bow, and said, "I am pleased to see you."[47]

In Truth's letter, she portrayed herself as presented by a white associate (Mrs. Colman) to the white President who is polite both to black and to white. According to Truth, Mrs. Colman presents her as if her chief claim to his attention is that she has come a long way: rather a homely presentation, not the announcement of a Presence, perhaps putting Truth at a bit of a disadvantage.[48] In her account, Truth shifts the terms of this unpromising opening by making a comparison that casts Lincoln as the vulnerable one:

> I said to him, "Mr. President, when you first took your seat I feared you would be torn to pieces, for I likened you unto Daniel, who was thrown into the lions' den; and if the lions did not tear you into pieces, I knew that it would be God that had saved you; and I said if He spared me I would see you before the four years expired, and He has done so, and now I am here to see you for myself."

Now Truth has a better introduction to Lincoln than Mrs. Colman's; God has spared Lincoln and God has spared Truth. They are equals under God.

> He then congratulated me on my having been spared. Then I said: "I appreciate you, for you are the best President who has ever taken the seat."

Lincoln does not, however, wish to share this much of Truth's ground. He now issues a demurral:

> He replied thus: "I expect you have reference to my having emancipated the slaves in my proclamation. But," said he, mentioning the names of several of his predecessors (and among them emphatically that of Washington), "they were all just as good, and would have done just as he had done if the time had come. If the people over the river (pointing

across the Potomac) had behaved themselves, I could not have done what I have; but they have not, and I was compelled to these things."[49]

In this account, Lincoln distances himself from the Emancipation Proclamation ("I expect you have reference"—as if there might be many more equivalently interesting items) by pointedly citing the names of former presidents, all of whom, except the Adamses, were slaveholders like Washington, good men who did not feel "the time had come" to end slavery. In 1852 Frederick Douglass had used his Fourth of July address to observe that Washington was revered especially by slave traders; in 1860 Robert Purvis had denounced Washington and Jefferson to the Pennsylvania Anti-Slavery Society, adding that "Thomas Jefferson sold his own daughter."[50] Lincoln instead blames those people "over the river" (the South), who had not "behaved themselves," so, like naughty children, they compelled Father Abraham to act as he did. Not very subtly, Lincoln repudiates Truth's cause. Much more subtly, Truth counters: "I then said: 'I thank God that you were the instrument selected by him and the people to do it.'" She felicitously accepts and now re-asserts Lincoln's own claim that he was not the *agent* of good: the *people* are sovereign under God and Lincoln is indeed only their *instrument*.[51]

Lincoln now attempts his master stroke:

> He then showed me the Bible presented to him by the colored people of Baltimore, of which you have no doubt seen a description. I have seen it for myself, and it is beautiful beyond description.[52]

The expensive book was decorated with a representation of the slave reaching upward toward the (emancipating) master.[53] Inside the elegant covers lay the Book. Truth knew that the Spirit was not bound by the wordings of its interpreters. She knew that it was used by the Christian churches to uphold the institution of slavery: "We have men-stealers for ministers, women-whippers for missionaries, and cradle-plunderers for church members," Frederick Douglass had written.[54] But that is not what she attacked in replying to Lincoln. She attacked the United States government of which he was the representative for sanctioning the laws that made it illegal for enslaved people to learn to read:

> After I had looked it over, I said to him: "This is beautiful indeed; the colored people have given this to the Head of the government, and that government once sanctioned laws that would not permit its people to learn enough to enable them to read this Book. And for what? Let them answer who can."[55]

The Book is its own reproach to the President, who, apparently, gave no answer.

Truth drew her account of the visit to a climax by describing Lincoln's autographing of her "Book of Life," in which she collected the signatures of celebrities she encountered. Lincoln may have intended a slight act of condescension by signing Truth's book "For Aunty" (Lucy Colman later noted "as he would his washerwoman"),[56] but Truth outmaneuvered him even here. In her record of the event, she affixed publicly to this act of signing Lincoln's previously disavowed identity as the slayer of slavery:

> He took my little book, and with *the same hand that signed the death-warrant of slavery,* he wrote as follows:
> "For Aunty Sojourner Truth,
> "Oct. 29, 1864 A. Lincoln."
> [emphasis added]

The letter describing her visit with Lincoln, which Truth intended for publication, went on to publicize her refugee relief work. In an earlier personal letter of November 1864 Truth wrote to Rochester from Mason's Island, an island in the Potomac, where she was already encountering incompetence and corruption in the relief efforts: "these office seekers tries to root *every* one out that try to elevate these people and make them *know* they are *free.*"

> I am going around among the colored folks and find out who it is sells the clothing to them that is sent to them from the North they will tell me for they think a good deal of me.

In her contempt for the white government overseers—"the people here (white) are only here for the *loaves* and *fishes* while the freedmen get the *scales* and crusts"[57]—Truth infused her echo of the Sermon on the Mount with the sarcasm of the Juba beater:

> We raise de wheat,
> Dey gib us de corn;
> We bake de bread,
> Dey gib us de crust;
> We sif de meal,
> Dey gib us de huss. . . .[58]

Not even freedpeople's persons were secure. In 1864 Truth found that Maryland slavers made kidnapping raids among the freedpeople, "seizing and carrying away their children" and threatening the distraught mothers with the guard-house. If the Marylanders "attempted to put her into the guard-house," Truth said, she "would make the United States rock like a cradle" (*NarBk*, 183). It seems characteristic of Truth that she stressed to the mothers their own *power* under the law, and that she fashioned her expression ("rock like a cradle") to identify the power in their hands. Although enslaved people in Maryland had been formally emancipated on 1 November 1864 some of them were the last to know, as Truth wrote in her letter of 3 November. The people at the Colored Home "*never* knew that Maryland was free until I told them." She remembered that "*one* old woman clung around my neck and most choked me she was so *glad.*" At a mass meeting to announce the news, Truth "had good chance to tell the colored people things that they had never heard."[59]

By December 1864 Truth had been appointed as a "counselor to the freed people at Arlington Heights, Va." by the New York office of the privately funded National Freedman's Relief Association. A letter dated 13 September 1865 from the government financed Bureau of Refugees, Freedmen, and Abandoned Lands, authorized her work at the Freedmen's Hospital (*NarBk*, 181-83). At the hospital Truth worked with her white friends Josephine Griffing, with whom she had lectured among the Copperheads of Indiana, and Laura Haviland, who would head relief efforts in Kansas during the Black Migration at the end of the 1870s.

At the end of the war, Washington experienced an influx of demobilized black soldiers and black laborers no longer employed in the war effort, joining the already vast ranks of the "contraband" men, women and children. Truth worked for the relocation of many of the black unemployed, arranging for some of them who could present themselves as promising workers to settle in Battle Creek and in Rochester. To her white audiences Truth often emphasized that government resettlement of the Washington freedpeople would constitute an economy, since the freedpeople would then work for themselves instead of being supported on government assistance. In both asking for funds for resettlement and in emphasizing her distaste for government assistance, Truth caught up the split consciousness of the Freedmen's Bureau, an embattled experiment in land reform, education, and economic reconstruction that had to constantly defend itself against political enemies determined to characterize blacks as unable to function without white surveillance and supervision. The Bureau's director General O. O. Howard had cautioned his assistants from June 1865 onward against excessive "charity"; he ordered the cutting of rations to the refugees to avoid "pauperizing" them, "as many people seem bound to do," insisting publicly that "there is not one word of truth" in reports of the "terrible suffering here in Washington."

While administrators of the Freedmen's Bureau were trying to diminish the public perception of the mass needs of the area freedpeople by lowering the numbers on relief, Josephine Griffing and Truth embarrassed the Bureau by publicizing dire conditions ("Mrs. Griffing is simply irrepressible: and yet she must be repressed," a correspondent wrote to Howard).[60] In her contacts with the Bureau, Truth was present at the construction of the racist narrative of the restless and shiftless freedperson, a drain on government resources, which was to accompany and justify the systematic exclusion of post-War blacks from economic opportunity.[61]

Truth worked with freedwomen, former field workers, who she realized were "very ignorant in relation to house-keeping, as most of them were instructed in field labor, but not in household duties."[62] Reform-minded whites in the North were willing to absorb some of the freedpeople when their own needs could be met simultaneously. During the war, for example, benevolent societies had resettled hundreds of black women as domestics with white families in the North. Dorothy Sterling gives some examples of the preferences of housewives who wrote to these societies:

> I should like a woman who understood cooking, washing and ironing and would be obliging and willing, age between 25 and 35 without a child with her.[63]

Sometimes a housewife would ask for the child without the mother. In their practical effects many of the benevolent attempts to get freedwomen employed took very little more notice of family structure than chattel slavery had. Truth found in trying to find employment for these people that "it cost a great amount of labor, time, and money to locate the young and strong, leaving the aged and little children still uncared for" (*NarBk*, 191).

The year before her great speech on equal pay to the Equal Rights Convention, Truth had written to Amy Post in Rochester from Campbell Hospital in Washington:

> I would like to know if you can find some good places for women that have children there has been a great many gone on to the west but there are yet some good women here that want homes these have all been slaves there are some that have no children also. I shall most likely leave here this month & would take them along if you or some of the friends of the Cause would find homes for them.[64]

In her early account of the refugees Harriet Jacobs wrote that "Single women hire at four dollars a month, a woman with one child two and a half or three dollars a month. Men's wages are ten dollars per month." She thought that "the little children, pine like prison birds for their native element."[65] The separation of women from their children, women's limited wage-earning opportunities, and the disparity between the pay of men and of women were constant themes in Truth's efforts to find employment for the freedpeople. She wrote to Amy Post:

> There has been about 140 sent west and we have heard that the men get 36 dollars a month & the women 1.25 a week these were from the Hospital & there are some here now full as smart as those that have gone I wish you would let me [know] what can be done for them in Rochester for I want to see them provided for before I leave here please be kind enough to write as soon as you get this remember me to My Children & accept my love & best respects for yourself.[66]

The anxieties and painful separations familiar to poor people moving around in search of work remained regular features of Truth's own experience during this period. She wrote to Post from Toledo on 25 August 1867 to ask about the freedwomen she had brought to Rochester:

> How is Aunt Mary and the women I brought you getting along, and the rest of the women, I do want very much to know and how is the little baby of Mrs. Willis's, it was so poorly when I came away, did it live or die?—I've bought me a lot with a barn on it and I'm going to fix the barn into a house and think I shall be very comfortable & then I shall want you to come and see me.—

Truth had paid for some of the transportation and other expenses for the refugees out of her own pocket, and she had difficulty getting reimbursement from the Government:

> Have you heard anything about the money I paid for those colored people from Washington to Baltimore—I wish I had the money, do write to me about it as soon as you can and please don't forget my three questions and direct it to the care of Richard Merrit Battle Creek I went to Adrian to try and raise a little money and came down here to see what I could do—I brought my grandson Sammy hoping to find a place for him tho' I hope to have him with me again by & by.—

"I want you to read this to Aunt Mary," Truth continued; "tell her I would write to her, but I have hard work to get so many letters written."[67]

Richard Merritt wrote for Truth from Battle Creek to the Freedmen's Bureau, protesting that "she has never received anything from the government in any shape while, on the other hand, she thinks she has given her time and considerable money, for the benefit of the freedpeople, and for the relief of the government." General Howard used his influence to get her a government award of $390, which amounted to "fifteen dollars per month for twenty-six months" (*NarBk*, 289). Truth used the money to pay one of the Merritts toward the mortgage on her house. Truth had, of course, been making her own way by working as a domestic in Battle Creek, helping to raise Richard Merritt and his brothers. Some of the family remembered that they were criticized for eating with her at the same table. It was for some of the Merritt children that Truth danced Juba.[68]

Payton Grayson was one of the children in a family resettled in Battle Creek by Truth in 1866. He remembered that "Aunt Sojourner wanted to help us help ourselves" and wished them to settle in small towns where work could be found. Grayson recalled her judgment that "We were too thick there," in Washington, "and she told us we wanted to go out west where we could get work."[69]

As the Southern counter-revolution opened with the institutionalization of the Black Codes, the organized structures of white abolitionism were being dismantled. At the end of the war when Garrison proposed dissolving the Anti-Slavery Society, he was merely expressing the common view of liberal reformers that the fundamental issues of black rights *within* American society had not formed part of the antislavery crusade. In 1867 Truth feared the intentions of the most committed former abolitionists. She wrote in desperation to the *Anti-Slavery Standard*, "I've just heard an extract of a letter read from Gerrit Smith to Mr. Garrison, which makes all my nerves quiver. It terrifies me to think that he should long for a heart union with rebels, thieves, robbers, and murderers." Perhaps she recalled her earlier more hopeful words to Harriet Tubman about how long it takes to turn the ship of state:

> When I think of Mr. Smith, I feel as if I was on board the ship of State, and one of the best anchor-cables had broken; but hope that the water is so shallow, that it can be got up again. This may seem harsh and out of place for me; but I must say something—for I can't help it. If I had not appreciated him so highly, I would not have said anything.[70]

On 9 May 1867, the day Truth delivered her great speech to the Equal
Rights Association meeting in New York City laying out the legacy of economic bondage left to her people, the New York *Daily Tribune* carried a
front page notice:

> Mr. William Lloyd Garrison, who may be truly named the apostle of
> Anti-Slavery, sailed yesterday for Europe to benefit his health. He takes
> deserved holiday after a long and earnest work well done. The thousands
> of Christian men and women whose good wishes will follow him will be
> glad to learn that, before sailing, it was made known to him that $30,000
> had been collected and deposited to his order as a tribute to his anti-
> Slavery labors.[71]

From the turn of the century, virtually no thought had been given to
assimilating black people into American society: all thought centered on
various removal schemes, especially the scheme for removal to Liberia. At
the end of the war virtually all blacks believed there would be land reform
based on the subdivision and redistribution of Southern plantations; black
thinkers had long argued for this. At the outset of the war, the *Anglo-
African* had a land after peace policy in its November 1861 editorial,
"What Shall Be Done with the Slaves?"

> When the war is ended, there will be few, if any slaves, for the gov-
> ernment to dispose of. There will be four million of free men and
> women and children, accustomed to toil, who have by their labor during
> sixty years past supported themselves, and in addition, an extravagant
> aristocracy.

The *Anglo-African* urged that lands confiscated from the rebels be
"turned into public lands," and that these lands should be given to "these
freed men who know best how to cultivate them, and will joyfully bring
their brawny arms, their willing hearts, and their skilled hands to the glori-
ous labor of cultivating as their OWN, the lands which they have bought
and paid for by their sweat and blood."[72]

Government promises of reclamation (land, houses) and reparations
("forty acres and a mule") were made, but retracted. In late 1864, General
Sherman's "Special Field Order No. 15" designating an area for exclusive
black settlement between Charleston and Jacksonville brought farm land
to forty thousand freedmen, who were mostly turned off the land by
President Andrew Johnson's order to return all confiscated lands to the
former rebels in August 1865.[73] Placing land reform in the South in the

international struggle between the poor and the rich, W. E. B. Du Bois argued that it should have been "an integral part of Emancipation."

> To emancipate four million laborers whose labor had been owned, and separate them from the land upon which they had worked for nearly two and a half centuries, was an operation such as no modern country had for a moment attempted or contemplated. The German and English and French serf, the Italian and Russian serf, were, on emancipation, given definite rights in the land. Only the American Negro slave was emancipated without such rights and in the end this spelled for him the continuation of slavery.[74]

But Congress would not overturn the "property rights" of the Southern landholders. Truth was present at a meeting in 1869 when Aaron Powell, the editor of the *National Anti-Slavery Standard*, urged listeners to send petitions to Senator Charles Sumner of Massachusetts, who was sponsoring legislation to obtain land for freedpeople in the South.[75] Perhaps Truth had already given up the dream of reparations for her people as a whole. She told a Boston audience in 1870 in the company of William Wells Brown that she believed in agitation but that she also believed in works (*NarBk*, 215). Working outward from her own experience among the displaced people in Washington, she began to press for a smaller-scale effort at resettlement specifically directed toward refugees.

The idea of an escape from the cruelties of urban life, of rural resettlement with land, tools, and farm animals seemed logical for a people that had worked the land, handled the tools, and raised the farm animals of generations of white slaveholders. In response to worsening urban employment conditions, Truth had urged a return to the land as early as 1853 in her speech to John T. Raymond's congregation in New York City:

> My colored brothers and sisters, there's a remedy for this; where I was lately lecturing out in Pennsylvania, the farmers wanted good men and women to work their farms on shares for them. Why can't you go out there?—and depend upon it, in the course of time you will get to be independent.[76]

Truth did not regard the Government grant of land and assistance as anything other than reparations. As Maria Stewart had said in 1831, "it is the blood of our fathers, and the tears of our brethren that have enriched your soils. AND WE CLAIM OUR RIGHTS."[77] In 1871 at an anniversary celebration of the Emancipation Proclamation in Boston, Truth invited her audience to sign the following petition:

To the Senate and House of Representatives, in Congress assembled:

Whereas, through the faithful and earnest representations of Sojourner Truth (who has personally investigated the matter), we believe that the freed colored people in and about Washington, dependent upon Government for support, would be greatly benefited and might become useful citizens by being placed in a position to support themselves:

We, the undersigned, therefore earnestly request your honorable body to set appart for them a portion of the public land in the West, and erect buildings thereon for the aged and infirm, and otherwise so to legislate as to secure the desired results.[78]

Truth had had fifty petitions printed at her own expense and had been taking them through the Eastern states, she wrote to the New York *Tribune:*

I made up my mind last Winter, when I saw able men and women taking dry bread from the Government to keep from starving, that I would devote myself to the cause of getting land for these people, where they can work and earn their own living in the West, where the land is so plenty.

"Instead of sending these people to Liberia, why can't they have a Colony in the West?" Truth asked; "This is why I am contending so in my old age. It is to teach the people that this Colony can just as well be in this country as in Liberia."[79] Truth's speaking of her proposed land grant for Washington-area refugees as comparable (if preferable) to Liberian colonization may have reflected the desperation of the moment rather than an actual belief in political separatism. Yet in campaigning for Grant both in 1868 and in 1872 she had expressed her belief that she would emigrate to Canada if he was not re-elected.[80] Optimism throughout the black community was fading. After 1871, with the rise of the White Leagues and the Klan, Nell Irvin Painter has written, "the South had begun to take on the feudal usages which shaped race relations economically and politically throughout the rest of the century."[81]

With her grandson Truth traveled throughout New England and into the Midwest lecturing and collecting signatures on her petitions, but by 1874 she had had only limited success. The death of Senator Sumner, the dissolution of the Freedmen's Bureau, and a general amnesty for Confederate leaders had intervened. No legislator presented her petition to Congress. In December 1874 Truth's grandson's illness forced their return to Battle Creek, where he died tragically a few months later.[82]

Nell Irvin Painter has described the Exodus, the rural-to-rural migration in early 1879 that brought thousands of blacks from the South into Kansas, as "the first, massive repudiation of the Democratic South."[83] In the Exodus Truth saw a vindication of her conviction that her people would find a home in the West at last: "The colored people is going to be a people. Do you think God has had them robbed and scourged all the days of their life for nothing?"[84]

In the fall of 1879, Truth and Frances Titus left Battle Creek to join Laura Haviland and Elizabeth Comstock in the privately funded relief effort of the Kansas Freedmen's Relief Association. Truth was past eighty years old, only four years away from death. In her Civil War song, "The Valiant Soldiers," she had sung hopefully that

> Father Abraham has spoken, and the message has been sent;
> The prison doors have opened, and out the prisoners went
> To join the sable army of African descent,
> As we go marching on. (*NarBk*, 126)

The hopeful freedmen marching off for the Union in 1863, who were to be joined by "prisoners" freed within the slave states, had been replaced by Southern freedpeople imprisoned and terrorized in the post-Reconstruction South. For the Exodusters, these new "Valiant Soldiers," Truth revised her verse:

> The word it has been spoken; the message has been sent;
> The prison doors have opened, and out the prisoners went.
> To join the sable army of African descent, for God is marching on.[85]

There is an implicit melancholy in this revision which no longer looks to "Father Abraham" (and certainly not to the post-Reconstruction President Hayes) to speak, and in which the hopeful "we are marching on" is replaced by a more resigned "God is marching on." It is as if the direction of history has once more been handed back into Divine, rather than black human hands, recalling the days of nonresistance when Douglass's call for active black resistance could be interrupted by reminding him of

God's superior management: "Is God dead?" But in what seems a direct repudiation of her earlier nonviolent question, Truth is reported to have told her black audience in a Topeka Baptist church that "God still lives and means to see the black people in full possession of all their rights, even if the entire white population of the South has to be annihilated in the accomplishment of His purpose."[86]

In their confrontation at the Western Anti-Slavery Society meeting in 1852, Douglass had advocated that blacks take their political fates into their own hands. He now opposed the Exodus as a "premature, disheartening surrender, since it would make freedom and free institutions depend upon migration rather than protection," and staked his faith on limiting the violence of Southern whites against blacks.[87] Truth rejected the argument that blacks should stand fast and fight for their rights under such unequal conditions:

> The blacks can never be much in the South. They cannot get up. As long as the whites have the reins in their hands, how can the colored people get up there?

The Exodus did not achieve "the regeneration, temporally and spiritually, of the American colored race" for which Truth had hoped.[88] For the black frontierspeople, the Kansas migration brought its own kind of bitter harvest. Some had made their lives better by the move, many had died, many survived in extreme poverty. Forming an unskilled labor pool in the urban areas, most were earning around $1.50 a day a decade after the Exodus, working on the average for only two-thirds of every year.[89] In the end, a tiny proportion of black people joined the westward migration or took their places among the European immigrants homesteading across the West. But Nell Irvin Painter has argued forcefully that although only a few thousand of the six million blacks in the South chose to migrate, the Exodus to Free Kansas was a significant political statement by African Americans lacking civil rights, public school education, and the hope of economic independence, and who had to function in the South without "the classic tool for public redress—the reasonably independent exercise of the vote."[90]

"For two hundred years we had toiled for them," wrote Susie King Taylor in 1902; "the war of 1861 came and was ended, and we thought our race was forever freed from bondage, and that the two races could live in unity with each other, but when we read almost every day of what is being done to my race by some whites in the South, I sometimes ask, 'Was the war in vain? Has it brought freedom, in the full sense of the word, or has it not made our condition more hopeless?'"[91]

Notes

1. [Holley], *A Life for Liberty*, 62-64.
2. Ibid., 80-81.
3. Lucy Colman, *Reminiscences*, 65.
4. Stowe, "Sojourner Truth, the Libyan Sibyl," 478. Stowe did not recall exactly which antislavery texts, so she used as her example "Proclaim liberty throughout all the land unto all the inhabitants thereof," the famous slogan of the American Anti Slavery Society. Truth spread the banner over the pulpit in 1853 when she lectured in New York City. According to the report in the *Tribune*, 8 November 1853, the slogans included the even more famous "Am I not a Woman and a Sister": "Pendant from the pulpit cushion was a banner of white satin, on which was inscribed: Ashtabula County. / Am I not a Woman and a Sister! / [Kneeling figure of a woman with uplifted hands.] / How long, O Lord! how long. / A Million-and-a-half of American Women in chains. / Shall we heed their wrongs? / Will not a righteous God be avenged upon / such a Nation as this!"
5. Wyman, *American Chivalry*, 107.
6. Douglas, *The Feminization of American Culture*, 317.
7. *Anti-Slavery Bugle*, 4 September 1852.
8. For an attempted reconstruction of this exchange through five contemporary newspaper accounts, see Mabee and Newhouse, *Sojourner Truth*, 83-88.
9. *Anti-Slavery Bugle*, 28 August 1852. For an analysis of the Constitutional debate between these factions, see Lewis Perry, *Radical Abolitionism: Anarchy and the Government of God in Anti-Slavery Thought* (Ithaca: Cornell University Press, 1973), 188-208.
10. The passage is our translation of the following dialect rendering of Truth's vision by Joseph Dugdale, which was printed in *National Anti-Slavery Standard*, 4 July 1863:

    > Children, I talks to God and God talks to me. I goes out and talks to God in de fields and de woods. [The weevil had destroyed thousands of acres of wheat in the West that year.] Dis morning I was walking out, and I got over de fence. I saw de wheat a holding up its head, looking very big. I goes up and takes holt ob it. You b'lieve it, dere was no wheat dare? I says, God [speaking the name in a voice of reverence peculiar to herself], what is de matter wid dis wheat? and he says to me, "Sojourner, dere is a little weasel in it." Now I hears talkin' about de Constitution and de rights of man. I comes up and I takes hold of dis Constitution. It looks *mighty big*, and I feels for *my* rights, but der aint any dare. Den I says, God, what *ails* dis Constitution? He says to me, "Sojourner, dere is a little *weasel* in it."

11. See John R. McKivigan, "The Frederick Douglass-Gerrit Smith Friendship and Political Abolitionism in the 1850s," in *Frederick Douglass: New Literary and Historical Essays*, edited by Eric J. Sundquist (Cambridge: Cambridge University Press, 1990), 205-32, for the stages of Douglass's evolution into political action and the presidential election year politics of 1852.

12. *Anti-Slavery Bugle*, 28 August 1852.

13. *Anti-Slavery Bugle*, 4 September 1852.

14. *Pennsylvania Freeman*, 4 September 1852.

15. Orange, New Jersey, *Journal*, 29 July 1876.

16. Douglass's statement is quoted in Lillie Buffum Chace Wyman, "Sojourner Truth," *New England Magazine* 24 (March 1901): 63.

17. *The Liberator*, 10 September 1852.

18. bell hooks, *Black Looks: Race and Representation* (Boston: South End Press, 1992), 90. In *Yearning: Race, Gender, and Cultural Politics* (Boston: South End Press, 1990), hooks writes that sexualized language established "a discursive practice . . . that links black male liberation with gaining the right to participate fully within patriarchy" (76).

19. See Eric J. Sundquist's Introduction in *Frederick Douglass: New Literary and Historical Essays*, edited by Eric J. Sundquist (Cambridge: Cambridge University Press, 1990), 9-10; McKivigan, "The Frederick Douglass-Gerrit Smith Friendship and Political Abolitionism in the 1850s," 208, 226n.

20. Frederick Douglass, *Life and Times of Frederick Douglass, written by himself* (New York: Pathway Press, 1941), 306. This quick mention of Truth, the only one in the book, is an aside in a chapter entitled "John Brown and Mrs. Stowe." Stowe gave the encounter national publicity, mistakenly setting it in Faneuil Hall in Boston (Stowe, "Sojourner Truth, the Libyan Sibyl," 480).

21. Perry, *Radical Abolitionism*, 189, 194.

22. Cora L. V. Daniels to Amy Post, 2 January 1866, IAPFP, UR.

23. Stanton, et al., *History of Woman Suffrage*, 1:553.

24. Ibid., 1:128.

25. Ibid., 1:547 and 1:567. During this week in September in New York City Truth also spoke with Garrison and C. C. Burleigh at an antislavery meeting in Metropolitan Hall; Garrison wrote that 1200 people paid "12$^1/_2$ cts. admission" (William Lloyd Garrison, *The Letters of William Lloyd Garrison*, edited by Walter M. Merrill and Louis Ruchames [Cambridge: Harvard University Press, 1971-81], 4:248-49).

26. Stanton, et al., *History of Woman Suffrage*, 1:568.

27. Angela Y. Davis, "Reflections on the Black Woman's Role in the Community of Slaves," *Black Scholar* 3 (December 1971): 3-15.

28. See Hazel V. Carby, "'On the Threshold of Woman's Era': Lynching, Empire, and Sexuality in Black Feminist Theory," in *"Race," Writing, and Difference*, edited by Henry Louis Gates, Jr. (Chicago: University of Chicago Press, 1986), 301-16; and Carby, *Reconstructing Womanhood*, especially 20-39. See also Frances Smith Foster, *Witnessing Slavery*, 131-32.

29. See Yee, *Black Women Abolitionists*, 40-59.

30. Stanton, et al., *History of Woman Suffrage*, 1:384.

31. Carby, *Reconstructing Womanhood*, 20.

32. Although racial incidents predominated in the south of Indiana where there was continuing black immigration, counties of the extreme north

allowed almost no black settlement. By 1900, there were twenty-nine
counties in northern Indiana with fewer than fifty blacks in residence
(Emma Lou Thornbrough, *The Negro in Indiana Before 1900: A Study of a
Minority* [Bloomington: Indiana University Press, 1993], 31, 227).

33. Elizabeth Keckley, *Behind The Scenes; or Thirty Years a Slave, and Four Years
in the White House* (New York: G. W. Carleton & Co., 1868), 33. See also
the fascinating discussion of Elizabeth Keckley in Frances Smith Foster,
*Written By Herself: Literary Production by African American Women, 1746-
1892* (Bloomington: Indiana University Press), 117-30.

34. Frederick Douglass, *My Bondage and My Freedom*, edited by Philip S.
Foner (New York: Dover Publications, 1969), 60. See also the analysis of
Douglass's rhetorical manipulation of the slave woman's body by Jenny
Franchot, "The Punishment of Esther," 141-65.

35. James M. McPherson, *The Negro's Civil War: How American Blacks Felt and
Acted During the War for the Union* (New York: Ballantine Books, 1991),
163, 166.

36. *Tribune*, 8 September 1865.

37. Earl Conrad, *Harriet Tubman* (New York: Paul S. Eriksson, 1969), 181.

38. *National Anti-Slavery Standard*, 27 April 1867.

39. *Tribune*, 8 September 1865. See McPherson, *The Negro's Civil War*, 183-
84, 195; Amanda Berry Smith had three brothers in the war (*An
Autobiography*, 65).

40. Norman B. Wood, *The White Side of a Black Subject Enlarged and Brought
Down to Date: A Vindication of the Afro-American Race* (Chicago: American
Publishing House, 1897), 247-48. See *NarBk*, 126. For a performance of
"Sojourner's Battle Hymn," listen to the 20th anniversary album of Sweet
Honey in the Rock, *Still On the Journey* (Redway, California: EarthBeat!
Records, 1993).

41. *The Liberator*, 3 September 1862. For a description of refugee work by black
women in the Washington area, see Sterling, *We Are Your Sisters*, 245-56.

42. Keckley, *Behind The Scenes*, 111-16, 245, 248-51. For a valuable picture of
the free black community in this area before the Civil War, see Letitia
Woods Brown, *Free Negroes in the District of Columbia 1790-1846* (New
York: Oxford University Press, 1972).

43. Letter from Truth to Rowland Johnson, *National Anti-Slavery Standard*, 17
December 1864. *The Liberator* printed a much edited version of the letter
23 December 1864.

44. *National Anti-Slavery Standard*, 17 December 1864.

45. Conrad, *Harriet Tubman*, 183-84.

46. In her somewhat self-promoting account Colman said that Truth had been
prevented from visiting the White House before Colman's intervention:
"Sojourner Truth, who was not allowed to enter the White House as an
equal with other visitors, was living at the village at that time, going
among the people and teaching them to make the best use of the little the
government gave them to live upon" (*Reminiscences*, 65-68).

47. *National Anti-Slavery Standard*, 17 December 1864. Frances Titus published Truth's letter in *NarBk* with the addition of two sentences discussed in note 51 below (176-80). The original letter is apparently lost.

48. Truth's account in this letter may reflect her awareness of the benevolent condescension that is obvious in Lucy Colman's later description of the visit; in her *Reminiscences*, Colman remembers a more formal and respectful introduction: "When the President was ready I said, "I am very happy, sir, to say to you that I have not come to ask any favor; my business is simply to present to you my friend, Sojourner Truth, a woman widely known, not only in our country, but abroad; she will say to you what she wishes without further help from me" (66).

49. *National Anti-Slavery Standard*, 17 December 1864.

50. Frederick Douglass, *Life and Writings of Frederick Douglass*, edited by Philip S. Foner (New York: International Publishers, 1950-75), 2:188; *National Anti-Slavery Standard*, 3 November 1860.

51. This is made emphatic in the version of Truth's letter printed by Frances Titus, which includes these lines: "I told him that I had never heard of him before he was talked of for president. He smilingly replied, 'I had heard of you many times before that'" (*NarBk*, 178). The newspaper editors may have considered these lines impolitic and deleted them. Since Truth is reported as describing this exchange with Lincoln in the Detroit *Post*, 12 January 1869, in 1878 in the New York *Herald*, and in 1879 in the Chicago *Daily Inter-Ocean*, there is no reason to assume that Titus added these sentences. Titus noted that Rowland Johnson had given her Truth's letter; without the letter itself it is impossible to say if it contained these lines.

52. Kathleen Collins has traced a well-known representation of this moment. In 1892, almost ten years after Truth's death, Frances Titus commissioned the subject from the painter Frank Courtner, a Professor of Art at Albion College in Michigan. Courtner had not known Truth, but he had a reputation for painting Lincoln. For his image of Truth, Courtner copied a photograph Truth had sold during the 1870s. Apparently, Titus paid $100 for the oil painting, *President Lincoln Showing Sojourner Truth the Bible Presented Him by the Colored People of Baltimore* (1893), proceeds from the posthumous edition of the expanded *Narrative* (1884). Titus had photographic copies of the painting made, with the notice on the back: "From the Original Painting by F. C. Courtner. Copies may be had from the owner, Mrs. F. W. Titus, Battle Creek, Michigan. Twenty-five cents each." In this way, Titus paid for the Sojourner Truth Memorial. A later oil painting (1913) by J. S. Jackson was made from the photograph of Courtner's oil painting (Collins, "Shadow and Substance," 192-93).

53. Benjamin Quarles describes the Bible and its presentation by a delegation of ministers on the White House lawn in *The Negro in the Civil War* (Boston: Little, Brown and Co., 1953), 254-55.

54. Frederick Douglass, *Narrative of the Life of Frederick Douglass, an African Slave, Written by Himself*, edited by Houston A. Baker, Jr. (New York: Penguin Books, 1982), 154.

55. *National Anti-Slavery Standard*, 17 December 1864

56. Lucy Colman wrote: "Mr. Lincoln was not himself with this colored woman; he had no funny story for her, he called her aunty, as he would his washerwoman, and when she complimented him as the first Antislavery President, he said 'I'm not an Abolitionist; I wouldn't free the slaves if I could save the Union any other way—I'm obliged to do it.'" Lincoln's awkwardness about a proper address for Truth was shared by many closer friends and admirers, as can be seen from the mix of forms of address in Titus's selections from letters and signatures in Truth's "Lamb's Book of Life," (*Reminiscences*, 67; *NarBk*, 256-99).

After Lincoln was assassinated, Lucy Colman took Truth to the White House again, as an honored representative of the National Freedmen's Relief Association, to visit President Andrew Johnson. Ironically, "Mr. Johnson was quite at home with his colored guest, asking her—Mrs Truth, he called her—to be seated, and refusing to be seated himself while she should stand" (*Reminiscences*, 68).

Berenice Lowe found Truth listed in Battle Creek's *City Directory* (1869-1870) as "Truth, Mrs. Sojourner (col.d)," with the occupation "Lecturer" ("Michigan Days of Sojourner Truth," 127-35).

57. Truth to "My dear daughter," 3 November 1864, IAPFP, UR. It has been argued that this letter was addressed to Amy Post, but it seems unlikely that Truth would have used this salutation to Post, and Truth did write to her daughters in care of Post. In mid-1866, for example, Truth wrote to Post to find out "if my daughter has recd money that I sent her some time ago," noting that "I sent the last letter in your care & I wish you would find out & let me know if it has been recd" (Truth to Amy Post, 3 July 1866, IAPFP, UR).

58. We know that Truth danced the Juba into her old age. See Sterling Stuckey's discussion of the Jubilee Beater in "'Ironic Tenacity': Frederick Douglass's Seizure of the Dialectic," in *Frederick Douglass: New Literary and Historical Essays*, edited by Eric J. Sundquist (Cambridge: Cambridge University Press, 1990), 37-38. For Truth's dancing Juba in Battle Creek, see Mabee and Newhouse, *Sojourner Truth*, 229-30.

59. Truth to "My Dear Daughter," 3 November 1864, IAPFP, UR. Truth apparently lectured publicly on the corruption of the relief operations; a Fall River, Massachusetts newspaper notice says that in her work among the Washington area freedpeople she "has discovered certain abuses which should be rectified. All who come to listen will learn how some of the public money goes that is nominally appropriated to feed the black paupers in Washington" (*NarBk*, 202).

60. George R. Bentley, *A History of the Freedmen's Bureau* (New York: Farrar, Straus and Giroux, 1974), 77-79.

61. See Jacqueline Jones, *The Dispossessed: America's Underclasses from the Civil War to the Present* (New York: Basic Books, 1992), 13-44.

62. Truth to Rowland Johnson, *National Anti-Slavery Standard*, 17 December 1864.
63. Sterling, *We Are Your Sisters*, 255.
64. Truth to Amy Post, 3 July 1866, IAPFP, UR.
65. *The Liberator*, 3 September 1862.
66. Truth to Amy Post, 3 July 1866, IAPFP, UR.
67. Truth to Amy Post, 25 August 1867, IAPFP, UR.
68. Mabee and Newhouse, *Sojourner Truth*, 100, 142, 147, 214, 229.
69. Interview in Battle Creek *Enquirer and Evening News*, 29 May 1929, quoted in Mabee and Newhouse, *Sojourner Truth*, 145.
70. *National Anti-Slavery Standard*, 27 April 1867.
71. *Tribune*, 9 May 1867.
72. See McPherson, *The Negro's Civil War*, 297-98.
73. See "Land for the Landless," in McPherson, *The Negro's Civil War*, 298-304.
74. W. E. B. DuBois, *Black Reconstruction*, 611.
75. *National Anti-Slavery Standard*, 27 November 1869 and 18 and 25 December 1869.
76. *Tribune*, 8 November 1853.
77. Stewart, *Maria W. Stewart*, 40.
78. *Zion's Herald*, 23 February 1871; this was printed by Titus in slightly different form (*NarBk*, 199).
79. *Tribune*, 13 March 1871.
80. Mabee and Newhouse, *Sojourner Truth*, 181.
81. Nell Irvin Painter, *Exodusters: Black Migration to Kansas after Reconstruction* (New York: Alfred A. Knopf, 1977), 16.
82. John E. Fleming, "Slavery, Civil War and Reconstruction: A Study of Black Women in Microcosm," *Negro History Bulletin* 38, no. 6 (August-September 1975): 432-33.
83. Painter, *Exodusters*, 4.
84. *Daily Inter-Ocean*, 13 August 1879.
85. Quoted in Painter, *Exodusters*, 247. Accounts of Truth's presence in Kansas appeared in St. Louis *Globe-Democrat*, 24 April 1879 and Chicago *Daily Inter-Ocean*, 25 October 1879. For a more negative evaluation of the migration, see Robert G. Athearn, *In Search of Canaan: Black Migration to Kansas 1879-80* (Lawrence: The Regents Press of Kansas, 1978).
86. *Colored Citizen*, 11 October 1879, quoted in Mabee and Newhouse, *Sojourner Truth*, 166.
87. Douglass, *Life and Writings of Frederick Douglass*, 4:336.
88. *Daily Inter-Ocean*, 13 August 1879.
89. Athearn, *In Search of Canaan*, 278; Athearn summarizes a report in the *Topeka Daily Capital*, 2 May 1889.
90. Painter, *Exodusters*, 260-61.
91. Susie King Taylor, *Reminiscences of My Life In Camp with the 33d United States Colored Troops Late 1st S. C. Volunteers* (Boston: Published by the Author, 1902), 61.

South Carolina;
Candy Merchant.

Six

Harvest Time for the Black Man, and Seed-Sowing Time for Woman: Nancy Works in the Cotton Field

But to be a woman of the Negro race in America, and to be able to grasp the deep significance of the possibilities of the crisis, is to have a heritage, it seems to me, unique in the ages.

Anna Julia Cooper,
A Voice from the South (1892)

The special plight and the role of black women is not something that just happened three years ago. We've had a special plight for 350 years.

Fannie Lou Hamer,
Speech to NAACP Legal Defense Fund Institute,
7 May 1971[1]

When Truth gathered the children around her in Elizabeth Cady Stanton's parlor in mid-May 1867 to hear the newspaper reports of her speeches at the Equal Rights Convention, the woman's rights movement led by white feminists was in painful transition. No woman's rights meetings had been held during the Civil War, while women, as Stanton later wrote, "held their own claims in abeyance to those of the slaves in the South."[2] At the end of the Civil War, white feminist reformers who had worked for the end of slavery viewed themselves as a full-fledged part of Reconstruction. Just as they had seen the constitutional conventions at the state levels as opportunities to secure the rights of women in new laws, they saw Reconstruction not merely as the reordering of relationships between the southern states and the federal government, but as an all-encompassing restructuring of the nation from which a new world for white women as well as for blacks could emerge. What they saw happening, instead, to their great disillusionment, was an attempt "to reconstruct our government on the basis of manhood suffrage," proposed by the Republican Party, and sanctioned by the American Anti-Slavery Society.[3]

White feminist leaders including Stanton, Susan B. Anthony, Lucy Stone, Amy Post, Lucy Colman, Antoinette Brown Blackwell, Ernestine Rose, and Angelina Grimké Weld had formed the Women's Loyal National League at a convention in May 1863. At the closing session Angelina Grimke Weld read her "Address to the Soldiers of our Second Revolution," a radical statement against race prejudice:

> This war is not, as the South falsely pretends, a war of races, nor of sections, nor of political parties, but a war of *Principles*; a war upon the working classes, whether white or black; against *Man*, the world over.

The League successfully passed, over the opposition of some of its members, a resolution stating that "There never can be a true peace in this Republic until the civil and political rights of all citizens of African descent and all women are practically established." Angelina Grimké Weld told the meeting: "I want to be identified with the negro; until he gets his rights, we never shall have ours."[4] Before the passage of the Thirteenth Amendment, the League had gathered 400,000 signatures on a petition to the Congress calling for an act emancipating "all persons of African descent held to involuntary service or labor in the United States."[5] It was to a meeting of the Women's Loyal National League in 1864 that Anthony had displayed a photograph of a living exemplar of the barbarity of slavery, "'Sojourner Truth,' the heroine of one of Mrs. H. B. Stowe's tales."[6]

With the passage of the Thirteenth Amendment abolishing slavery in 1865, woman's rights leaders looked forward to legislation that would extend the franchise to blacks and to white women. Instead, the legislation proposed as the Fourteenth Amendment, which passed Congress in June 1866 and was ratified two years later, became the terrain on which were fought the battles that destroyed the coalition of white feminists and black rights activists. The sexism in the antislavery movement activated the racism in the white feminist movement for mutually destructive ends. Sojourner Truth was a pivotal figure in the fateful struggle that evolved, standing at the intersection of the two movements yet not entirely with either.[7]

The Fourteenth Amendment guaranteed due process of law to persons born or naturalized in the United States; prohibited insurrectionists from taking public office except by approval of the Congress; and absolved the government of Confederate debt and denied compensation for the loss of slaves. It also contained a controversial section that read as follows:

> Representatives shall be apportioned among the several States according to their respective numbers, counting the whole number of persons in each State, excluding Indians not taxed. But when the right to vote at any election for the choice of electors for President and Vice President of the United States, Representatives in Congress, the Executive and Judicial officers of a State, or the members of the Legislature thereof, is denied to any of the male inhabitants of such State, being twenty-one years of age, and citizens of the United States, or in any way abridged, except for participation in rebellion or other crime, the basis or representation therein shall be reduced in the proportion which the number of such male citizens shall bear to the whole number of male citizens twenty-one years of age in such State.

Women had been kept from voting by the actions of the states because the Constitution was silent about sex, a situation that woman's rights advocates had hoped to remedy by Constitutional amendment. The passage of the Fourteenth Amendment would for the first time explicitly inscribe gender in the Constitution, with the inference that the ballot was the unconditional right only of *male* citizens. Feminists were confronted with a constitutional sanction of gendered suffrage.

The Republican proposal did not guarantee black men the right to vote; it simply said that Southerners could not count blacks for the purpose of representation in Congress unless they allowed black men to vote. Indeed some abolitionists, among them Wendell Phillips, rejected the Fourteenth Amendment because by sanctioning a penalty for states that limited suffrage to white men, it tacitly accepted the right of those states to limit voting on racial grounds.

While black male suffrage was the culmination of a Radical Republican dream, the party's strategy was only a political expedient intended to secure Republican political dominance in the postwar South. As Thaddeus Stevens explained, "If impartial suffrage is excluded in the rebel States then every one of them is sure to send a solid rebel representative delegation to Congress, and cast a solid rebel electoral vote. They, with their kindred Copperheads of the North, would always elect the President and control Congress."[8] Counting "the whole number of persons in each State" meant counting the freedpeople as full persons rather than as 3/5 of a person, as under slavery; if all blacks were to be counted, the South would have received new representatives in Congress, shifting the balance of national power to the South.

Republicans counted on black men to vote for their party; but under their proposal, if the South prevented black men from voting, Republicans would control Congress because of the resulting reduction in Southern representation. Women were customarily counted in apportionment, though barred from voting, so their numbers were not at issue here. But it must have been obvious that if white women in the South got the vote, they would not be voting Republican. Robert Dale Owen reported back to the Loyal League the behind-the-scenes talk in Washington; the amendment had to specify "males," some legislators were saying, otherwise "it would enfranchise all the Southern wenches."[9] Some leaders in the woman's rights movement, including Lucy Stone's husband, Henry B. Blackwell, brazenly lobbied for support for woman suffrage among white supremacists by pointing out that the votes of Southern white women could cancel out the votes of both black women and black men: "Your 4,000,000 of Southern white women will counterbalance your 4,000,000 of negro men and women, and thus the political supremacy of your white race will remain unchanged."[10]

In December 1865 Elizabeth Cady Stanton published an angry letter in which she assumed a stance that would come to characterize the hierarchical exclusionary politics of the white feminist movement:

> The representative women of the nation have done their uttermost for the last thirty years to secure freedom for the negro; and as long as he was lowest in the scale of being, we were willing to press his claims; but now, as the celestial gate to civil rights is slowly moving on its hinges, it becomes a serious question whether we had better stand aside and see "Sambo" walk into the kingdom first.[11]

The Emersonian "representative [wo]men" were "educated white women"; *their* efforts, not the efforts of blacks, were seen as paramount in the struggle for black freedom; the generic black man ("Sambo") was "lowest in the scale of being," a vicious reference to a position nearest apes and monkeys on the Great Chain of Being. Truth had once said that answering such an argument from a proslavery male speaker was the "scullionest" of all the "dirty scullion work" she had ever done (*NarBk*, 149).

Identifying her constituency with the Wise Virgins of the parable, Stanton argued that "self-preservation" was the "first law of nature," and that women should "keep our lamps trimmed and burning" and enter the "constitutional door" on the arm of "the black soldier." She feared "the negro's hour," which could only add more men as oppressors. "In fact," she said, purporting to speak for black women and leaving behind the image of the Virgin escorted by the black man in Union blue, "it is better to be the slave of an educated white man, than of a degraded, ignorant black one."[12]

Susan B. Anthony, working with black refugees in the Midwest, had addressed a largely black audience in Chicago, where she had been introduced as "one of their old and firm friends; not one who had believed in sitting down to the communion first, and letting the negro come last."[13] Now she returned to fight the Fourteenth Amendment. In January 1866, Anthony had written to Truth urging her to sign a petition opposing the explicit introduction of gender into the Constitution:

> I know you will be glad to put your mark to the inclosed petition, and get a good many to join it, and send or take it to some member of Congress to present. Do you know there are three men, Schench, Jenkes, and Broomall, who have dared to propose to amend the United States Constitution by inserting in it the word "male," thus shutting all women out by constitution from voting for president, vice-president, and congressmen, even though they may have the right to vote in the State for State officers. It is a most atrocious proposition, and I know Sojourner Truth will say, No, to it. (*NarBk*, 282)

For the first time the woman's rights movement, which had previously worked through state legislatures, petitioned the U.S. Congress for legislation prohibiting states from abridging the right to vote on grounds of sex or of race. Republicans accepted the petitions as support for the concept of universal suffrage, then proceeded to interpret that as manhood suffrage, ignoring the issue of votes for women, which they insisted had no general public support; Democrats, who opposed black male suffrage, offered themselves as allies of the women. To achieve their own ends the two major political parties were prepared, cynically, to pit the two causes against each other.

At the Eleventh National Woman's Rights Convention in New York City in May 1866, the first woman's rights meeting held since before the Civil War, a coalition of feminists and abolitionists established the American Equal Rights Association (ERA) to unify the campaigns for black and woman suffrage under the broad concept of "a Human Rights platform."[14] From the beginning, there was a refusal to acknowledge the disparity of the conditions of blacks and white middle-class women, evidenced in Susan B. Anthony's resolution that "by the act of Emancipation and the

Civil Rights bill, the negro and woman now hold the same civil and political *status*, alike needing only the ballot."[15] There was something both ludicrous and tragic in the contention that the abolition of slavery had placed blacks in a position of parity with white middle-class women. The conflicting needs of the two groups were eloquently voiced by Frances Watkins Harper, who described the racist economic discrimination directed even against free blacks to explain why she "did not feel as keenly as others, that I had these rights, in common with other women, which are now demanded." Harper's great speech is not reprinted in the official *History of Woman Suffrage*, perhaps because the editors afterward felt that Harper's subjects, unequal justice before the law, segregated schools, the disgrace of a segregated public transportation system, and the indifference of white women to all of these, did not speak to their specialized issue of woman suffrage. "I do not believe," Harper said with majestic understatement, "that giving the woman the ballot is immediately going to cure all the ills of life."[16]

In the call to the anniversary meeting of the Equal Rights Association to be held in New York City, Lucretia Mott wrote that the association's aim was "to secure Equal Rights to all American Citizens, especially the Right of Suffrage, irrespective of race, color or sex."

> The recent war has unsettled all our governmental foundations. Let us see that in their restoration, all these unjust proscriptions are avoided. Let Democracy be defined anew, as *the Government of the people*, AND THE WHOLE PEOPLE.

When the convention met 10 May 1867, Susan B. Anthony defined the difference between two uneasily allied camps, the one moving toward suffrage for black males and urging delay for woman suffrage, and the other moving simply toward equal rights for all:

> As I understand the difference between Abolitionists, some think this is harvest time for the black man, and seed-sowing time for woman. Others with whom I agree, think we have been sowing the seed of individual rights, the foundation idea of a republic for the last century, and that this is the harvest time for all citizens who pay taxes, obey the laws and are loyal to the government.[17]

In December of 1866, at a state equal rights convention in Rochester, Anthony had introduced Truth as the person who "had done more than any other in the room for the cause of freedom,"[18] a strategic acknowledgment of the value Truth represented to both sides of the abolitionist-feminist alliance. Early in 1867, Elizabeth Cady Stanton wrote to ask Truth to be present at the ERA convention in New York City to help create "a genuine republic" in New York state.[19] Truth agreed, staying at Stanton's house during the convention week. But when Truth appeared on the platform to the obvious acclaim of the convention, she demarcated areas of difference between herself and her largely white audience:

> My friends, I am rejoiced that you are glad, but I don't know how you will feel when I get through. I come from another field—the country of the slave. They have got their liberty—so much good luck to have slavery partly destroyed; not entirely. I want it root and branch destroyed. Then we will all be free indeed.[20]

Against the beliefs of the white feminists that emancipation had created a situation of parity in the civil and political status of blacks and women, Truth asserted that slavery had been only "partly destroyed; not entirely." Against their arguments that all could be free only when women had their rights, Truth argued that we would "all be free indeed" only when slavery was "root and branch destroyed." At the close of the speech, she brought in her relief work in Washington, recognizing that the ballot as a measure of freedom had to be placed in the context of the desperate economic condition of the freedpeople:

> I have been in Washington about three years, seeing about these colored people. Now colored men have the right to vote. There ought to be equal rights now more than ever, since colored people have got their freedom.[21]

Over the President's veto, Congress had just passed a bill extending suffrage to blacks of the District of Columbia. In April, Josephine Griffing had written to Truth about the uncertainties of the freedmen, animated by the anxiety of the refugee and the hope of the emergent citizen:

> As to sending you people, it is impossible to promise anything. We have been trying to get some people to go the last week, but all who go incline to go to Providence, Battle Creek, or some place where already several have gone.

Griffing wrote that the freedmen were reluctant to leave the Washington area to look for work "in any considerable numbers till after the first of June, when they will vote" (*NarBk*, 275). Griffing told the convention that she welcomed "the enfranchisement of the negro as a step toward the enfranchisement of women."[22]

Truth's assertion to the ERA convention that "since colored people have got their freedom" the possibility of equal rights would increase was pointedly polemical. Against a rising chorus decrying his people's fitness for democracy, Charles Lenox Remond reminded the convention that black men had historically served as patriots and even as legislators: "People seem to have forgotten our past history. The first blood shed in the Revolutionary war ran from the veins of a black man; and it is remarkable that the first blood shed in the recent rebellion also ran from the veins of a black man." Although Remond, who had refused to be seated at the World Anti-Slavery Conference in London in 1840 when it had denied seating to the American women, had been among the white feminists' strongest allies, his assurance that if black men received the suffrage before women they would as a group "heartily acquiesce in admitting women also to the right of suffrage" fell on deaf ears.[23]

White feminists were arguing instead that the creation of a pool of black male voters would jeopardize their own chances of getting rights. Although anecdotes hinting at the repressive nature of black middle class men were told, the white feminists' rhetoric attached itself to the shadowy mass of unknown freedmen out of which they projected the rise of barbarian patriarchs.

To argue of the black freedman, as Stanton did, that "degraded, oppressed himself, he would be more despotic with the governing power than even our Saxon rulers are,"[24] was unwarranted. As Herbert J. Gutman has argued, the black family had withstood the oppression of slavery with great resilience, and the complex experience of black families in which every member functioned as a productive worker had discouraged the rigid gender roles of white male supremacy.[25] Domestic life for enslaved black women had provided them, as Angela Davis has said, "with the only space where they could truly experience themselves as human beings."[26] In this domestic space, where they labored for themselves, enslaved women and men translated their equality of oppression into a level of sexual equality rarely experienced in white male supremacist society. Ironically, the paranoid argument that white feminists made, that women seeking expanded rights had more to fear from the "degraded" male freedman than from the educated white former master, was precisely contrary to the social reality.

Once freedwomen's marriage arrangements began to come under white patriarchal laws, the discriminatory nature of these laws could affect black women just as much as white women, but this had to do with the laws, not with the special nature of black family relations. White feminists were interested in pointing out the abuses in the institution of marriage wherever they found them, but their analyses shifted more and more of the blame for bad treatment of black women onto individual black men who were then extracted from the social fabric to serve as types.

Frances Gage believed that she was bringing the voices of freedwomen she had known in South Carolina and in the Mississippi valley to the convention: "You give us a nominal freedom, but you leave us under the heel of our husbands, who are tyrants almost equal to our masters." Gage travestied what were the very real desires of freedpeople to legalize their slave marriages. Freedmen, she argued, wanted legal marriage so that they could "manage the women, and take care of their money, but if they were not married in the church the women took their own wages and did just as they had a mind to."[27] Gage's picture of women taking "their own wages" and doing "just as they had a mind to" attributes both economic independence and sass to these black women; probably only the latter was true. In Georgia, Frances Watkins Harper had heard "that often during the war men hired out their wives and drew their pay," but Harper had implicated whites in the social chaos nourished by "ignorance and poverty" in "one of the lowest down States in the South, as far as civilization has been concerned."[28]

On another seemingly contradictory front, Gage attacked the freedman's reputed inability to value his wife's domesticity:

> The biggest quarrel I had with the colored people down there, was with a plantation man because I would not furnish a nurse for his child. "No, Nero," said I, "I can not hire a nurse for your child while Nancy works in the cotton-field." "But what is we to do? I'se a poor miserable man and can't work half the time, and Nancy is a good strong hand; and we must have a nurse." He went away in utter disgust, and declared to the people outside that I had got the miserablest notion he had ever heard, to spoil a good field hand like his Nancy to nurse her own baby.[29]

The man needs his wife's field work; to make this possible he asks for child care for the family. Gage portrays him instead as dismissive of his wife's caring for her own child. We never get to hear from Nancy: did she send her husband to ask for a nurse? Gage shapes the anecdote to imply that the husband has a low valuation of his wife's maternal role; she achieves an attitudinal slant in her use of the phrase "to nurse her own baby," as if she could discredit the black man back through time by implying his acquiescence in the old reality under slavery, when a black woman had to nurse someone else's baby as part of her forced labor. Many largely unconscious elements in a long-lived racist narrative are constituted here.

Gage's story of Nancy hints at the difficulties of black women but subordinates them to the rhetorical stereotyping of the discredited Nero. In the years after the War, both black women and men in the South wished to remove women and children from the fields to the home. Out of necessity, even those women who described themselves as homemakers in the census of 1870 seem to have worked in the fields during cotton-picking season, forming part of the family laboring unit that, as Jacqueline Jones has shown, was one of the adaptive survival mechanisms of postwar freedpeople.[30]

In her stated determination to "not give up the slave woman into the hands of man, to do with her as he pleases hereafter," Frances Gage adopted a common device, denigrating the freedman in order to praise the freedwoman.[31] The condition of black women was more and more employed as a useful counter in the argument that black men should not be masters over white women. The use of minstrelized anecdotes of the family life of freedpeople as a device to portray black men as unworthy citizens had the extraordinary effect of enhancing the status of the brutal white patriarchy that had instigated and superintended slavery. Seldom have so many words favorable to the relative good status of white men been uttered by white women desperate to end their subjugation to them, as expediency brought them to identify themselves as women of culture and refinement with white men of their own class. Their most telling appeal was made to white men in power on the grounds of familiarity. Powerful white men *knew* them; they were their wives, sisters, daughters, mothers. White men in power would admit no such intimate relation to blacks, even when it existed.

Examining the underlying assumptions of the arguments white feminists made during this crucial series of meetings, it becomes clear that although their avowed aim was equal rights for blacks and women, the white feminists felt the two groups could be critically compared and contrasted on the basis of the binary oppositions they were used to in the imprisoning definitions of their own womanhood: pure/impure, uplifted/degraded. To this they added their own class-related oppositions, in which literacy equaled intelligence and illiteracy equaled its lack. Black men were morally degraded, uneducated, and either innately or by conditioning given to despotism (unfit to govern). The women contrasted their high level of culture and refinement to what they saw as a primitive lack of any culture. The benevolent work many of these women had done with poor black populations seemed to redound against the blacks, who could be seen as a people under the tutelage of educated white women. The white women's generosity underwent a transvaluation into a moral superiority that fitted them, but not their pupils, for suffrage.

By first conceptualizing blacks and white women as allied groups and then shifting to a rhetoric of contrast, white feminists contributed to the stereotyping of the black voter, and inevitably this stereotype injured the black woman as much as the black man. The corollary of Frances Gage's argument that "the former slave man of the South has learned his lesson of oppression and wrong of his old master," was Paulina Wright Davis's awful observation that "the black women are more intelligent than the men, because they have learned something from their mistresses."[32]

Sojourner Truth spoke directly to these assumptions, each of which had been reached in response to the sexism that oppressed all women, but each of which showed the impossibility of separating sexism from the race and class discrimination that compounded it. In three separate performances, Truth argued that sexism was grounded in economic inequality; that women had to be freed of their own stereotypes of pure womanhood in order to realize themselves as women; that voting rights, while they should not have to do with gender, should not have to do with class or race. In doing so, Truth shaped and enriched a tradition of black feminist activism extending into our own time.

In her great statement of the problems of black working women in their families, Truth recognized a critical juncture in the relations of black women and black men, emerging from changes in their legal and economic conditions. At the beginning of the violent 1830s, Maria Stewart publicly urged black women to escape the disabilities of rigid gender roles by becoming economically independent. Stewart had enraged some of her mixed audience by telling black men "to flee from the gambling board and the dance-hall; for we are poor, and have no money to throw away,"[33] linking women's economic welfare with the control of male behaviors. Like Stewart thirty-five years earlier, Truth signaled her willingness to attack within the black community for what she perceived to be its greater good, excoriating men who controlled the earnings of women.

There is a great stir about colored men getting their rights, but not a word about the colored women; and if colored men get their rights, and not colored women theirs, you see the colored men will be masters over the women, and it will be just as bad as it was before.

In her attack on sexism in the black working family, Truth argued that the solution to structural problems in the postwar black family was a radical economic one: equal pay for equal work. Grounded in the conditions of labor of black women both enslaved and free, Truth's feminism always expressed her solidarity with the brigades who labored in the fields and went out washing, cooking, and cleaning for other people. In judging male-female inequity, Truth emphasized that the inequity within the black family was part of the greater inequity in society, which showed itself dramatically in the inequity between white and black women.

> White women are a great deal smarter, and know more than colored women, while colored women do not know scarcely anything. They go out washing, which is about as high as a colored woman gets, and their men go about idle, strutting up and down; and when the women come home, they ask for their money and take it all, and then scold because there is no food.[34]

Truth argued that sexism would yield to economic equality; women who received decent pay for their work, at least equal to men's, would not be subordinated in gender relations. Further, she placed the subordination of black women to black men in the context of their subordination to white women.

The washerwomen Truth chose as her example, whose skills she, Harriet Tubman, and Susie King Taylor practiced, were integral to the modern economy. Amanda Berry Smith was taking in washing on Amity Street in New York City around 1865:

> Many nights I have stood at my wash-tub all night, from six in the morning till six the next morning, and so at my ironing table, night and day. I would get so sleepy I could hardly stand on my feet, then I would lean my head on the window ledge and sleep a little till the first deep sleep would pass off, then I would work on till daylight with perfect ease. I had to use all the economy I could, and I know just how much ironing I could do with a ten cent pail of coal. If I lay down I would oversleep myself, and my fire would burn out, and my coal would be gone. I worked hard day and night, did all I could to help my husband, but he was one of those poor unfortunate dispositions that are hard to satisfy, and many a day and night my poor heart ached as I wept and prayed God to help me.[35]

These were working women of a heroic sort, who showed a formidable independence within the confines of their poverty. Some had already begun to voice group solidarity. In 1866, one year before Truth's speech, the black washerwomen in Jackson, Mississippi had tried to organize to set uniform rates for their labor ($1.50 daily, $10.00 and $15.00 monthly for individual and family washing).[36]

In a far-reaching analysis that went beyond the protests about low-status work voiced by Maria Stewart and Martin Delany, Truth argued both for decent work and for according a kind of dignity-status to the worker.

> I feel that if I have to answer for the deeds done in my body just as much as a man I have a right to have just as much as a man.[37]

"Sojourner Truth gave us the whole truth in about fifteen words," Frances Gage said later in the day, "'If I am responsible for the deeds done in my body, the same as the white male citizen is, I have a right to all the rights he has to help him through the world.'"[38]

In arguing for equal pay, Truth represented herself as a field worker, as she had at Akron in 1851; this was the occupation of the great majority of black women workers at the end of the war.

> I have done a great deal of work; as much as a man, but did not get so much pay. I used to work in the field and bind grain, keeping up with the cradler; but men doing no more, got twice as much pay; so with the German women. They work in the field and do as much work, but do not get the pay. We do as much, we eat as much, we want as much.[39]

In her phrase "keeping up with the cradler," Truth's fierce pride showed through (equal to Amanda Berry Smith's pride in her father—"he was a great cradler and mower in those days"), evoking countless spirited women like herself, including those forty women Frederic Law Olmsted saw before emancipation in Mississippi who "carried themselves loftily, each having a hoe over the shoulder, and walking with a free, powerful swing like chasseurs on the march."[40]

Truth conflated gendered liberty with "a little money" as a beginning, looking toward economic independence at the end.[41] Fascinatingly, she turned to the writer as a concrete example of the inequitable compensation of women and men. This is Truth's public assertion of her pride in authorship, to set beside her accomplishments as washerwoman and field worker:

> What we want is a little money. You men know that you get as much again as women when you write, or for what you do. When we get our rights we shall not have to come to you for money, for then we shall have money enough in our own pockets; and may be you will ask us for money.[42]

The writing of black women, from Lucy Terry and Phillis Wheatley to Ann Plato and Sarah Forten, from Frances Watkins Harper to Harriet E. Wilson, Harriet Jacobs, Elizabeth Keckley, and Charlotte Forten, both sustained them personally and sustained a communal tradition within which black identity could be nurtured and defined.[43] "Writing as hard as ever," Frances Rollin confided to her diary in 1868 as she worked on the biography of Martin Delany that would appear under the name "Frank A. Rollin" because the publisher felt readers would not accept a black woman writer.[44] Truth, who more than any other woman of the nineteenth century, spoke aloud and on paper to honor the communal in the individual, seems to call a community of black women worker-writers to her side, as if Elizabeth the Colored Evangelist, Maria Stewart, Jarena Lee, Zilpha Elaw, Mary Prince and Nancy Gardner Prince, and other powerful sisters have all come at once to join Truth in selling their narratives; perhaps Harriet Tubman, who barely made ends meet by telling her life into Sarah Bradford's prose in 1868, is there in spirit too.

Alice Walker has asked, "What did it mean for a black woman to be an artist in our grandmothers' time? In our great-grandmothers' day? It is a question with an answer cruel enough to stop the blood."[45] On this platform the blues groans of Mau Mau Bett are more than background music.

Equal pay was as elusive for educated black women as for their uneducated sisters: "Miss Weston and Miss Rollin are much above the average and deserve I think $30.00 and Mr. Weston, being a Male, will get, I suppose $60.00 at least," wrote the superintendent of the American Missionary Association school in South Carolina where Frances Rollin was teaching in 1865.[46]

The range of opportunity was limited, for both black and white working women. Discouraged with her work as a school teacher, Frances Watkins Harper wrote to a friend, "What would you do if you were in my place? Would you give up and go back and work at your trade (dress-making)?"[47] Bostonian E. H. Heywood told the Equal Rights Convention in 1867 that "Woman wanted not merely the right to vote, but the right to labor." Urging "new avenues for labor," he noted that "the average life of the factory girl in Lowell was only four years."[48] But black women faced the added disadvantages created by racism. "And of all Lowell's multitudinous factories," a story in the *North Star* asserted, "we presume there is not one in which the presence of a colored person would be tolerated even if he would work for nothing and board himself."[49]

Because of the "force of prejudice" against black women, Maria Stewart had protested in 1832, "it is impossible for scarce an individual of them to rise above the condition of servants."[50] After delegates from the Working

Women's Associations of Boston and of New York tried to bring their concerns before the convention in 1869, Frances Watkins Harper questioned whether the white feminists' "idea of working women" was sufficiently "broad enough to take colored women." When Susan B. Anthony and others responded that it was, Harper demurred: "Mrs. Harper said that when she was at Boston there were sixty women who left work because one colored woman went to gain a livelihood in their midst."[51]

The Seneca Falls convention had concentrated on the disabilities of white middle-class women, their restriction from the public domain by marriage and family institutions, and discrimination against them in education and the newly professionalized occupations. Black women occupied a different space. Marriage had had neither the economic advantages nor many of the psychological disadvantages for black women. Most free black women by necessity worked outside the home, and some were independent owners of their own businesses. The great majority of both enslaved and free women worked for low wages, and their economic conditions made advanced education and the professions largely irrelevant to them. Working as wage laborers, tenant farmers, sharecroppers, domestics, seamstresses, often separated from their families, for subsistence wages, always far below even the pitifully low wages of black men, black women both worked in a public world and were invisible in it. As white women tried to break out of the suffocating structure of the middle-class nuclear family, many free black women were trying to survive in poverty-level jobs; freedwomen moved from their experience of vulnerable family life under slavery, in which their status as wife or mother was always subordinate to their status as forced laborer, to the difficult life of the "free" working wife and mother.

The extent to which preoccupation with class rights dominated the 1867 ERA convention is apparent in Frances Gage's extraordinary testimonial, or confession, from the platform, after a pioneering career as an abolitionist and woman's rights speaker, that she had had her own history as an undereducated working woman, braving public opinion, reviving herself from "fainting weakness," and that supporting herself she had found "her womanhood not one bit degraded." But "these are things I do not often tell in public," she admitted.[52] Being undereducated and working at low-status jobs made it difficult to achieve respectability as a "true woman."

The necessity for the black community to counter the racist stereotypes of the black woman as the matriarchal mammy, the unfeminine field laborer, the drudging domestic servant, and the sexually violable body had increased the tyranny over the black woman's image by imposing on it the requirements of middle class gentility.[53] Truth saw that to some extent

black men collaborated with white men and women in constructing a
newly constricting image for black women based on respectability and reputation.

At the 1867 ERA convention, Truth devoted one of her speeches to signifying on the idea of reputation. Taking off on the argument that women
were spiritually unfit to vote, Truth took several of her characteristic turns
on the concept of spirit:

> I am glad to see that men are getting their rights, but I want women to
> get theirs, and while the water is stirring I will step into the pool. Now
> that there is a great stir about colored men getting their rights it is the
> time for women to step in and have theirs.[54]

Pressing the need to seize the moment, Truth compared the political
waters stirred by the effort for black male suffrage to the biblical pool of
Bethesda where the sick were healed if they could step into the pool at the
right moment:

> For an angel went down at a certain season into the pool, and troubled
> the water: whosoever then first after the troubling of the water stepped in
> was made whole of whatsoever disease he had (John 5:4).

Convinced that the crucial moment for woman suffrage had come, the
waters stirring as if from the angel's touch, Truth extended the biblical
parallels to examine the arguments about women's fitness to vote:

> I am sometimes told that "Women ain't fit to vote. Why, don't you
> know that a woman had seven devils in her; and do you suppose a woman
> is fit to rule the nation?"[55]

In extending her biblical parallels beyond the pool of Bethesda, Truth
returned to a profoundly felt assertion about the nature of spirits. It was, of
course, Mary Magdalene who had had seven devils (Luke 8:2); choosing
her as an exemplar allowed the opposition to characterize woman as both
sinful (she was thought of as a prostitute), and, being possessed of devils,
lacking in self-agency. In contrast, Truth offered the Gadarene man with
innumerable devils ("Legion"), which Jesus sent into a herd of swine (Luke
8:30-33):

> Seven devils ain't no account; a man had a legion in him. (great laugh-
> ter) The devils didn't know where to go; and so they asked that they

might go into the swine. They thought that was as good a place as they came out from. (renewed laughter).[56]

Although the pool of Bethesda stood near the sheep market in Jerusalem, Jesus sent the man's devils into swine. In Truth's retelling, men were not merely sheep (as in the Northampton camp meeting, when she had needed to separate the sheep from the goats) but swine.

> They didn't ask to go into sheep—no, into the hog; that was the self-ishest beast; and man is so selfish that he has got women's rights and his own too, and yet he won't give women their rights. He keeps them all to himself.[57]

Reversing the pattern in which the woman stayed at home and the man took to the road, Mary Magdalene, the scorned woman relieved of seven devils, was favored by Jesus and was allowed to follow him, while Jesus sent the Gadarene man away: "Return to thine own house"(Luke 8:38-39).

> If a woman did have seven devils, see how lovely she was when they were cast out, how much she loved Jesus, how she followed him. When the devils were gone out of the man, he wanted to follow Jesus, too, but Jesus told him to go home, and didn't seem to want to have him around.[58]

In contrast to the unfit nature posited for fallen woman by Christians, the true qualities of woman's spirit are the tenacity and assertiveness shown by Mary Magdalene, whose unwavering dedication to her object made her fitter for the task of finding Jesus than his male disciples were. When he arose, Jesus appeared first to her (Mark 16:9).

> And when the men went to look for Jesus at the sepulchre they didn't stop long enough to find out whether he was there or not; but Mary stood there and waited, and said to Him, thinking it was the gardener, "Tell me where they have laid Him and I will carry Him away." See what a spirit there is. Just so let women be true to this object, and the truth will reign triumphant.[59]

In her nimbly crafted performance Truth responded to the political argument about the timing of the campaign for woman suffrage, the religious argument about the fitness of fallen woman to set the world right, and the cultural argument about the relative competence of women to men. In valorizing the Magdalene, Truth signified on middle-class respectability,

black or white: its class orientation, its obsession with essences such as
purity and spiritual cleanliness rather than with transformative lived experience, and its determination to thread everything spiritual through the nee-
dle's eye of reputation. Truth never went for the purity of the Virgin, but
for the progressive self-realization of the Magdalene.

In 1900, the day after the convention of the National American Woman
Suffrage Association, Coralie Franklin Cook presented the greetings of
black women to Susan B. Anthony, who was eighty. In her bold remarks
Cook made an identification of people of color with the Magdalene that
could have come down in a direct line from Truth:

> Not until the suffrage movement had awakened woman to her respon-
> sibility and power, did she come to appreciate the true significance of
> Christ's pity for Magdalene as well as of His love for Mary; not till then
> was the work of Pundita Ramabai in far away India as sacred as that of
> Frances Willard at home in America; not till she had suffered under the
> burden of her own wrongs and abuses did she realize the all-important
> truth that no woman and no class of women can be degraded and all
> womankind not suffer thereby.[60]

Although Stanton and her allies supported Truth's appearance, intending, as Stanton had written to Truth "to bury the woman & the negro in
the citizen,"[61] Truth emphasized to the Association that there had not
been "a word about the colored woman." Truth seems to have felt her isolation not only from white women activists at this point but also from
blacks within the feminist-abolitionist movement; she is reported to have
said at this meeting "I suppose that I am about the only colored woman
that goes about to speak for the rights of the colored woman."[62] Truth was
not singling herself out from black feminists in the black abolitionist
movement so much as acknowledging her solitary position on this issue.

Frances Watkins Harper, who was working with freedpeople in
Darlington, South Carolina in May 1867 during the week of the Equal
Rights Convention, had already accepted delaying woman's suffrage in
order to secure black male suffrage. "I am glad that the colored man gets
his freedom and suffrage together; that he is not forced to go through the
same condition of things here, that has inclined him so much to apathy,
isolation, and indifference, in the North," Harper wrote to William Still
from South Carolina. Things were a little more hopeful in the South, she
wrote, "some of the colored people are getting better contracts, and, I
understand, that there's less murdering."[63] At the 1869 Equal Rights

Convention in New York City, Harper—"Mrs. Harper (colored)," as she is described—was recorded as saying that "When it was a question of race, she let the lesser question of sex go. But the white women all go for sex, letting race occupy a minor position."[64]

There were few black male activists who would say with Charles Lenox Remond that "all I ask for myself I claim for my wife and sister," or with Robert Purvis that "he would rather his son should never be enfranchised, unless his daughter could be also, that, as she bore the double curse of sex and color, on every principle of justice she should first be protected."[65] The prevailing black male judgment developed over many years in the black abolitionist movement was that woman's rights activism was a strictly separate activity that had already damaged the antislavery cause. In 1855 Frederick Douglass expressed his own anger at the historical tendency of woman's rights agitation to interfere with abolitionism. In a speech to the Rochester Ladies' Anti-Slavery Society, Douglass pointed to the split in the American Anti-Slavery Society precipitated in 1840 by the election of Abby Kelley Foster to the executive committee as a bitter cautionary tale.

> God forbid! that I should open here those bitter fountains. I may say, however, that the first grand division took place fourteen years ago, and on the very minor question—Shall a woman be a member of a committee in company with men? The majority said she should be; and the minority seceded. Thus was a grand philanthropic movement rent asunder by a side issue, having nothing, whatever to do with the great object which the American Anti-Slavery Society was organized to carry forward.

Douglass believed that Abby Kelley Foster should have reasoned that "the battle of Woman's Rights should be fought on its own ground; as it is, the slave's cause, already too heavy laden, had to bear up under this new addition."[66] During the entire period, Douglass was the most vocal male public advocate of woman's rights, including woman suffrage, but his separatist view encouraged many less committed black activists to disregard woman's issues in their political agendas.

There was no tradition among black male abolitionists of arguing for woman's rights on the basis of citizenship. Even Douglass's advocacy often sounded the wrong themes for woman's rights, emphasizing women's superior "benevolence and kindness" and their full equality in "moral, mental and intellectual endowments,"[67] rather than their rights as citizens, which should be recognized without regard to such endowments. As Truth had said at Akron, there was no need for comparisons; however much a woman could hold she should still have her "half-measure full."[68]

A critical turn for the alliance of feminists and abolitionists came in Kansas, where in March 1867 the legislature authorized that woman suffrage and black male suffrage be placed on the ballot as popular referenda for a November vote. During the Kansas campaign the refusal of old Republican allies, including long-time abolitionist supporters, to identify themselves with woman suffrage led Anthony and Stanton to align themselves with the racist Democrat George Francis Train in lecturing campaigns that made race (black, Asian, and Indian) the fundamental issue.

It has been argued that, in the long run, the schism that developed out of the Kansas campaign resulted in the formulation of an autonomous political critique advanced through the new journal *Revolution* financed for Stanton and Anthony by George Francis Train.[69] The heavy cost of the breaking of the link between black male suffrage and woman suffrage was the enhancement of a white supremacist narrative through its adoption by white feminists who had been abolitionists. In their anti-black male rhetoric, which was at heart simply anti-black rhetoric, two positions were adumbrated that achieved general acceptance in the later history of the white feminist movement. The articulation of a complex of attitudes relating white women's superiority to black male inferiority contributed to a scenario of white female endangerment. In her manipulative contention that the Republican strategy of manhood suffrage "creates an antagonism between black men and all women that will culminate in fearful outrages on womanhood, especially in the Southern states," Stanton invoked what Ida B. Wells, in *Southern Horrors*, her early pamphlet on lynching, called the "screen of defending the honor of women."[70] Further, the white feminist willingness to be compromised on the issue of universal suffrage by the qualification argument prepared them for their compromised alliance with white Southern women who rejected universal *female* suffrage because it would include black women. *The Revolution* was not entirely devoid of mention of black women: Stanton said that she would rather see "Bridget" and "Dinah" voting than "Patrick" and "Sambo," linking the stereotypes of the immigrant Irish and of blacks and showing that it was often difficult for her to see beyond them to the poor white or to any black woman.[71]

Truth's determination to keep the issue of woman suffrage within the larger context of economic injustice was in sharp contrast to the direction chosen by white feminists, for whom the old opposition between the enfranchised white male and proponents of universal suffrage was replaced by a bitter and embittering opposition between a (low) black or immigrant and a (high) white woman of culture and privilege. Stanton argued that educated and elevated women had the power "to develop the Saxon race into a higher and nobler life."[72] "Patrick and Sambo and Hans and Ung

Tung," she said, should not be "making laws for Lydia Maria Child, Lucretia Mott, or Fanny Kemble."[73]

Eric Foner has argued that the white supremacist power structure served by the Fifteenth Amendment, which did not expand the definition of citizenship, was as determined to retain forms of inequality that affected the white immigrant working class as to extend suffrage to blacks.[74] White feminists' nativist rhetoric ultimately served this white male cause without winning any rights for themselves. At the Worcester Woman Suffrage Convention at the end of 1869, Julia Ward Howe and Lucy Stone referred nostalgically to the first Worcester Convention nearly two decades past; then Stone's husband, Henry Blackwell, rose to argue that "For every Chinaman there would be a Chinese woman to vote. There were more Irish women came to this country than Irishmen. If the ballot were given to women, a large proportion of power would pass into the hands of these ignorant, foreign women."[75]

At the May 1869 meeting of the Equal Rights Association in New York City, Frederick Douglass challenged Stanton's rhetorical "employment of certain names, such as 'Sambo,' and the gardener, and the bootblack, and the daughters of Jefferson and Washington" in *The Revolution*: "I have asked what difference there is between the daughters of Jefferson and Washington and other daughters." Douglass argued that rising violence against blacks constituted an emergency justifying the immediate granting of black suffrage.

> I must say that I do not see how any one can pretend that there is the same urgency in giving the ballot to woman as to the negro. With us, the matter is a question of life and death, at least, in fifteen States of the Union. When women, because they are women, are hunted down through the cities of New York and New Orleans; when they are dragged from their houses and hung upon lamp-posts; when their children are torn from their arms, and their brains dashed out upon the pavement; when they are objects of insult and outrage at every turn; when they are in danger of having their homes burnt down over their heads; when their children are not allowed to enter schools; then they will have an urgency to obtain the ballot equal to our own. (Great applause.)

When a voice called out from the Convention floor, "Is that not all true about black women?" Douglass replied, "Yes, yes, yes; it is true of the black woman, but not because she is a woman, but because she is black."[76] In a bizarre mirror image of Douglass's argument, the white leaders of the twentieth-century National Woman's Party recognized the illegal disenfranchisement of black women, but argued "that since black women were discriminated against in the same way as black men, it was not a question of woman's rights and, therefore, their organization had no obligation to defend the rights of black women."[77] Although Douglass evoked recent anti-black terrorism in Memphis and New Orleans, the terms of his argument had evolved within the antislavery movement long before. In 1837, Angelina Grimké had been enraged by the argument of her future husband Theodore Weld that "What is done for the *slave* and *human rights* in this country must be done now, now, now. Delay is madness, ruin, whereas woman's rights are not a life and death business, *now or never.*"[78] Black men had not much helped black women in their fight for the vote, but black women had suffered both from that indifference and from the white feminist onslaught on black male suffrage.

Susan B. Anthony's dangerous rejoinder to Douglass was that "if you will not give the whole loaf of suffrage to the entire people, give it to the most intelligent first." Giving precedence to intelligence (clearly conceived of as a racial, ethnic, and class concept) Anthony argued, would elevate the woman question and place black suffrage last.[79] The divisive argument that "intelligent," that is, educated, white women should not be classed with all black men and women in agitating for equal rights threatened the "whole loaf of suffrage" just as surely as the argument that suffrage should be granted to black males and not to all women.[80]

At a culminating point in Stanton's clash with George Downing, one of the key political organizers in the black male suffrage campaign, Downing stated that women "had no right to refuse an act of justice upon the assumption that it would be followed by an act of injustice," to which Stanton made her well-known inflammatory reply:

> Mrs. Stanton replied she demanded the ballot for all. She asked for reconstruction on the basis of self-government; but if we are to have further class legislation, she thought the wisest order of enfranchisement was to take the educated classes first. If women are still to be represented by men, then I say let only the highest type of manhood stand at the helm of State. But if all men are to vote, black and white, lettered and unlettered, washed and unwashed, the safety of the nation as well as the interests of woman demand that we outweigh this incoming tide of ignorance, poverty, and vice, with the virtue, wealth, and education of the women of the country.

"Would Horace Greeley, Wendell Phillips, Gerrit Smith, or Theodore Tilton be willing to stand aside and trust their individual interests, and the whole welfare of the nation, to the lowest strata of manhood?" Stanton asked Downing.[81] Probably not; although in New Orleans, the male intellectual leaders of the free black community had rejected a white scheme to grant equal rights to them while denying these rights to the rural freedmen. They refused to allow "the oppressors [to] represent the free colored population which has sacrificed so much for the noble cause of liberty as being the enemy of black men who have been held in slavery until now."[82]

In her third and final appearance before the Equal Rights Convention, Truth placed the struggle for woman's rights in the context of the long bloody battle for "the colored people" to "own their soul and body." This other struggle could achieve "liberty without blood":

> I have lived on through all that has taken place these forty years in the anti-slavery cause, and I have plead with all the force I had that the day might come that the colored people might own their soul and body. Well, the day has come, although it came through blood. It makes no difference how it came—it did come. (applause) I am sorry it came in that way. We are now trying for liberty that requires no blood—that women shall have their rights—not rights from you.[83]

In saying that "women shall have their rights—not rights from you," Truth reasserted Lucretia Mott's defining statement in her "Discourse on Woman" that women wanted "nothing as a favor" from man, but intended to gain the right "not to be governed by laws not her own."[84] But in the context of the prevailing rhetorical identification of slave with woman, Truth's distinction between the struggle that required blood, in which rights were wrested from unwilling masters, and this other struggle for "liberty that requires no blood" is significant. In her earlier argument about sexist subordination in the black family, Truth had said that "the man claims her money, body, and everything for himself."[85] Advancing on Stanton's suggestion that the movement "bury the negro & the woman in the citizen," Truth buried the black woman in the whole people; she had struggled so that "the day might come that the colored people might own their soul and body."

Truth was toying with the distinction between the slave master and the master of the house when she switched from the elevated tone of her opening to the ironic "kindness" of her call for woman's suffrage:

> Give them what belong to them; they ask it kindly too. (laughter) I ask it kindly. Now I want it done very quick. It can be done in a few years. How good it would be.

Voting rights were hedged with special qualifications; a person might own property, might pay taxes, might meet any number of special requirements and still be denied voting rights because of some other requirement, such as race or gender; conversely, property qualifications or special taxes meant the "colored people might own their soul and body," yet not own enough else to qualify to vote. Property requirements enshrined the discrimination toward working class people, blacks, immigrants, and poor native born whites.

Class-based educational requirements did the same thing. Had Truth been able to vote as a black and as a woman, and as a property owner, and as a taxpayer, she would not have been allowed to vote in many states because she could not have met the literacy requirement. A gulf between Truth and her audience can be seen opening up, gauged by the increasing laughter:

> I would like to go up to the polls myself. (laughter) I own a little house in Battle Creek, Michigan. Well, every year I got a tax to pay. Taxes, you see, be taxes. Well, a road tax sounds large. Road tax, school tax and all these things. Well, there was women there that had a house as well as I. They taxed them to build a road, and they went on the road and worked. It took them a good while to get a stump up. (laughter) Now, that shows that women can work. If they can dig up stumps they can vote. (laughter) It is easier to vote than dig stumps. (laughter) It doesn't seem hard work to vote, though I have seen some men that had a hard time of it. (laughter) But I believe that when women can vote there won't be so many men that have a rough time getting to the polls. (great laughter)[86]

The "hard work" of voting was harder for blacks, who had not completely gained those aspects of personal freedom that distinguish freedom from slavery—freedom of movement, freedom of economic activity, and personal inviolability—without which blacks could hardly function as emancipated citizens in the political realm. "There is danger of their life sometimes," Truth said of black citizens trying to vote, perhaps momentarily diminishing the laughter. "I guess many have seen it in this city."

In 1865 Frederick Douglass had argued in *The Liberator* for the ballot as an emergency measure, for without the ballot, emancipation accomplished only a transfer of ownership: "Individual ownership has been abolished," but without black suffrage "we shall establish an ownership of the blacks by the community among which they live."[87] In South Carolina in 1867 Frances Harper saw the great difficulty the black man would have in exercising the franchise without some economic security:

While I am writing, a colored man stands here, with a tale of wrong—he has worked a whole year, year before last, and now he has been put off with fifteen bushels of corn and his food; yesterday he went to see about getting his money, and the person to whom he went, threatened to kick him off, and accused him of stealing. I don't know how the colored man will vote, but perhaps many of them will be intimidated at the polls.[88]

The fight for ratification of the Fifteenth Amendment, which prohibited racial discrimination in voting, but not gender discrimination, left the alliance between abolitionists and feminists moribund. The Equal Rights Association split, with the Stanton-Anthony faction forming the National Woman Suffrage Association, radically isolating themselves to work only for woman's rights. The more traditional reformist elements of the New England faction led by Lucy Stone, Henry Blackwell, Thomas Wentworth Higginson, and Julia Ward Howe created the American Woman Suffrage Association, which hoped first to secure black male suffrage through the ratification of the Fifteenth Amendment and then to agitate for another amendment granting women the vote.

Although Truth's differences with both factions were great enough, she continued to speak at meetings; now more than ever she used the woman's rights platforms to argue for land reform. At a session of the New England contingent of the American Woman Suffrage Association, Thomas Wentworth Higginson's speech rallying the women "to come forward in the defense of their own rights" was followed by Paulina W. Davis's introduction of Truth. Truth was not introduced as a campaigner for woman's rights but as one who "had labored for the emancipation of her race." She began by protesting the limited time she had been allotted:

Sojourner Truth, who seems to carry her weight of years very heartily, said she was somewhat pleased to come before them to bear testimony, although she had a limited time—only a few minutes—but as many friends wanted to hear Sojourner's voice, she thought she would accept the offer. She spoke when the spirit moved her—not when the people moved her, but when she was limited to a few minutes, the people moved her. (*NarBk*, 218)

Rather waspishly, Truth challenged the conception of woman's rights as a self-contained movement. "She was in the woman movement," she said, "for she was a woman herself," implying that there was a universal condition of eligibility for the movement rather than an ideological one. Beginning by differentiating her position from that of other speakers, she argued for the communal benefit of woman's suffrage because of the connectedness of women and men:

> The Friend said that woman ought to have her rights for her own benefit, she ought to have them, not only for her own benefit, but for the benefit of the whole creation, not only the women, but all the men on the face of the earth, for they were the mothers of them. Therefore she ought to have her God-given right, and be the equal of men, for she was the resurrection of them. (*NarBk*, 218)

Truth then implicitly addressed the animating issue of educational qualification by arguing not just for land but also for education for the black refugees, "favoring a grant of land to the freedmen of Washington, and such a provision of educational privileges as will tend to the elevation of this unfortunate class" (*NarBk*, 217). She then said "that she would stop before she was stopped" (*NarBk*, 218).

The extent of Truth's differences with middle-class white feminists was probably reflected in her attack on the leaders of the Rhode Island suffragists after their October 1870 convention. At an unrelated meeting of her own to promote her plan for land for the freedpeople, Truth denounced the fashionable excesses of the feminists (among whom none was more fashionable than their president, Paulina Wright Davis):

> When I saw them women on the stage at the Woman's Suffrage Convention, the other day, I thought, what kind of reformers be you, with goose-wings on your heads, as if you were going to fly, and dressed in such ridiculous fashion, talking about reform and women's rights? 'Pears to me you had better reform yourselves first. (*NarBk*, 243)

Recuperating her argument that women were "the mothers of creation" whose "sons were cut off like grass by the war and the land was covered with their blood," Truth situated the factionalized woman's rights movement as a human rights concern. Under this altered criterion, even affluent educated white women might be seen as unqualified reformers: "What will such lives as you live do for humanity?"

When Truth met Grant in the White House 31 March 1870, the day after the ratification of the Fifteenth Amendment, she told him she was grateful that "colored people had gained the right of suffrage" (*NarBk*, 274). Grant was probably grateful for black male suffrage as well. His popular majority in the election was only 309,584, and he is thought to have received 450,000 votes from black men.[89] The Amendment did not establish uniform voting requirements, thus allowing states to institute literacy, property, and educational tests as they desired, tests that would effectively disfranchise the majority of black voters. Suffrage qualifications favored by Northerners would continue to abridge the right to vote of the white poor, immigrants, and those citizens who were illiterate.

White southerners who had participated in the Civil War were largely disfranchised from 1870 to 1877; and from 1877 to 1890 black southerners were disfranchised by intimidation and election devices. After 1890 state constitutional amendments in the South restricted black suffrage by requiring that a prospective voter must have paid full taxes, must own a certain amount of property, be able to pass an educational test, or be accepted under a grandfather clause, which allowed suffrage to (white) men who could not satisfy the educational or property tests.[90] Jacqueline Jones has shown that the disfranchisement of "unworthy citizens" entrapped poor whites as well as blacks.

> Between 1890 and 1903 white landowners' efforts to limit political opposition to the Democratic party—efforts achieved through constitutional restrictions on voting by way of the literacy clause and poll tax, for example—reduced white voting strength by an average of 25 percent (and black strength by 62 percent) throughout the South.[91]

What Pauli Murray has called "a century of illusive citizenship" had begun.[92] Contrary to Susan B. Anthony's flourish, the black man had not harvested; and for a long time after the white woman's seed-sowing, the black woman worked on in symbolic cotton-fields.

"Who can hesitate to decide, when the question lies between educated women and ignorant negroes?" Stanton heard the voters in Kansas asking.[93] By invoking the strategy of superior qualification, middle-class feminists had set themselves in opposition to black suffrage, whether male or female. Black women's interests had been split off and used as a subset for strategic positioning; in its later history, using the same qualification argument, the white suffrage movement would dissociate itself from the rights of black women. By 1919 Mary Church Terrell had come to believe that white suffragists would be willing to see a Nineteenth Amendment that did not include black women.[94]

Only five years after the Civil War, Frances Watkins Harper had become discouraged about the prospects for black voters in the South. She wrote to William Still from Greenville, Georgia:

> The political heavens are getting somewhat overcast. Some of this old rebel element, I think, are in favor of taking away the colored man's vote, and if he loses it now it may be generations before he gets it again.

Harper showed herself, in her disillusionment, not unaffected by the nearly universal acceptance of special intellectual requirements for voting, but she also clearly grasped the future consequences of such a position:

> Well, after all perhaps the colored man generally is not really developed enough to value his vote and equality with other races, so he gets enough to eat and drink, and be comfortable, perhaps the loss of his vote would not be a serious grievance to many; but his children differently educated and trained by circumstances might feel political inferiority rather a bitter cup."[95]

In 1871 William Wells Brown, the president of the National Association for the Spread of Temperance and Night Schools among the Freed People of the South, organized a meeting in Fremont Temple in Boston on the eighth anniversary of the Emancipation Proclamation. Truth shared the platform with J. D. Fulton, Gilbert Haven, and Brown. Fulton, in keeping with the views of the organization, supported education for the freedpeople, going so far as to argue that "the freedmen of the South without education will be cursed rather than blessed by the ballot." He said that he did not believe "in anybody casting a vote in this land that cannot read and write" (*NarBk*, 210). But the rate of illiteracy among freedpeople, according to W. E. B. DuBois was as high as 95 percent.[96] Had illiterate people no knowledge of their own vital interests? When Truth's turn came, she spoke both for land reform and for government-sponsored education, connecting economic improvement to literacy. But she insisted, even on this occasion, in disconnecting literacy from the ability to understand politics, and, by implication, to vote: "I tell you I can't read a book, but I can read de people" (*NarBk*, 216).

The reform measures advanced in the mid-1860s by radical Republicans, land reform, the enforcement of civil rights legislation and the establishment and protection of voting rights, had been successfully circumvented by the mid-1870s as Reconstruction drew to a halting end. The relief programs and civil rights activities of the Freedmen's Bureau had disappeared. Moderate reformers had seized upon educational programs as the more traditional, more acceptable means to black achievement; black (segregated) education was also the least costly reform, in every sense, to whites. Everything in Truth's experience had taught her that rights should come first. In a racist society, education for blacks could not bring economic and political power; it was whites who needed to be educated against racism. As James Oliver Horton has argued in his study of the Washington, D.C. black community after the war,

The social program designed by the post-Civil War liberal Republican reformers for the benefit of the newly free people of color triumphed in its attempt to bring literacy. Yet as social reformers endorsed a gradualist approach to betterment focusing largely on education, political forces were depriving blacks of the franchise, thus denying them the power that might have made their educational accomplishments economically meaningful. Education was then acceptable to both liberal reformers and political moderates, partly because the removal of the potential of black political power guaranteed that its acquisition would not appreciably alter the economic relationships or threaten the security of social authority in Reconstruction Washington.[97]

"The ballot is a *schoolmaster*," Charles Sumner told the Senate in 1866.[98] "It is certainly desirable that our brethren recently redeemed from bondage and called to the blessings of freedom should have a certain degree of education," the black financed and edited New Orleans *Tribune* editorialized in opposition to a literacy qualification for black (male) voters; "However we can only see in this subject a distinct and collateral question, which has no direct bearing upon the right of voting." The newspaper argued that "the actual enjoyment of new rights is the only way to get accustomed to and become fit for their exercise."[99]

Black men meeting in Kansas in 1863 had rejected the argument that ignorance or "the want of intelligence" could result in the "forfeiture of a *natural* and *inherent* right," the right to vote, which rested "upon the fact of our being born in this country, and upon the form of government under which we live."[100] Of course, they were not talking about women.

In 1867 in Stanton's parlor, Truth had satirized the national obsession with the difference in women's and men's votes:

> I must sojourn once to the ballot-box before I die. I hear the ballot-box is a beautiful glass globe, so you can see all the votes as they go in. Now, the first time I vote I'll see if a woman's vote looks any different from the rest— if it makes any stir or commotion. If it don't inside, it need not outside.[101]

Contrary to the rhetoric at the Equal Rights Association meetings in which suffrage had appeared to be a badge of class rather than of citizenship, the argument that suffrage was the inherent and natural right of citizenship in a democracy was advanced by some black and white feminists when they tried to vote under the citizenship provision of the Fourteenth Amendment. White feminist Portia Gage, who wrote of Truth, "she has been a wonderful teacher to me" (*NarBk*, 290), and some other women citizens tried to vote in Vineland, New Jersey in 1868. In March 1869, black feminist Louisa Rollin spoke to the Reconstruction legislature in Columbia, South Carolina; according to the *New York Times*, "her argument (so-called) was to the effect that inasmuch as the Constitution did not define the voter as male, the intent and scope of that paper were that sex was unknown to the Constitution, and that, accordingly, women have as much right to vote as men have."[102] In October of that year, Virginia Minor, President of the Woman Suffrage Association of Missouri, presented this argument to the suffrage convention in St. Louis; it became the official stance of NWSA. Without the sanction of either of the white feminist factions, Victoria Claflin Woodhull put the argument to a congressional committee in 1871.[103]

Mary Ann Shadd Cary heard Woodhull speak at the Washington Woman Suffrage Convention in 1870. A student at Howard University Law School, Cary prepared a statement for the House Judiciary Committee advancing the citizenship argument. In 1871 Cary registered to vote in the District.[104] In Michigan, white feminist Nanette B. Gardner succeeded in casting a vote in the state election of 1871. "Dear Sojourner," Gardner wrote from Detroit, "at your request I record the fact that I succeeded in registering my name in the First Precinct of the Ninth Ward, and on Tuesday, the 4th of April, cast the first vote for a state officer deposited in an American ballot-box by a woman for the last half century" (*NarBk*, 285). Susan B. Anthony and other women registered and voted in the presidential election of 1872, but following the vote Anthony was arrested. When the St. Louis registrar refused her registration in the same year, Virginia Minor sued, claiming her constitutional rights had been denied.

In November 1872 the Battle Creek *Daily Journal* reported that Truth, who had campaigned aggressively before black audiences for the reelection of Grant, had tried to register in the third ward in Battle Creek:

> Sojourner Truth, on the Saturday before the recent election, appeared before the Board of Registration, in the third ward where she resides, and claimed the right to have her name entered upon the list of electors. Upon being refused, she repaired to the polls on election day in the same ward and again asserted her right to the ballot. She was politely received by the authorities in both instances, but did not succeed in her effort, though she sustained her claim by many original and quaintly put arguments. (*NarBk*, 231)

In 1875, in *Minor v. Happersett*, the Supreme Court ruled that although women were indeed citizens the Constitution did not guarantee suffrage to citizens; states could decide which citizens voted and under what conditions.

In 1890, seven years after Truth's death, the two factions of the white feminist movement that had split over the Fourteenth and Fifteenth Amendments merged into the National American Woman Suffrage Association, presided over by first Stanton, then Anthony. Like Truth, some black feminists continued to work with some white feminists after the split in the white feminist movement. In 1870, the interracial South Carolina Woman's Rights Association was organized by blacks, including Katherine Rollin and Charlotte Rollin, asking for woman suffrage not as a favor or privilege "but as a right based on the ground that we are human beings, and as such, entitled to all human rights."[105] Charlotte Rollin represented the group at the AWSA convention in 1872. Her sisters, Frances Rollin Whipper, the biographer of Martin Delany, and Louisa, were active feminists. Frances Watkins Harper spoke at the AWSA in 1876. Harriet Tubman, who had spoken at pre-war meetings before the split in the movement, retained her personal loyalty to Susan B. Anthony. In 1878 Truth attended NWSA's convention in Rochester celebrating the fiftieth anniversary of Seneca Falls as a delegate from Battle Creek. But the direction had shifted now for black women. While Mary Ann Shadd Cary continued to attend meetings of the NWSA during the 1870s, in 1880 she organized the Colored Women's Progressive Association, asserting a broadly-based concept of woman's rights, including suffrage. Black women were beginning to organize to articulate and advance their own claims.[106]

Sojourner Truth and Mary Ann Shadd Cary were dead and Harriet Jacobs was too ill to attend the historic meeting in Washington in 1896 at which the National Association of Colored Women was formed. Nurtured in the tradition of women like Sarah Mapps Douglass, Maria Stewart, Sarah Parker Remond, Sarah and Margaretta Forten and Harriet Forten Purvis, Susan Paul, Grace Douglass, and Hattie Purvis, the activist generation of Rosetta Douglass Sprague, Fanny Jackson Coppin, Louisa Jacobs, Frances Watkins Harper, Charlotte Forten Grimké, and Ella Sheppard Moore would join forces with younger activists like Josephine St. Pierre Ruffin, Rebecca Cole, Mary Church Terrell, Margaret Murray Washington, Alice Moore Dunbar, and Victoria Earle Mathews. Across the generations, Harriet Tubman would join Ida B. Wells Barnett.[107]

The federal amendment that would prohibit the abridgment of suffrage on account of sex was introduced into the Senate in 1878 and into the House in 1883, the year of Truth's death. In 1920, when the Nineteenth Amendment became law, there were three million black women among the twenty-five million women constitutionally guaranteed the right to vote.

The white woman's movement had for some time been sympathetic to educational and property qualifications as a means of keeping down the black vote. In South Carolina, where fifty-one years earlier Louisa Rollin had taken her argument for woman suffrage to the floor of the House, white election officials tried to intimidate and prevent black women from registering to vote in the weeks leading up to the 1920 election; the women "defied all opposition."[108] The registrar who disqualified Fannie Lou Hamer in 1962 after asking her to interpret the 16th section of the Mississippi state constitution had not grasped that he was dealing with a woman who could feel within herself, as Truth had, "the *power of a nation.*"[109]

In Akron in 1851 Truth had embodied the woman in the black. In her path-breaking performances in New York City in 1867 she embodied the sophisticated and seasoned political activist in a radically inclusive form. She said that people who are black, who are poor, who are illiterate, who are not true women, could be empowered to choose for themselves the leaders who govern them. When Harriet Tubman had felt the call to "take care of my people," she at first told the Lord to "get some better edicated person—get a person wid more cultur dan I have"; the Lord had demurred. When asked if she really believed that women should vote, she replied, "I suffered enough to believe it," but she did not live to see it.[110] Truth, like Tubman, had matured as a political activist over a long and turbulent career that had taught them both the multitudinous paths by which people become qualified for anything. They had both grounded gendered black power in the vitality of the working woman. Always disturbing the hierarchies, Truth honored the shaping energy of labor as the defining human activity. She honored God as the spirit of creative labor, working the world into being and sustaining it by constant ceaseless endeavor. In the 1850 *Narrative*, Truth had examined the Creation story in Genesis with the skeptical eye of an ill-paid laborer who was used to "keeping up with the cradler":

> Why, if God works by the day, and one day's work tires him, and he is obliged to rest, either from weariness or on account of darkness, or if he waited for the "cool of the day to walk in the garden," because he was inconvenienced by the heat of the sun, why then it seems that God cannot do as much as *I* can; for *I* can bear the sun at noon, and work several days and nights in succession without being much tired. Or, if he rested nights because of the darkness, it is very queer that he should make the night so dark that he could not see himself. If *I* had been God, I would have made the night light enough for my own convenience, surely. (*NarBk*, 107)

Valuing the lively defining human ability to create over the dead things that weighed on human spirits, Truth might have respected Marx's belief that "labor is the living, shaping fire; it represents the impermanence of things, their temporality."[111] In Elizabeth Cady Stanton's living room in 1867 the day after the Equal Rights Convention, Truth said something like this:

> You know, children, I don't read such small stuff as letters, I read men and nations. I can see through a millstone, though I can't see through a spelling-book. What a narrow idea a reading qualification is for a voter! I know and do what is right better than many big men who read. And there's that property qualification! just as bad. As if men and women themselves, who made money, were not of more value than the thing they made.[112]

Notes

1. Anna Julia Cooper, *A Voice from the South; By a Black Woman of the South* (Xenia, Ohio, 1892), 144; Fannie Lou Hamer, "The Special Plight and the Role of Black Woman," in *Black Women in White America: A Documentary History*, edited by Gerda Lerner (New York: Vintage Books, 1992), 609.
2. Elizabeth Cady Stanton, *Eighty Years and More: Reminiscences 1815-1897* (New York: Schocken Books, 1917), 240. Angela Davis notes that Stanton considered the subordination of women's advocacy to antislavery during the war as an error in strategy (*Women, Race & Class*, [New York: Vintage Books, 1983], 73).
3. Stanton, et al., *History of Woman Suffrage*, 2:190-91.
4. Stanton, et al., *History of Woman Suffrage*, 2:890, 57n., 61. For the significance of Grimké Weld's presence at these meetings representing "the close link between women's rights and Negro rights," see Lerner, *The Grimké Sisters from South Carolina*, 351-55.
5. Stanton, et al., *History of Woman Suffrage*, 2:892.
6. Ibid., 2:898.
7. For analyses of the opposition to the Fourteenth and Fifteenth Amendments, to which our discussion is indebted, see Pamela Allen, "Woman Suffrage: Feminism and White Supremacy," in *Reluctant Reformers: Racism and Social Reform Movements in the United States*, by Robert L. Allen with Pamela P. Allen (Washington, D.C.: Howard University Press, 1983), 139-49; Davis, *Women, Race & Class*, 30-86; Eric Foner, *Reconstruction*, 251-61; Barbara Hilkert Andolsen, *Daughters of Jefferson, Daughters of Bootblacks: Racism and American Feminism* (Macon: Mercer University Press, 1986), 1-80.

8. Bentley, *A History of the Freedmen's Bureau*, 35. See 199 and 261n.102, for the initially successful Republicanizing of the South. In 1868 seven formerly Confederate states were rewarded for enfranchising black males and ratifying the Fourteenth Amendment by having their Congressional representation restored. These seven states elected twelve Republican senators; of their thirty-two congressmen only two were Democrats.

9. Stanton, et al., *History of Woman Suffrage*, 2:91.

10. Ibid., 2:930.

11. Ibid., 2:94n.

12. Ibid.

13. Ibid., 2:899.

14. Ibid., 2:172.

15. Ibid., 2:171.

16. *Proceedings of the Eleventh Woman's Rights Convention*, May 1866, 45-48, quoted from Frances Ellen Watkins Harper, *A Brighter Coming Day: A Frances Ellen Watkins Harper Reader*, edited by Frances Smith Foster (New York: The Feminist Press, 1990), 217-19.

17. Stanton, et al., *History of Woman Suffrage*, 2:220

18. Quoted in Mabee and Newhouse, *Sojourner Truth*, 183.

19. Stanton to Truth, 24 March 1867, IAPFP, UR. The official call to the convention was signed by Lucretia Mott (Stanton, et al., *History of Woman Suffrage*, 2:182).

20. Stanton, et al., *History of Woman Suffrage*, 2:193.

21. Ibid., 2:194.

22. Ibid., 2:221.

23. Ibid., 2:214 and 225.

24. Ibid., 2:214.

25. See Herbert J. Gutman, *The Black Family in Slavery and Freedom, 1750-1925* (New York: Pantheon Books, 1976), 412-31 and passim; Jacqueline Jones, *The Dispossessed*, 1-44; Jones, *Labor of Love, Labor of Sorrow*, 11-43; Davis, *Women, Race & Class*, 3-29. For an opposing argument that "enslaved black people accepted patriarchal definitions of male-female sex roles," see "Sexism and the Black Female Slave Experience," in bell hooks, *Ain't I a Woman: Black Women and Feminism* (Boston: South End Press, 1981) 15-49. Also see hooks' discussion of differences in the way black men responded to white patriarchal expectations in *Black Looks*, 89-93.

26. Davis, *Women, Race & Class*, 16.

27. Stanton, et al., *History of Woman Suffrage*, 2:197.

28. Still, *The Underground Railroad*, 773.

29. Stanton, et al., *History of Woman Suffrage*, 2:197.

30. Gutman, *The Black Family in Slavery and Freedom*, 224-29; Jacqueline Jones, *Labor of Love, Labor of Sorrow*, 58-68.

31. Stanton, et al., *History of Woman Suffrage*, 2:197.

32. Ibid., 2:197 and 391.

33. Stewart, *Maria W. Stewart*, 44, 59-60.

34. Stanton, et al., *History of Woman Suffrage*, 2:193.

35. Smith, *An Autobiography*, 68.

36. Gutman has shown that married women with children in the South chose this occupation over other kinds of service because it gave them flexibility in staying with their children (*The Black Family in Slavery and Freedom*, 628-32). For post-war efforts of washerwomen to organize, see Sterling, *We Are Your Sisters*, 355-58. For the status of washerwomen in the black community see Sharon Harley, "Northern Black Female Workers: Jacksonian Era," in *The Afro-American Woman: Struggles and Images*, edited by Sharon Harley and Rosalyn Terborg Penn (Port Washington, New York: Kennikat Press, 1978), 10 and two studies by Elsa Barkley Brown, "Womanist Consciousness: Maggie Lena Walker and the Independent Order of St. Luke," *Signs: Journal of Women in Culture and Society* 14 (Spring 1989): 610-33 and "Mothers of Mind," *Sage* 6, no. 1 (Summer 1989): 7.

37. Stanton, et al., *History of Woman Suffrage*, 2:193.

38. Ibid., 2:197.

39. Ibid., 2:194.

40. Amanda Berry Smith, *An Autobiography*, 32; Frederick Law Olmsted, *A Journey in the Back Country* (New York, 1860), 14-15.

41. Houston A. Baker, Jr., found in Olaudah Equiano a "conflation of getting 'a little money' and freedom" (*Blues, Ideology, and Afro-American Literature: A Vernacular Theory* [Chicago: University of Chicago Press, 1984], 34). In his Introduction to *Narrative of Sojourner Truth; A Bondswoman of Olden Time, With a History of Her Labors and Correspondence Drawn from Her "Book of Life"* (New York: Oxford University Press, 1991) Jeffrey C. Stewart argued that Truth "preached a labor theory of human equality" (xxxvi).

42. Stanton, et al., *History of Woman Suffrage*, 2:194.

43. For the black woman writer as a worker see Hazel Carby, *Reconstructing Womanhood*, 40-43. For a personal view of some of the difficulties of black women worker-writers, see Erlene Stetson, "Silence: Access and Aspiration," in *Between Women: Biographers, Novelists, Critics, Teachers and Artists Write About Their Work on Women*, edited by Carol Ascher, Louise DeSalvo, and Sara Ruddick (New York: Routledge, 1994), 237-51.

44. Sterling, *We Are Your Sisters*, 455 and 461.

45. Alice Walker, "In Search of Our Mothers' Gardens," in *In Search of Our Mothers' Gardens: Womanist Prose* (San Diego: Harcourt Brace & Co., 1984), 233.

46. Sterling, *We Are Your Sisters*, 265n.

47. Still, *The Underground Railroad*, 757.

48. Stanton, et al., *History of Woman Suffrage*, 2:223.

49. *North Star*, 20 October 1848; Harley, "Northern Black Female Workers," 5-16.

50. Stewart, *Maria W. Stewart*, 46.

51. Stanton, et al., *History of Woman Suffrage*, 2:391-92. In 1869, under pressure from black women delegates, the National Colored Labor Union

heard Mary Ann Shadd Cary speak on woman's rights and suffrage and voted to include women workers in its organizations (Paula Giddings, *When and Where I Enter: The Impact of Black Women on Race and Sex in America* [New York: William Morrow and Co., 1984], 68-70).

52. Stanton, et al., *History of Woman Suffrage*, 2:199.
53. See Yee, *Black Women Abolitionists*, 40-59. See an extension of this form of social control in Hazel V. Carby, "Policing the Black Woman's Body in an Urban Context," *Critical Inquiry* 18 (Summer 1992): 738-75.
54. Stanton, et al., *History of Woman Suffrage*, 2:222.
55. Ibid., 2:222.
56. Ibid.
57. Ibid.
58. Ibid.
59. Ibid.
60. Ibid., 4:399.
61. Stanton to Truth, 24 March 1867, IAPFP, UR.
62. Stanton, et al., *History of Woman Suffrage*, 2:193, 194.
63. Still, *The Underground Railroad*, 767-68.
64. Stanton, et al., *History of Woman Suffrage*, 2:391.
65. Ibid., 2:220 and 265.
66. Douglass, *Life and Writings of Frederick Douglass*, 2:349-50. See Yee, *Black Women Abolitionists*, 146-47. Yee discusses the interesting political development immediately after Abby Kelley Foster's election, in which after the dissenters withdrew, Lucretia Mott and Lydia Maria Child were accepted on the executive committee while black activist Hester Lane was rejected on the advice of a black male activist who objected to her supposedly anti-Garrisonian views (*Black Women Abolitionists*, 105-7).
67. *North Star*, 10 August 1848.
68. *National Anti-Slavery Standard*, 2 May 1853.
69. See for example Ellen Carol DuBois, *Feminism and Suffrage: The Emergence of an Independent Women's Movement in America, 1848-1869* (Ithaca: Cornell University Press, 1978). Ample contrary evidence is assembled in the path-breaking study by Rosalyn Terborg-Penn, "Afro-Americans in the Struggle for Woman Suffrage," Ph.D. dissertation, Howard University, 1977, 73-90 and passim.
70. Davis, *Women, Race & Class*, 76, quoting Eleanor Flexner, *Century of Struggle: The Women's Rights Movement in the U. S.* (New York: Atheneum, 1973), 144. For the extension of this rhetoric of implied sexual danger into the era of lynch law, see Carby, "'On the Threshold of Woman's Era,'" 307-9.
71. *The Revolution*, 26 February 1868, 120-21; see Andolsen, *Daughters of Jefferson, Daughters of Bootblacks*, 18 and 70.
72. Stanton, et al., *History of Woman Suffrage*, 2:188; Mary Ann Shadd Cary in *Provincial Freeman*, 27 May 1854, Ripley, et al., *The Black Abolitionist Papers*, 2:286.

73. Foner, *Reconstruction*, 448.
74. Ibid., 447.
75. *National Anti-Slavery Standard*, 25 December 1869.
76. Stanton, et al., *History of Woman Suffrage*, 2:382.
77. Robert L. Allen with Pamela P. Allen, *Reluctant Reformers: Racism and Social Reform Movements in the United States* (Washington, D.C.: Howard University Press, 1983), 163. See William L. O'Neill, *Everyone Was Brave: The Rise and Fall of Feminism in America* (Chicago: Quadrangle Books, 1969), 275.
78. Catherine H. Birney, *The Grimké Sisters, Sarah and Angelina Grimké: The First American Women Advocates of Abolition and Woman's Rights* (Boston: Lee and Shepard, 1885), 211-13.
79. Stanton, et al., *History of Woman Suffrage*, 2:383.
80. See Eric Foner, *Reconstruction*, for Lincoln's last speech before his assassination in 1865, which recommended black male suffrage for "the very intelligent" and for those who served the Union as soldiers (74).
81. Stanton, et al., *History of Woman Suffrage*, 2:215-16.
82. See McPherson, *The Negro's Civil War*, 286.
83. Stanton, et al., *History of Woman Suffrage*, 2:224-25.
84. Quoted in Lillian O'Connor, *Pioneer Women Orators* (New York: Columbia University Press, 1954), 199.
85. *World*, 10 May 1867.
86. Stanton, et al., *History of Woman Suffrage*, 2:225.
87. Quoted in Davis, *Women, Race & Class*, 78.
88. Still, *The Underground Railroad*, 768.
89. Charles H. Coleman, *The Election of 1868: The Democratic Effort to Regain Control* (New York: Columbia University Studies in History, Economics and Public Law, 1933), 369, 384.
90. Foner, *Reconstruction*, 446.
91. Jones, *The Dispossessed*, 78.
92. Pauli Murray, "The Negro Woman in the Quest for Equality," in *The Female Experience: An American Documentary*, edited by Gerda Lerner (Indianapolis: Bobbs-Merrill, 1977), 592.
93. Stanton, et al., *History of Woman Suffrage*, 2:248.
94. Rosalyn Terborg-Penn, "Discrimination Against Afro-American Women in the Woman's Movement, 1830-1920," in *The Afro-American Woman: Struggles and Images*, edited by Sharon Harley and Rosalyn Terborg-Penn (Port Washington, NY: Kennikat Press, 1978), 25.
95. Still, *The Underground Railroad*, 772-73.
96. W.E.B. DuBois, *Black Reconstruction*, 638.
97. Horton, *Free People of Color*, 167. This argument is developed in chapter nine, "Race, Occupation, and Literacy in Reconstruction Washington, D.C." (185-97).
98. DuBois, *Black Reconstruction*, 195.
99. McPherson, *The Negro's Civil War*, 288-89.

100. "Address of the Colored Convention to the Citizens of Kansas," 1863, quoted in McPherson, *The Negro's Civil War*, 278-79. Eric Foner has argued that "blacks who commented on the [Fifteenth] Amendment preferred language explicitly guaranteeing all male citizens the right to vote. Not for the first time in the nation's history, their commitment to the ideal of equal citizenship exceeded that of other Americans" (*Reconstruction*, 447).

101. Stanton, et al., *History of Woman Suffrage*, 2:928.

102. See Sterling, *We Are Your Sisters*, 366n; Giddings, *When and Where I Enter*, 70.

103. Lerner, *The Female Experience*, 347-54.

104. Giddings, *When and Where I Enter*, 70-71.

105. Stanton, et al., *History of Woman Suffrage*, 3:828.

106. Giddings, *When and Where I Enter*, 75.

107. Sterling, *We Are Your Sisters*, 398-99.

108. William Pickens, "The Woman Voter Hits the Color Line," in *A Documentary History of the Negro People in the United States, 1910-1932*, edited by Herbert Aptheker (Secaucus, New Jersey: The Citadel Press, 1977), 305-9.

109. *NarBk*, 45; Kay Mills, *This Little Light of Mine: The Life of Fannie Lou Hamer* (New York: Dalton, 1993), 36-39.

110. Sterling, *We Are Your Sisters*, 397 and 411.

111. Davis, *Women, Race & Class*, 11, quoting from Karl Marx, *Grundrisse der Kritik der politischen Ökonomie*.

112. Stanton, et al., *History of Woman Suffrage*, 2:926-27.

Appendices

Early Ohio

I Am Pleading For My People
(To the Tune of "Auld Lang Syne")

I am pleading for my people—
A poor, down-trodden race,
Who dwell in freedom's boasted land,
With no abiding place.

I am pleading that my people
May have their rights astored;
For they have long been toiling,
And yet had no reward.

They are forced the crops to culture,
But not for them they yield,
Although both late and early
They labor in the field.

Whilst I bear upon my body
The scars of many a gash,
I am pleading for my people
Who groan beneath the lash.

I am pleading for the mothers
Who gaze in wild despair
Upon the hated auction-block,
And see their children there.

I feel for those in bondage—
Well may I feel for them;
I know how fiendish hearts can be
That sell their fellow-men.

Yet those oppressors steeped in guilt—
I still would have them live;
For I have learned of Jesus
To suffer and forgive.

I want no carnal weapons,
No enginery of death;
For I love not to hear the sound
Of war's tempestuous breath.

I do not ask you to engage
In death and bloody strife,
I do not dare insult my God
By asking for their life.

But while your kindest sympathies
To foreign lands do roam,
I would ask you to remember
Your own oppressed at home.

I plead with you to sympathize
With sighs and groans and scars,
And note how base the tyranny
Beneath the stripes and stars.

(*NarBk* 302-3)

Letter from Sojourner Truth to Amy Post

> [Ravenna, Ohio, a few days after
> the Woman's Rights Convention
> in Akron, Ohio, ca. 29 May 1851]

Dear Mrs. Post

I have arrived safe in Ohio. I got to Buffaloe on the evening of the same day I left you. I left Buffalo Friday night and arrived in Cleaveland on Saturday. Had a beautiful passage up the lake. Stopped among the colored friends and was treated with great kindness until Tuesday. Attended a meeting and sold three dollars worth of books. And on Tuesday went to Akron to the Convention where I found plenty of kind friends just like you & they gave me so many kind invitations I hardly knew which to accept of first. But I left Akron this morning and got to Hudson in time to take the cars for Ravenna where I came to the house of Mrs Skinner who was at the convention and invited me to her house to remain until Mrs Treat comes to make arrangement for me. The Lord has directed me to this quiet family, and here I shall probably remain some days. If there are any letters there for me direct them to Mrs Mary Ann B. Skinner Ravenna Portage Co. Ohio

I sold a good many books at the Convention and have thus far been greatly prospered—Tell dear Abby Fair [i. e., Thayer] I wish she was here and she must come in the fall with Garrison and friends

With love you and all kind friends Abby especialy and her dear mother and sister I remember all your kindness

This from your friend Sojourner Truth

To Mr Post I would say I have found some kind spirits like you. Dear Edmund I remember you still bathing you with water spiritually.

Sojourner

(The Isaac and Amy Post Family Papers, University of Rochester Library)

Letter from Sojourner Truth to William Lloyd Garrison

Salem [Ohio] August 28 [18]51

Dear Mr Garrison

Will you please inform me How how much I am now indebted to Mr Yerrington for the printing Please send Mr Yerrington's bill in full & all receipts upon it—I wish to know precisely how the matter stands Also please let me know how many books James W. Walker received of of Mr Yerington & how much money has been forwarded by Mr Walker on their account. Mr Walker says he sent the some money either to you or Mr Yerrington—but how much he could not tell when I saw him Please be particuler about Mr Yerrington account as I want to know how much I have got to pay him

I wrote to you for a report of the no of books on hand but have as yet received no answer. I am anxious to know just what is the amount of my indebtedness what my means for paying it.

I have sold but few books during the summer but now the way seems opened for me to do better at the conventions which are now being held— Will you please forward to me care of *John Skinner Ravenna* 600 of the books. My last box cost me $7.00 It was nearly half full of paper & shavings—Don't send so much next time I don't like to pay transportation on it

Since I gave the fifty dollars to you I have only made $30 which I sent to Mr. Hill—before this which I now send you. MKost of this last I received at the late anniversary of the Anti Slavery Society.

When you write, direct to the care of M. R. Robinson Salem Columbiana Co. Ohio—

I dont know but I shall stay in Ohio all winter I have heard that Mr Parker & his family have moved to Cleveland. So that I shall have a good comfortable place to winter.

Don't *fail to send the books without delay*—I may get out of books before they arrive—Pack them tight—Send by the most speedy safe conveyance Dont get any more books bound—I cant sell the bound volumes—I am now in Salem— My health is pretty good. I should like to hear from you all I saw Mrs Boyle at the anniversary— Mr. Boyle is boarding at Mr Bensons in Williamsburgh while Mrs. Boyle is visiting her friends in Ohio

Affectionately your Friend

Sojourner Truth

(Department of Rare Books and Manuscripts, Boston Public Library)

Two New York City Speeches

Address by a Slave Mother

Mrs. Sojourner Truth, a colored woman, and a slave until emancipated by this State in 1827, delivered a very interesting discourse last evening at the First Congregational Church in Sixth st. between 3rd and 4th avs.

Mrs. Truth, in consequence of her unhappy situation in early life, is totally uneducated, but speaks very fluently in tolerably correct and certainly very forcible style, and the latter quality of her address is rather enhanced by her occasional homely and therefore natural expressions. The audience was not so numerous as was expected, owing probably to a misdescription of the locality in the announcement, but those present (principally colored, with a sprinkling of white folks,) made a decent display in the body of the church, and listened with attention to the address and the proceedings.

These were opened by a Hymn well sung to the accompaniment of the organ, after which the Pastor of the Church, Rev. Mr. Tillon, offered a very excellent and appropriate Prayer.

Mrs. Truth being introduced to the meeting expressed some disappointment at the thinness of the meeting, but hoped a blessing would be extended to it by Him who had promised where two or three were gathered together in His name He would be in the midst. She felt thankful that she had lived to see the day she stood before her own people. She had held a great many meetings, and it seemed to her that the spirit of God had come upon her and enabled her to plead to her race, and not only to her own race but to the slave owners. She had always felt this difficulty: What was she to say to her own race on the subject of Slavery? They were the sufferers, and as strangers in the land, who had had little of God's footstool under their control.

She had been robbed of education—her rights; robbed of her children, her father, mother, sister and brother; yet she lived; and not only lived, but God lived in her. [Applause] Why was her race despised? What had they done that they should be hated? She had frequently asked this question, but never had received any answer. Was it because they were black? They had not made themselves black, and if they had done anything wrong why not let them know, that they might repent of that wrong. It had been said that the colored people were careless, and regardless of their rights and liberties; and this was partly true, though she hoped for better things in future. And why had they been careless and unheard? It was indeed hard that their oppressors should bind them hand and foot, and ask them why did they not run.

She was about 24 [i.e. 32?] years of age when she came to New-York, ignorant, and could not speak English very well; but she would not bow to the filth of the City. As a slave she had never been allowed to go anywhere, but then she went round with the lady who brought her here, and she was determined if she was despised she would go among the white people and learn all she could. She had known nothing of religion a few months before—not even that Jesus Christ was the Son of God. She found her religion as she was at her work, as she washed her dishes, and all she could say or think was Jesus. She wanted to get among her own colored people and teach them this, but they repulsed and shoved her off, yet she felt she wanted to be doing.

She used to go and hold prayer meetings at the houses of the people in the Five Points, then Chapel st, but she found they were always more inclined to hear great people, and she instanced the case of one colored woman who declining her prayers, said she had two or three ministers about. She (the Speaker) went off weeping while her dying sister was looked upon as a "glory of Zion."

She had learnt of Jesus and had become strengthened, and if they all had learned religion of Jesus and were of one mind, what would become of the slave-holder? How stood the case between them? The colored people had given to the white all their labor, their children, husbands, and all. She used to say, "why was I black, when if I was white I could have plenty of food and clothes?" But now she gloried in her color. She rejoiced in the color that God had been pleased to give her, and she was well satisfied with it.

She used to say she wished God would kill all the white people and not leave one for seed. Her mother had taught her to pray to make her master good, and she did so, but she was tied up and whipped till the blood trickled down her back and she used to think if she was God she would have made them good, and if God were she, she would not allow it. Such were her ideas, and how could she, or how could slaves be good while masters and mistresses were so bad? What she said to the whites she said to her own people.

She had been tied up and flogged; her husband's blood had flowed till it could be traced for a mile on the snow; and her father had been allowed to freeze to death. What could they say on the Day of Judgment in reply to the question "why do they hate us?" She did not wish unduly to ridicule the whites, but the blood and sweat and tears drawn from the black people were sufficient to cover the earth all over the United States. Still she desired to advocate their cause in a Christian spirit and in one of forgiveness, and had high hopes of their success; but she exhorted the people to stir and not let the white people have it all to themselves in their World's Conventions.

She deprecated the people who were satisfied with their enslaved lot, and as a colored woman, she wanted *all* the rights she was entitled to. Her address occupied a considerable time, and at its conclusion an interesting narrative of hers was handed round, and several copies sold for her benefit. She intends to hold other meetings in New-York, and bids fair to excite considerable interest and popularity.

(New York *Tribune*, 7 September 1853)

Lecture by Sojourner Truth

A respectable audience of colored people assembled at their church, in Anthony st., last evening, to listen to an address from a woman of their race, named Sojourner Truth. Pendant from the pulpit cushion was a banner of white satin, on which was inscribed:

> ASHTABULA COUNTY.
> Am I not a Woman and a Sister?
> [Kneeling figure of a woman with uplifted hands.]
> How long, O Lord! how long.
> A Million-and-a-half of American Women in chains.
> Shall we heed their wrongs?
> Will not a righteous God be avenged upon
> such a Nation as this?

At 8 o'clock, Sojourner arose and asked some person present who possessed the spirit of prayer to give utterance to it. An elderly colored man responded to her invitation.

Mrs. Truth commenced her discourse by singing a hymn beginning with

"I am pleading for my people,
A poor, down-trodden race"

After her hymn was finished, she detailed much of her practical experience as a slave. Some twenty-five years have elapsed since she received her freedom, but the brutality of the Dutch family, whose slave she was, had not been effaced by time. In her heathen despair she used to pray to God that he would kill all the white people. She prayed to God, but she did not know what or who the Divine being was. In her mind he was like Napoleon, or General Washington. When her soul was lighted by the influx of celestial love, her nature changed; where she had before showered curses, she called down blessings. She went on to talk of the condition of the colored people and their prospects. They were gradually being thrust out from every menial occupation by their white brethren; but she believed this was ominous of a better future. They were being prepared for some great change that would take place ere long. She was decidedly opposed to the colonization project; they must stay, and a short time would show that that was the best course. When the colored people were waiters, and did all the common and lower kinds of work the streets were clean; the servants scraped the dirt from the corners, swept out the gutters and half-way across the streets. Now, white folk clean boots, wait at table, lie about lazy, and beg cold victuals. The colored people did that sometimes too—but not to keep boarders on it! [Laughter.] Well, in those times, twenty-five or thirty years ago, the streets were kept nice and clean without costing the people a penny. Now the white people have taken it in hand, the dirt lies in the streets till it gets too thick, and flies all about into the shops and people's eyes, and then they sift water all over it, make it into mud, and that's what they do over and over again, without ever dreaming of such an easy thing as taking it away. In the course of time it becomes too thick, and too big a nuisance and then they go to work right straight off with picks and crow bars, and pull up the stones, above the dirt, and then go on again! [Laughter.] Not long ago nobody but colored people were coachmen and barbers, but now they have white Pompeys, with the livery coats on, and poor black Pompey goes to the wall. My colored brothers and sisters, there's a remedy for this; where I was lately lecturing out in Pennsylvania, the farmers wanted good men and women to work their farms on shares for them. Why can't you go out there?—and depend upon it, in the course of time you will get to be independent. She asked the audience to review the history of the past fifty years, and although the course was slow, the colored race had vastly improved, and that menial position to which nature seemed to have consigned them was rapidly being changed for the better. How long ago was it that a colored woman could address a white audience of a thousand people, and be listened to with respectful attention. These things were signs of the times. The papers rarely recorded crimes committed by her race, though they often teemed with those committed against them. She hoped her people would thus continue to put the white people to the blush. Mrs. Truth is something of a reformer in her way. She commented somewhat severely on the modern style of preaching the Gospel. The parsons went away into Egypt among the bones of dead Pharaohs and mummies, and talked about what happened thousands of years ago, but quite forgot that the living present around them teemed with the sternest realities. Many of the churches were big, lumbering things, covering up costly space and doing good to no one. While many of the citizens of this metropolis were living in low dens and sky-lighted garrets, these immense buildings, which would comfortably lodge them, were about one third filled once in the week, and for the other six days allowed to lie unoccupied, and a dead loss. And then the preachers, too, came in for a share of her satire. Big Greek-crammed, mouthing men, who, for many a long century, had been befogging the world, and getting its affairs into the most terrible snarl and confusion, and then when women came in to their assistance, cried "shame on the women!" They liked the fat and easy work of preaching and entangling too well, not to feel alarmed when woman attempted to set matters aright. She conceived that women were peculiarly adapted to fill the talking professions, and men should no longer unsex themselves by leaving the plow and the plane, for the pulpit and the platform. She hoped all of her sex would set to work and drag the world right side up, disentangle it from the snarl which men have willfully got it into, and set matters in general aright, and then keep them so. They could only do this by being united and resolutely putting their shoulders to the wheel.

A resolution supporting the Free Democracy ticket was then read and adopted.

After her address she did a considerable business in the way of selling the first part of her life, done up in some 120 pages, 12mo., to support the remainder.

(New York *Tribune*, 8 November 1853)

Civil War Era

The Valiant Soldiers
(To the Tune of "John Brown")

We are the valiant soldiers who've 'listed for the war;
We are fighting for the Union, we are fighting for the law;
We can shoot a rebel farther than a white man ever saw,
 As we go marching on.

 Chorus—
 Glory, glory, hallelujah! Glory, glory, hallelujah!
 Glory, glory, hallelujah, as we go marching on.

Look there above the center, where the flag is waving bright;
We are going out of slavery, we are bound for freedom's light;
We mean to show Jeff Davis how the Africans can fight,
 As we go marching on.—CHORUS

We are done with hoeing cotton, we are done with hoeing corn;
We are colored Yankee soldiers as sure as you are born.
When massa hears us shouting, he will think 'tis Gabriel's horn,
 As we go marching on.—CHORUS

They will have to pay us wages, the wages of their sin;
They will have to bow their foreheads to their colored kith and kin;
They will have to give us house-room, or the roof will tumble in,
 As we go marching on.—CHORUS

We hear the proclamation, massa, hush it as you will;
The birds will sing it to us, hopping on the cotton hill;
The possum up the gum tree could n't keep it still,
    As he went climbing on.—CHORUS

Father Abraham has spoken, and the message has been sent;
The prison doors have opened, and out the prisoners went
To join the sable army of African descent,
    As we go marching on.—CHORUS

(NarBk, 126)

Letter from Sojourner Truth to William Lloyd Garrison

Detroit April 11th '64

Mr Garrison
My dear friend

I have just been hearing of the Subscription Testimonial to George Thompson. I hope the friends of Liberty and the Uenion will pour out to him a cup of blessing—*full & running over*. My heart is glowing just now with the remembrance of his kindness to me in 1851. I had been publishing my Narrative and owed for the whole edition. A great debt for me! Every cent I could obtain went to pay it. You said to me "I am going with George Thompson on a lecturing tour. Come with us and you will have a good chance to dispose of your book". I replied that I had no money. You generously offered to bear my expenses and it was arranged that I should meet you in Springfield. On the appointed day I was there but you were not at the Hotel. I enquired for Mr Thompson & was shown into his room. He received & seated me with as much courtesy and cordiality as if I had been the highest lady in the land, informing me that you were too ill to leave home but if I would go with himself and Mr. Putnam it would be all the same. But said I, I have no money & Mr Garrison offered to pay my passage. "I'll bear your expenses Sojourner" said he. "Come with us!" And so I went. He accompanied me to the cars and carried my bag. At the Hotel tables he seated me beside him-self & never seemed to know that I was poor and a black woman At the meetings he reccommended my books. "Sojourner Truth has a narrative of her life—'Tis very interesting. Buy largely friends"! Good man! genuine gentleman! God bless George Thompson! the great hearted friend of my race.

Many have been kind to me. Among others, yourself, Oliver Johnson, Gerrit Smith, Dr Boyle, & Mr Hill. When I think of you all, a great blessing swells my soul—it only amounts to empty thanks here but when I reach my father's house, I'll return you "full measure, heaped up and running over.

Mr Garrison you say that small sums will be welcome for this testimonial—"the more that participate the better". I want to send a little—my mite—just to have a hand in it. So I enclose $2. made from my shadow. Put it beside Gerrit Smith's 200—that will make $202

Your friend
Sojourner Truth

P. S. Mr Thompson once promised me his picture—Will you tell him that I would be very glad to receive it. Perhaps he would like to see old Sojourner once more—so I enclose my shadow.

(Department of Rare Books and Manuscripts, Boston Public Library)

Equal Rights Speeches

(Truth's speeches at the Equal Rights Association Convention in New York City at the Church of the Puritans, 9-10 May 1867, as reported in *National Anti-Slavery Standard*, 1 June 1867)

[Thursday evening, 9 May]

Sojourner Truth was introduced and said:

My friends, I am rejoiced that you are glad, but I don't know how you will feel when I get through, I come from another field—the country of the slave. They have got their rights—so much good luck: now what is to be done about it? I feel that I have got as much responsibility as anybody else. I have got as good rights as anybody. There is a great stir about colored men getting their rights, but not a word about the colored women; and if colored men get their rights, and not colored women get theirs, there will be a bad time about it. So I am for keeping the thing going while things are stirring; because if we wait till it is still, it will take a great while to get it going again. White women are a great deal smarter, and know more than colored women, while colored women do not know scarcely anything. They go out washing, which is about as high as a colored woman gets, and their men go about idle, strutting up and down; and when the women come home, they ask for their money and take it all, and then scold because there is no food. I want you to consider on that, chil'n. I want women to have their rights. In the Courts women have no right, no voice; nobody speaks for them. I wish woman to have her voice there among the pettifoggers. If it is not a fit place for women, it is unfit for men to be there. I am above 80 years old; it is about time for me to be going. But I suppose I am kept here because something remains for me to do; I suppose I am yet to help break the chain. I have done a great deal of work; as much as a man, but did not get so much pay. I used to work in the field and bind grain, keeping up with the cradler; but men never doing no more, got twice as much pay. So with the German women. They work in the field and do as much work, but do not get the pay. We do as much, we eat as much, we want as much. I suppose I am about the only colored woman that goes about to speak for the rights of the colored woman. I want to keep the thing stirring, now that the ice is broken. What we want is a little money. You men know that you get as much again as women when you write, or for what you do. When we get our rights, we shall not have to come to you for money, for then we shall have money enough of our own. It is a good consolation to know that when we have got this we shall not be coming to you any more. You have been having our right so long, that you think, like a slaveholder, that you own us. I know that it is hard for one who has held the reins for so long to give up; it cuts like a knife. It will feel all the better when it closes up again. I have been in Washington about three years, seeing about these colored people. Now colored men have a right to vote; and what I want is to have colored women have the right to vote. There ought to be equal rights more than ever, since colored people have got their freedom. I am going to talk several times while I am here; so now I will do a little singing. I have not heard any singing since I came here. Accordingly, suiting the action to the word, Sojourner sang, "We are going home." There, children, said she, we shall rest from all our labors; first do all we have to do here. There I am determined to go, not to stop till I get there to that beautiful place, and I do not mean to stop till I get there.

[Friday morning, 10 May]

Sojourner Truth again addressed the meeting. She said: Well, children—I know it is hard for men to give up entirely. They must run in the old track. (Laughter.) I was amused how men speaks up for one another. They cannot bear that a woman should say anything about the man, but they will stand here and take up the time in man's cause. But we are going, tremble or no tremble. (Laughter.) Men is trying to help us. I know that all—the spirit they have got; and they cannot help us much until some of the spirit is taken out of them that belongs among the women. (Laughter.) Men have got their rights, and women has not got their rights. That is the trouble. When woman gets her rights man will be right. How beautiful that will be. Then it will be peace on earth and good will to men. (Laughter and applause.) But it cannot be that until it be right. I am glad that men got here. They have to do it. I know why they edge off, for there is a power they cannot gainsay or resist. It will come. A woman said to me, "Do you think it will come in ten or twenty years?" Yes, it will come quickly. (Applause.) It must come. (Applause.) And now then the waters is troubled and now is the time to step into the pool. There is a great deal now with the minds, and now is the time to start forth. I was going to say that it was said to me some time ago that "a woman was not fit to have any rule. Do you want women to rule? They ain't fit. Don't you know that a woman had seven devils in her, and do you suppose that a man should put her to rule in the government?" "Seven devils is of no account"—(laughter)—said I, "just behold, the man had a legion." (Loud laughter.) They never thought about that. A man had a legion—(laughter)—and the devils didn't know where to go. That was the trouble. (Laughter and applause.) They asked if they might get among the swine; they thought it was about as good a place as where they came from. (Laughter.) Why didn't the devils ask to go among the sheep? (Laughter.) But no. But that may have been selfish of the devils—(laughter)—and certainly a man has a little touch of that selfishness that don't want to give the women their right. I have been twitted many times about this, and I thought how queer it is that men don't think of that. Never mind. Look at the woman after all, the woman when they were cast out, and see how much she loved Jesus, and how she followed, and stood and waited for him. That was the faithfulness of a woman. You cannot find any faith of man like that, go where you will. After those devils had gone out of the man he wanted to follow Jesus. But what did Jesus say? He said: "Better go back and tell what had been done for you!" (Laughter.) He didn't seem as he wanted him to come along right away. (Laughter.) He was to be clean after that. Look at that and look at the woman; what a mighty courage. When Mary stood and looked for Jesus, the man looked and didn't stop long enough to find out whether He was there or not; but when the woman stood there (blessed be God, I think I can see her!) she staid until she knew where He was, and said: "I will carry Him away!" Was woman true? She guarded it. The truth will reign triumphant. I want to see, before I leave here—I want to see equality. I want to see women have their rights, and then there will be no more war. All the fighting has been for selfishness. They wanted something more than their own, or to hold something that was not their own; but when we have woman's rights, there is nothing to fight for. I have got all I want, and you have got all you want, and what do you fight for? All the battles that have ever been was for selfishness—for a right that belonged to some one else, or fighting for his own right. The great fight was to keep the rights of the poor colored people. That made a great battle. And now I hope that this will be the last battle that will be in the world. Fighting for rights. And there never will be a fight without it is a fight for rights. See how beautiful it is! It covers the whole ground. We ought to have it all finished up now. Let us finish it up so that there be no more fighting. I have faith in God, and there is truth in humanity. Be strong women! blush not! tremble not! I know men will get up and brat, brat, brat, brat (laughter) about something which does not amount to anything except talk. We want to carry the point to one particular thing, and that is woman's rights, for nobody has any business with a right that belongs to her. I can make use of my own right. I want the same use of the same right. Do you want it? Then get it. If men had not taken something that did not belong to them they would not fear. But they tremble! They dodge! (Laughter.) We will have nothing owned by anybody. That is the time you will be a man, if you don't get scared before it goes to parties. (Laughter.) I want you to look at it and be men and women. Men speak great lies, and it has made a great sore, but it will soon heal up. For I know when men, good men, discuss sometimes, that they say something or another and then take it half back. You must make a little allowance. I hear them say good enough at first, but then there was a going back a little more like the old times. It is hard for them to get out of it. Now we will help you out, if you want to get out. I want you to keep a good faith and good courage. And I am going round after I get my business settled and get more equality. People in the North, I am going round to lecture on human rights. I will shake every place I go to. (Loud laughter and applause.)

[Friday evening, 10 May]

Sojourner Truth made a speech, in which she dwelt upon the circumstance that there was no interruption at the meeting, and that all seemed to acquiesce in the principles of the meeting, and that this was a good sign. She would like to go up to the polls herself. (Laughter.) She did not believe it to be very hard work to vote, and did not see why women could not do it. (Laughter.)

Bibliography

Editions of Narrative

[Truth, Sojourner with Olive Gilbert]. *Narrative of Sojourner Truth, A Northern Slave Emancipated From Bodily Servitude By The State of New York in 1828.* Boston: Printed for the author, 1850.

[Truth, Sojourner with Olive Gilbert]. *Narrative of Sojourner Truth.* Edited by Margaret Washington. New York: Vintage Classics, 1993.

[Truth, Sojourner with Olive Gilbert and Frances Titus]. *Narrative of Sojourner Truth; A Bondswoman of Olden Time, Emancipated by the New York Legislature in the Early Part of the Present Century; With a History of Her Labors and Correspondence Drawn from Her "Book of Life."* New York: Arno Press and The New York Times, 1968 [1878].

[Truth, Sojourner with Olive Gilbert and Frances Titus]. *Narrative of Sojourner Truth: A Bondswoman of Olden Time, Emancipated by the New York Legislature in the Early Part of the Present Century With a History of Her Labors and Correspondence Drawn from her Book of Life.* Edited by Sterling Stuckey. Chicago: Johnson Publishing Company, 1970 [1878].

[Truth, Sojourner, Olive Gilbert and Frances Titus]. *Narrative of Sojourner Truth; A Bondswoman of Olden Time, With a History of Her Labors and Correspondence Drawn from Her "Book of Life."* New York: Oxford University Press, 1991 [1878].

Manuscript Collections

Department of Rare Books and Manuscripts, Boston Public Library, Boston, Massachusetts.

The Isaac and Amy Post Family Papers, Department of Rare Books and Special Collections, University of Rochester Library, Rochester, New York.

Newspapers

Anti-Slavery Bugle (Salem, Ohio)
  3 May 1851
17 May 1851
21 June 1851
13 December 1851
28 August 1852
  4 September 1852
  8 November 1856

Colored American (New York City, New York)
13 April 1837
23 November 1839
28 March 1840

Colored Citizen (Topeka, Kansas)
11 October 1879

The Commonwealth (Boston, Massachusetts)
  3 July 1863
12 August 1864
19 August 1864

Daily Inter-Ocean (Chicago, Illinois)
13 August 1879
25 October 1879

Daily Journal (Battle Creek, Michigan)
25 October 1904

Enquirer and Evening News (Battle Creek)
29 May 1929

Evening Bulletin (Philadelphia, Pennsylvania)
28 July 1876

Frederick Douglass' Paper (Rochester, New York)
  9 November 1855

Globe-Democrat (St Louis, Missouri)
  24 April 1879

Herald (New York City, New York)
  25 October 1850
  26 October 1850
  28 October 1850

Journal (Orange, New Jersey)
  29 July 1876

The Liberator (Boston, Massachusetts)
  6 August 1836
  13 August 1841
  3 January 1851
  28 February 1851
  4 April 1851
  13 June 1851
  10 September 1852
  3 September 1862
  3 December 1862
  23 December 1864

National Anti-Slavery Standard (New York City, New York)
  28 November 1850
  8 May 1851
  10 September 1853
  3 November 1860
  3 September 1862
  2 May 1863
  4 July 1863
  17 December 1864
  27 April 1867
  27 November 1869
  18 December 1869
  25 December 1869

North Star (Rochester, New York)
  10 August 1848
  20 October 1848

Pennsylvania Freeman (Philadelphia, Pennsylvania)
  29 April 1852
   4 September 1852
  12 May 1853

Post (Detroit, Michigan)
  12 January 1869

Provincial Freeman (Windsor, Canada)
  27 May 1854

The Revolution
  26 February 1868

Topeka Daily Capital (Topeka, Kansas)
   2 May 1889

Tribune (New York City, New York)
  26 October 1850
   7 September 1853
  16 September 1853
   8 November 1853
   8 September 1865
   9 May 1867
  13 March 1871
   7 December 1878
  27 November 1883

Woman's Journal (Boston, Massachusetts)
   5 August 1876

World (New York, New York)
  10 May 1867

Zion's Herald (Boston, Massachusetts)
  23 February 1871

Books

Allen, Robert L. with Pamela P. Allen. *Reluctant Reformers: Racism and Social Reform Movements in the United States.* Washington, D.C.: Howard University Press, 1983.
Andolsen, Barbara Hilkert. *"Daughters of Jefferson, Daughters of Bootblacks": Racism and American Feminism.* Macon: Mercer University Press, 1986.

Andrews, William L. *To Tell A Free Story: The First Century of Afro-American Autobiography, 1760-1865.* Chicago: University of Illinois Press, 1988.

———. ed. *Sisters of the Spirit: Three Black Women's Autobiographies of the Nineteenth Century.* Bloomington: Indiana University Press, 1986.

Athearn, Robert G. *In Search of Canaan: Black Migration to Kansas 1879-80.* Lawrence: The Regents Press of Kansas, 1978.

Baker, Houston A., Jr. *Blues, Ideology, and Afro-American Literature: A Vernacular Theory.* Chicago: University of Chicago Press, 1984.

Bentley, George R. *A History of the Freedmen's Bureau.* New York: Farrar, Straus and Giroux, 1974.

Birney, Catherine H. *The Grimké Sisters, Sarah and Angelina Grimké: The First American Women Advocates of Abolition and Woman's Rights.* Boston: Lee and Shepard, 1885.

Bradford, Sarah. *Harriet Tubman: The Moses of Her People.* Secaucus, New Jersey: The Citadel Press, 1974 [1886].

Braude, Ann. *Radical Spirits: Spiritualism and Women's Rights in Nineteenth-Century America.* Boston: Beacon Press, 1989.

Brown, Letitia Woods. *Free Negroes in the District of Columbia 1790-1846.* New York: Oxford University Press, 1972.

Burritt, Elihu. *The Learned Blacksmith: The Letters and Journals of Elihu Burritt.* Edited by Merle Curti. New York: Wilson-Erickson, 1937.

Carby, Hazel V. *Reconstructing Womanhood: The Emergence of the Afro-American Woman Novelist.* New York: Oxford University Press, 1987.

A Chapter in The History of Robert Matthews, Otherwise Known as Matthias, The Prophet, Together with His Trial for The Murder of Mr. Pierson. Anonymous pamphlet, Utica,1835.

Child, Lydia Maria. *Letters of Lydia Maria Child.* Boston: Houghton Mifflin, 1883.

Clearwater, Alphonso T. *The History of Ulster County, New York.* New York: W. J. Van Deusen, 1967.

Coleman, Charles H. *The Election of 1868: The Democratic Effort to Regain Control.* New York: Columbia University Studies in History, Economics and Public Law, 1933.

Colman, Lucy N. *Reminiscences.* Buffalo: H. L. Green, 1891.

Conrad, Earl. *Harriet Tubman.* New York: Paul S. Eriksson, 1969.

Cooper, Anna Julia. *A Voice from the South; By a Black Woman of the South.* Xenia, Ohio, 1892.

Cooper, James Fenimore. *Satanstoe.* Lincoln: University of Nebraska Press, 1962.

The Cries of New-York, with Fifteen Illustrations, Drawn from Life by a Distinguished Artist; [with] the Poetry by Frances S. Osgood. New York: John Doggett, Jr., 1846.

Cross, Whitney R. *The Burned-over District: The Social and Intellectual History of Enthusiastic Religion in Western New York, 1800-1850.* New York: Cornell University Press, 1950.

Curry, Leonard P. *The Free Black in Urban America 1800-1850: The Shadow of the Dream.* Chicago: University of Chicago Press, 1981.

Davis, Angela Y. *Women, Race & Class.* New York: Vintage Books, 1983.

Dickens, Charles. *American Notes.* Gloucester, Massachusetts: Peter Smith, 1968.

Douglas, Ann. *The Feminization of American Culture.* New York: Avon Books, 1977.

Douglass, Frederick. *Life and Times of Frederick Douglass, written by himself.* New York: Pathway Press, 1941.

———. *Life and Writings of Frederick Douglass.* 5 vols. Edited by Philip S. Foner. New York: International Publishers, 1950-75.

———. *My Bondage and My Freedom.* Edited by Philip S. Foner. New York: Dover Publications, 1969.

———. *Narrative of the Life of Frederick Douglass, an African Slave, Written by Himself.* Edited by Houston A. Baker, Jr. New York: Penguin Books, 1982.

DuBois, W.E.B. *Black Reconstruction.* Millwood, New York: Kraus-Thomson, 1976.

DuBois, Ellen Carol. *Feminism and Suffrage: The Emergence of an Independent Women's Movement in America, 1848-1869.* Ithaca: Cornell University Press, 1978.

Elaw, Zilpha. *Memoirs of the Life, Religious Experience, Ministerial Travels and Labours of Mrs. Zilpha Elaw, An American Female of Colour; Together with Some Account of the Great Religious Revivals in America.* In *Sisters of the Spirit: Three Black Women's Autobiographies of the Nineteenth Century.* Edited by William L. Andrews. Bloomington: Indiana University Press, 1986.

[Elizabeth] *Elizabeth: A Colored Minister of the Gospel Born in Slavery.* In *Black Women in Nineteenth-Century American Life.* Edited by Bert J. Loewenberg and Ruth Bogin. University Park: Pennsylvania State University Press, 1978.

Flexner, Eleanor. *Century of Struggle: The Women's Rights Movement in the U. S.* New York: Atheneum, 1973.

Foner, Eric. *Reconstruction: America's Unfinished Revolution 1863-1877.* New York: Harper & Row, 1988.

Foote, Julia A. J. *A Brand Plucked from the Fire: An Autobiographical Sketch by Mrs. Julia A. J. Foote.* In *Sisters of the Spirit: Three Black Women's Autobiographies of the Nineteenth Century.* Edited by William L. Andrews. Bloomington: Indiana University Press, 1986.

Forten, Charlotte. *The Journal of Charlotte Forten.* Edited by Ray Allen Billington. New York: Collier Books, 1961.

Foster, Frances Smith. *Witnessing Slavery: The Development of Ante-bellum Slave Narratives.* Westport: Greenwood Press, 1979.

————. *Written By Herself: Literary Production by African American Women, 1746-1892.* Bloomington: Indiana University Press, 1993.

Garrison, William Lloyd. *The Letters of William Lloyd Garrison.* Edited by Walter M. Merrill and Louis Ruchames. 6 vols. Cambridge: Harvard University Press, 1971-81.

Gates, Henry Louis, Jr. *The Signifying Monkey: A Theory of Afro-American Literary Criticism.* New York: Oxford University Press, 1988.

Giddings, Paula. *When and Where I Enter: The Impact of Black Women on Race and Sex in America.* New York: William Morrow and Co., 1984.

Gold, Arthur and Robert Fizdale. *The Divine Sarah: A Life of Sarah Bernhardt.* New York: Vintage Books, 1992.

Grant, Anne MacVicar. *Memoirs of An American Lady. With Sketches of Manners and Scenes in America As They Existed Previous to the Revolution.* New York: Dodd, Mead and Co., 1903.

Gutman, Herbert J. *The Black Family in Slavery and Freedom, 1750-1925.* New York: Pantheon Books, 1976.

Hansen, Debra Gold. *Strained Sisterhood: Gender and Class in the Boston Female Anti-Slavery Society.* Amherst: University of Massachusetts, 1993.

Harper, Frances Ellen Watkins. *A Brighter Coming Day: A Frances Ellen Watkins Harper Reader.* Edited by Frances Smith Foster. New York: The Feminist Press, 1990.

Haviland, Laura S. *A Woman's Life-Work.* Chicago: Publishing Association of Friends, 1889.

Hedrick, Joan D. *Harriet Beecher Stowe: A Life.* New York: Oxford University Press, 1994.

Hewitt, Nancy. *Women's Activism and Social Change: Rochester, New York, 1822-1872.* Ithaca: Cornell University Press, 1984.

Higginson, Thomas Wentworth. *Army Life in a Black Regiment.* East Lansing: Michigan State University Press, 1960 [1870].

Holley, Sallie. *A Life for Liberty: Anti-Slavery and Other Letters of Sallie Holley.* Edited by John White Chadwick. New York: G.P. Putnam's Sons, 1899.

hooks, bell. *Ain't I A Woman: Black Women and Feminism*. Boston: South End Press, 1981.

———. *Black Looks: Race and Representation*. Boston: South End Press, 1992.

———. *Talking Back: Thinking Feminist, Thinking Black*. Boston: South End Press, 1989.

———. *Yearning: Race, Gender, and Cultural Politics*. Boston: South End Press, 1990.

Horton, James Oliver. *Free People of Color: Inside the African American Community*. Washington, D.C.: Smithsonian Institution Press, 1993.

Hurston, Zora Neale. *Their Eyes Were Watching God*. New York: Harper & Row, 1990 [1937].

Jackson, Rebecca Cox. *Gifts of Power: The Writings of Rebecca Jackson, Black Visionary, Shaker Eldress*. Edited by Jean McMahon Humez. Amherst: University of Massachusetts Press, 1981.

Jacobs, Harriet A. *Incidents in the Life of a Slave Girl, Written by Herself*. Edited by Jean Fagan Yellin. Cambridge: Harvard University Press, 1987.

James, Henry. *William Wetmore Story and His Friends*. 2 vols. Boston: Houghton, Mifflin & Co., 1904.

Jones, Gayl. *Liberating Voices: Oral Tradition in African American Literature*. New York: Penguin Books, 1991.

Jones, Jacqueline. *The Dispossessed: America's Underclasses from the Civil War to the Present*. New York: Basic Books, 1992.

———. *Labor of Love, Labor of Sorrow: Black Women, Work, and the Family from Slavery to the Present*. New York: Basic Books, 1985.

Keckley, Elizabeth. *Behind The Scenes; or Thirty Years a Slave, and Four Years in the White House*. New York: G. W. Carleton & Co., 1868.

Kemble, Frances Anne. *Journal of a Residence on a Georgian Plantation in 1838-1839*. London: Longman, Green, 1863.

Lee, Jarena. *The Life and Religious Experience of Jarena Lee, A Coloured Lady, Giving an Account of her Call to Preach the Gospel*. In *Sisters of the Spirit: Three Black Women's Autobiographies of the Nineteenth Century*. Edited by William L. Andrews. Bloomington: Indiana University Press, 1986.

Lerner, Gerda, ed. *Black Women in White America: A Documentary History*. New York: Vintage Books, 1992.

———, ed. *The Female Experience: An American Documentary*. Indianapolis: Bobbs-Merrill, 1977.

———. *The Grimké Sisters from South Carolina: Pioneers for Woman's Rights and Abolition*. New York: Schocken Books, 1971.

Levine, Lawrence W. *Black Culture and Black Consciousness: Afro-American Folk Thought from Slavery to Freedom.* New York: Oxford University Press, 1977.

Lincoln, C. Eric and Lawrence H. Mamiya. *The Black Church in the African American Experience.* Durham: Duke University Press, 1990.

Lochrie, Karma. *Margery Kempe and Translations of the Flesh.* Philadelphia: University of Pennsylvania Press, 1991.

Loewenberg, Bert J. and Ruth Bogin, eds. *Black Women in Nineteenth-Century American Life.* University Park: Pennsylvania State University Press, 1978.

Lorde, Audre. *Sister Outsider: Essays & Speeches.* Freedom, California: The Crossing Press, 1984.

Lott, Eric. *Love and Theft: Blackface Minstrelsy and the American Working Class.* New York: Oxford University Press, 1993.

McBee, Alice Eaton, 2nd. *From Utopia to Florence: The Story of a Transcendentalist Community in Northampton, Mass., 1830-1852.* Northampton: Smith College Studies in History, 1947.

McPherson, James M. *The Negro's Civil War: How American Blacks Felt and Acted During the War For the Union.* New York: Ballantine Books, 1991.

Mabee, Carlton and Susan Mabee Newhouse. *Sojourner Truth: Slave, Prophet, Legend.* New York: New York University Press, 1993.

Margherita, Gayle. *The Romance of Origins: Language and Sexual Difference in Middle English Literature.* Philadelphia: University of Pennsylvania Press, 1994.

Matthews, Margaret. *Matthias, by His Wife: With Notes on the Book of Mr. Stone on Matthias.* New York, 1835.

Matthews, Robert. *Memoirs of Matthias the Prophet.* New York, 1835.

Mills, Kay. *This Little Light of Mine: The Life of Fannie Lou Hamer.* New York: Dalton, 1993.

Montgomery, Janey Weinhold. *A Comparative Analysis of the Rhetoric of Two Negro Women Orators—Sojourner Truth and Frances E. Watkins Harper.* Hays: Fort Hays Kansas State College, 1968.

The New York Street Cries, in Rhyme. New York: Mahlon Day, ca. 1840.

O'Connor, Lillian. *Pioneer Women Orators.* New York: Columbia University Press, 1954.

O'Neill, William L. *Everyone Was Brave: The Rise and Fall of Feminism in America.* Chicago: Quadrangle Books, 1969.

Olmsted, Frederick Law. *A Journey in the Back Country.* New York, 1860.

Ottley, Roi and William J. Weatherby, eds. *The Negro in New York: An Informal Social History.* Dobbs Ferry, New York: Oceana Publications, 1967.

Painter, Nell Irvin. *Exodusters: Black Migration to Kansas after Reconstruction.* New York: Alfred A. Knopf, 1977.

Payne, Daniel. *Recollections of Seventy Years.* Nashville: A.M.E. Sunday School Union, 1888.

Pease, Jane H. and William H. Pease. *They Who Would Be Free: Blacks' Search for Freedom, 1830-1861.* New York: Atheneum, 1974.

Perry, Lewis. *Radical Abolitionism: Anarchy and the Government of God in Anti-Slavery Thought.* Ithaca: Cornell University Press, 1973.

Piersen, William D. *Black Yankees: The Development of an Afro-American Subculture in Eighteenth-Century New England.* Amherst: The University of Massachusetts Press, 1988.

Quarles, Benjamin. *The Negro in the Civil War.* Boston: Little, Brown and Co., 1953.

Rich, Adrienne. *On Lies, Secrets, and Silence.* New York: Norton, 1979.

Ripley, C. Peter, et al., eds. *The Black Abolitionist Papers.* 5 vols. Chapel Hill: University of North Carolina Press, 1985.

Sernett, Milton C., ed. *Afro-American Religious History: A Documentary Witness.* Durham: Duke University Press, 1985.

Sheffield, Charles A. *The History of Florence, Massachusetts.* Florence: The Editor, 1895

Sherman, Joan R. *Invisible Poets: Afro-Americans of the Nineteenth Century.* 2nd ed. Chicago: University of Illinois Press, 1989.

Shipps, Jan. *Mormonism: The Story of a New Religious Tradition.* Chicago: University of Illinois Press, 1985.

Smith, Amanda Berry. *An Autobiography: The Story of the Lord's Dealings with Mrs. Amanda Smith the Colored Evangelist.* Chicago: Meyer & Brother, 1893.

Smith, James McCune. *Introduction to a Memorial Discourse; by Rev. Henry Highland Garnet.* Philadelphia: Joseph M. Wilson, 1865.

[Smith, Joseph]. *History of the Church of Jesus Christ of Latter-Day Saints.* Salt Lake City: Published by the Church, 1904.

Smith-Rosenberg, Carroll. *Disorderly Conduct: Visions of Gender in Victorian America.* New York: Alfred A. Knopf, 1985.

Stanton, Elizabeth Cady. *Eighty Years and More: Reminiscences 1815-1897.* New York: Schocken Books, 1917.

Stanton, Elizabeth Cady, et al., eds. *History of Woman Suffrage.* 6 vols. New York: Fowler & Wells, 1881-1922.

Sterling, Dorothy, ed. *We Are Your Sisters: Black Women in the Nineteenth Century.* New York: W. W. Norton, 1984.

Stetson, Erlene, ed. *Black Sister: Poetry by Black American Women, 1746-1980.* Bloomington: Indiana University Press, 1981.

Stewart, Maria W. *Maria W. Stewart, America's First Black Woman Political Writer: Essays and Speeches.* Edited by Marilyn Richardson. Bloomington: Indiana University Press, 1987.

——. *Meditations.* 1879.

Still, William. *The Underground Railroad.* Philadelphia: Porter & Coates, 1872.

Stone, William L. *Matthias and His Impostures; or the Progress of Fanaticism.* New York, 1835.

Stuckey, Sterling. *Going Through the Storm: The Influence of African American Art in History.* New York: Oxford University Press, 1994.

——. *Slave Culture: Nationalist Theory and the Foundations of Black America.* New York: Oxford University Press, 1987.

Taylor, Susie King. *Reminiscences of My Life In Camp with the 33d United States Colored Troops Late 1st S. C. Volunteers.* Boston: Published by the Author, 1902.

Terborg-Penn, Rosalyn. "Afro-Americans in the Struggle for Woman Suffrage." Ph.D. dissertation, Howard University, 1977. Ann Arbor, University Microfilms International.

Thompson, E.P. *The Making of the English Working Class.* New York: Vintage Books, 1966.

Thornbrough, Emma Lou. *The Negro in Indiana Before 1900: A Study of a Minority.* Bloomington: Indiana University Press, 1993.

Turning The World Upside Down: The Anti-Slavery Convention of American Women Held in New York City, May 9-12, 1837. New York: The Feminist Press, 1987.

Vale, Gilbert. *Fanaticism; Its Source and Influence, Illustrated by the Simple Narrative of Isabella, in the case of Matthias, Mr. and Mrs. B. Folger, Mr. Pierson, Mr. Mills, Catherine, Isabella, &c. &c.* New York: Published by G. Vale, 1835.

Walker, Alice. *The Color Purple.* New York: Pocket Books, 1982.

Washington, Mary Helen. *Invented Lives: Narratives of Black Women 1860-1960.* New York: Anchor Doubleday, 1987.

Wheatley, Phillis. *Poems on Various Subjects, Religious and Moral.* London: A. Bell, 1773.

Williams, Sherley Anne. *Some One Sweet Angel Chile.* New York: William Morrow, 1982.

Wood, Norman B. *The White Side of a Black Subject Enlarged and Brought Down to Date: A Vindication of the Afro-American Race.* Chicago: American Publishing House, 1897.

Woodward, Helen Beal. *The Bold Women.* New York: Farrar, Straus and Young, 1953.

Wyman, Lillie Buffum Chace. *American Chivalry.* Boston: Clarke, 1913.

Yee, Shirley J. *Black Women Abolitionists: A Study in Activism, 1828-1860.* Knoxville: University of Tennessee Press, 1992.

Yellin, Jean Fagan. *Women & Sisters: The Antislavery Feminists in American Culture.* New Haven: Yale University Press, 1989.

Articles

Alford, Terry. "Islam." In *Dictionary of Afro-American Slavery.* Edited by Randall M. Miller and John D. Smith. Westport: Greenwood Press, 1988.

Allen, Pamela. "Woman Suffrage: Feminism and White Supremacy." In *Reluctant Reformers: Racism and Social Reform Movements in the United States.* By Robert L. Allen with Pamela P. Allen. Washington, D.C.: Howard University Press, 1983.

Andrews, William L. "Reunion in the Postbellum Slave Narrative: Frederick Douglass and Elizabeth Keckley." *Black American Literature Forum* 23, no. 1 (Spring 1989).

Bolster, W. Jeffrey "'To Feel Like a Man': Black Seamen in the Northern States, 1800-1860." *Journal of American History* 76 (March 1990).

Brown, Elsa Barkley. "Mothers of Mind." *Sage* 6, no. 1 (Summer 1989).

———. "Womanist Consciousness: Maggie Lena Walker and the Independent Order of St. Luke." *Signs: Journal of Women in Culture and Society* 14 (Spring 1989).

Carby, Hazel V. "'On the Threshold of Woman's Era': Lynching, Empire, and Sexuality in Black Feminist Theory." In *"Race," Writing, and Difference.* Edited by Henry Louis Gates, Jr. Chicago: University of Chicago Press, 1986.

———. "Policing the Black Woman's Body in an Urban Context." *Critical Inquiry* 18 (Summer 1992).

Collins, Kathleen. "Shadow and Substance: Sojourner Truth." *History of Photography* 7, no. 3 (July-September 1983).

Crossthwaite, Jane. "Women and Wild Beasts: Versions of the Exotic in Nineteenth Century American Art." *Southern Humanities Review* 19 (1985).

Davis, Angela Y. "Black Women and Music: A Historical Legacy of Struggle." In *Wild Women in the Whirlwind: Afra-American Culture and the Contemporary Literary Renaissance.* Edited by Joanne M. Braxton and Andrée Nicola McLaughlin. New Brunswick: Rutgers University Press, 1990.

———. "Reflections on the Black Woman's Role in the Community of Slaves." *Black Scholar* 3 (December 1971).

Douglass Frederick. "What I Found at the Northampton Association." In *The History of Florence, Massachusetts.* By Charles A. Sheffield. Florence: The Editor, 1895.

Fleming, John E. "Slavery, Civil War and Reconstruction: A Study of Black Women in Microcosm." *Negro History Bulletin* 38, no. 6 (August-September 1975).

Foster, Frances Smith. "Adding Color and Contour to Early American Self-Portraitures: Autobiographical Writings of Afro-American Women." In *Conjuring: Black Women, Fiction, and Literary Tradition.* Edited by Marjorie Pryse and Hortense J. Spillers. Bloomington: Indiana University Press, 1985.

Franchot, Jenny. "The Punishment of Esther: Frederick Douglass and the Construction of the Feminine." In *Frederick Douglass: New Literary and Historical Essays.* Edited by Eric J. Sundquist. Cambridge: Cambridge University Press, 1990.

Gwin, Minrose C. "Green-eyed Monsters of the Slavocracy: Jealous Mistresses in Two Slave Narratives." In *Conjuring: Black Women, Fiction, and Literary Tradition.* Edited by Marjorie Pryse and Hortense J. Spillers. Bloomington: Indiana University Press, 1985.

Hamer, Fannie Lou. "The Special Plight and the Role of Black Woman." In *Black Women in White America: A Documentary History.* Edited by Gerda Lerner. New York: Vintage Books, 1992.

Harley, Sharon. "Northern Black Female Workers: Jacksonian Era." In *The Afro-American Woman: Struggles and Images.* Edited by Sharon Harley and Rosalyn Terborg-Penn. Port Washington, New York: Kennikat Press, 1978.

Hewitt, Nancy. "Amy Kirby Post." *University of Rochester Library Bulletin* 37 (1984).

Hine, Darlene Clark. "Lifting the Veil, Shattering the Silence: Black Women's History in Slavery and Freedom." In *The State of Afro-American History: Past, Present, and Future.* Edited by Darlene Clark Hine. Baton Rouge: Louisiana State University Press, 1986.

Joseph, Gloria I. "Sojourner Truth: Archetypal Black Feminist." In *Wild Women in the Whirlwind: Afra-American Culture and the Contemporary Literary Renaissance.* Edited by Joanne M. Braxton and Andrée Nicola McLaughlin. New Brunswick: Rutgers University Press, 1989.

Kaplan, Sidney. "Sojourner Truth's Son Peter." *The Negro History Bulletin* 19 (November 1955).

Kerber, Linda K. "Abolitionists and Amalgamators: The New York City Race Riots of 1834." *New York History* 48 (January 1967).

Lorde, Audre. "The Master's Tools Will Never Dismantle The Master's House." In *Sister Outsider: Essays & Speeches.* Edited by Audre Lorde. Freedom, California: The Crossing Press, 1984.

Lowe, Berenice. "Michigan Days of Sojourner Truth." *New York Folklore Quarterly* 12 (Summer 1956).

McDade, Thomas. "Matthias, Prophet without Honor." *New York Historical Society Quarterly* 62 (October 1978).

McKivigan, John R. "The Frederick Douglass-Gerrit Smith Friendship and Political Abolitionism in the 1850s." In *Frederick Douglass: New Literary and Historical Essays*. Edited by Eric J. Sundquist. Cambridge: Cambridge University Press, 1990.

Murray, Pauli. "The Negro Woman in the Quest for Equality." In *The Female Experience: An American Documentary*. Edited by Gerda Lerner. Indianapolis: Bobbs-Merrill, 1977.

Painter, Nell Irvin. "Sojourner Truth in Life and Memory: Writing the Biography of an American Exotic." *Gender and History* 2, no. 1 (Spring 1990).

Perlman, Daniel. "Organizations of the Free Negro in New York City, 1800-1860." *Journal of Negro History* 56 (July 1971).

Pickens, William. "The Woman Voter Hits the Color Line." In *A Documentary History of the Negro People in the United States, 1910-1932*. Edited by Herbert Aptheker. Secaucus, New Jersey: The Citadel Press, 1977.

Porter, Dorothy B. "Anti-Slavery Movement in Northampton." *The Negro History Bulletin* 24, no. 2 (November 1960).

Ray, Charles B. "Colored Churches in This City." *The Colored American*, 28 March 1840.

Rose, Willie Lee. "Childhood in Bondage." In *Slavery and Freedom*. Edited by William W. Freehling. New York: Oxford University Press, 1982.

———. "The Domestication of Domestic Slavery." In *Slavery and Freedom*. Edited by William W. Freehling. New York: Oxford University Press, 1982.

Smith-Rosenberg, Carroll. "Beauty, the Beast and the Militant Woman: A Case Study in Sex Roles and Social Stress in Jacksonian America." *American Quarterly* 23 (October 1971): 561-84.

Squier, Effie J. "Sojourner Truth." *Christian at Work* (28 September 1882).

Stetson, Erlene. "Silence: Access and Aspiration." In *Between Women: Biographers, Novelists, Critics, Teachers and Artists Write About Their Work on Women*. Edited by Carol Ascher, Louise DeSalvo, and Sara Ruddick. New York: Routledge, 1994.

———. "Studying Slavery: Some Literary and Pedagogical Considerations on the Black Female Slave." In *All the Women Are White, All the Blacks Are Men, But Some of Us Are Brave*. Edited by Gloria T. Hull, Patricia

Bell Scott, and Barbara Smith. Old Westbury, New York: The Feminist Press, 1982.

Stowe, Harriet Beecher. "Sojourner Truth, the Libyan Sibyl." *Atlantic Monthly* 11 (April 1863).

Stuckey, Sterling. "'Ironic Tenacity': Frederick Douglass's Seizure of the Dialectic." In *Frederick Douglass: New Literary and Historical Essays*. Edited by Eric J. Sundquist. Cambridge: Cambridge University Press, 1990.

———. "The Skies of Consciousness: African Dance at Pinkster in New York, 1750-1840." In *Going Through the Storm: The Influence of African American Art in History*. Edited by Sterling Stuckey. New York: Oxford University Press, 1994.

Sundquist, Eric J. Introduction. In *Frederick Douglass: New Literary and Historical Essays*. Edited by Eric J. Sundquist. Cambridge: Cambridge University Press, 1990.

Terborg-Penn, Rosalyn. "Discrimination Against Afro-American Women in the Woman's Movement, 1830-1920." In *The Afro-American Woman: Struggles and Images*. Edited by Sharon Harley and Rosalyn Terborg-Penn. Port Washington, New York: Kennikat Press, 1978.

Walker, Alice. "Gifts of Power: The Writings of Rebecca Jackson." In *In Search of Our Mothers' Gardens: Womanist Prose*. San Diego: Harcourt Brace & Co., 1984.

———. "In Search of Our Mothers' Gardens." In *In Search of Our Mothers' Gardens: Womanist Prose*. San Diego: Harcourt Brace & Co., 1984.

Wheatley, Phillis. "On the Death of the Rev. Mr. George Whitefield. 1770." In *Poems on Various Subjects, Religious and Moral*. By Phillis Wheatley. London: A. Bell, 1773.

Wideman, John. "Frame and Dialect: The Evolution of the Black Voice." *The American Poetry Review* (September-October 1976)

Williams, Sherley Anne. "The Blues Roots of Contemporary Afro-American Poetry." In *Chant of Saints: A Gathering of Afro-American Literature, Art, and Scholarship*. Edited by Michael S. Harper and Robert B. Stepto. Urbana: University of Illinois Press, 1979.

Williams-Myers, A. J. "Pinkster Carnival: Africanisms in the Hudson River Valley." *Afro-Americans in New York Life and History* 9 (January 1985).

Wyman, Lillie Buffum Chace. "Sojourner Truth." *New England Magazine* 24 (March 1901).

Yellin, Jean Fagan. "Texts and Contexts of Harriet Jacobs' Incidents in the Life of a Slave Girl: Written by Herself." In *The Slave's Narrative: Texts and Contexts*. Edited by Charles T. Davis and Henry Louis Gates, Jr. New York: Oxford University Press, 1985.

Index